GUIDE TO THE WATERWAYS ⑦
Thames, Wey, Kennet & Avon

Recommended by
British Waterways

Nicholson
An imprint of HarperCollins*Publishers*

Also available:

Nicholson/Ordnance Survey Guide to the Waterways

1. **London, Grand Union, Oxford & Lee**
2. **Severn, Avon & Birmingham**
3. **Birmingham & the Heart of England**
4. **Four Counties & the Welsh Canals**
5. **North West & the Pennines**
6. **Nottingham, York & the North East**

Nicholson/Ordnance Survey Inland Waterways Map of Great Britain

First published in 1997 by
Nicholson
An imprint of HarperCollins*Publishers*
77-85 Fulham Palace Road
Hammersmith, London W6 8JB
and
Ordnance Survey
Romsey Road, Maybush
Southampton SO16 4GU

The mapping in this publication is based upon Ordnance Survey® Pathfinder®,
Outdoor Leisure™ and Explorer™ maps.

Ordnance Survey and Pathfinder are registered trade marks and Outdoor Leisure and
Explorer are trade marks of Ordnance Survey, the National Mapping Agency of Great Britain.

The representation in this publication of a road, track or path is no evidence of the existence of a
right of way.

Researched and written by David Perrott, Jonathan Mosse and Jane Mosse.
Design by Bob Vickers.

The publishers gratefully acknowledge the assistance given by British Waterways
and its staff in the preparation of this guide.

Photographs reproduced by kind permission of the following picture libraries:
Bill Meadows Picture Library pages 50, 74; Derek Pratt Photography pages 28, 36, 37, 42, 146.

Thanks is also due to CAMRA representatives and branch members.

Great care has been taken throughout this book to be accurate, but the publishers
cannot accept responsibility for any errors which appear, or their consequences.

Printed in Italy.

ISBN 0 7028 3302 9
JN 8539
97/1/15.5

The canals and river navigations of Britain were built as a system of new trade routes, at a time when roads were virtually non-existent. After their desperately short boom period in the late 18th and early 19th centuries, they gracefully declined in the face of competition from the railways. A few canals disappeared completely, but thankfully most just decayed gently, carrying the odd working boat, and becoming havens for wildlife and the retreat of the waterways devotee.

It was two such enthusiasts, L.T.C. Rolt and Robert Aickman who, in 1946, formed the Inland Waterways Association, bringing together like-minded people from all walks of life to campaign for the preservation and restoration of the inland waterways. Their far-sightedness has at last seen its reward for, all over the country, an amazing transformation has taken place. British Waterways, the IWA, local councils, canal societies and volunteers have brought back to life great lengths of canal, and much of the dereliction which was once commonplace has been replaced with a network of 'linear parks'.

The canals provide something for everyone to enjoy: engineering feats such as aqueducts, tunnels and flights of locks; the brightly decorated narrow boats; a wealth of birds, animals and plants; the mellow unpretentious architecture of canalside buildings; friendly waterside pubs and the sheer beauty and quiet isolation that is a feature of so much of our inland waterways.

It is easy to enjoy this remarkable facet of our history, either on foot, often by bicycle, or on a boat. This book, with its splendid Ordnance Survey mapping, is one of a series covering the waterways network, and gives you all the information you need.

▍CONTENTS

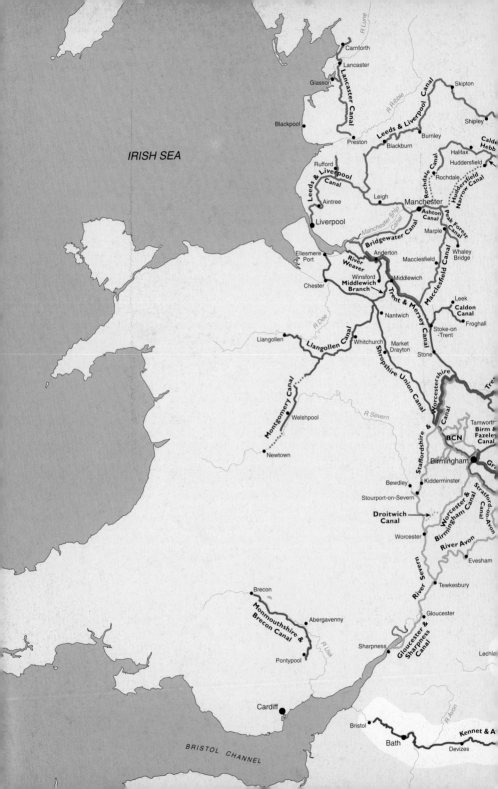

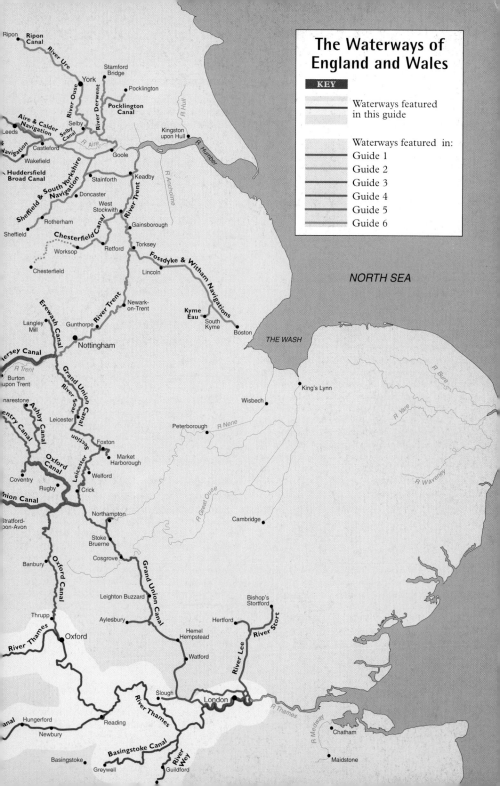

GENERAL INFORMATION FOR CANAL USERS

The slogan 'Waterways For All' was aptly coined to take account of the wide diversity of people using the inland waterways for recreation.

Today boaters, walkers, fishermen, cyclists and 'gongoozlers' (on-lookers) throng our canals and rivers anxious, in one way or another, to share in the enjoyment of our quite amazing waterway heritage. British Waterways, along with other navigation authorities, is empowered to develop, maintain and control this resource in order to maximise its potential: namely our enjoyment. It is to this end that a series of guides, codes, and regulations have come into existence over the years, evolving to match a burgeoning – and occasionally conflicting – demand. Set out below are the key points as they relate to everyone wishing to enjoy the waterways.

LICENSING – BOATS

The majority of the navigations covered in this series of books are controlled by British Waterways and are administered on first a regional and then on a local basis. Individual Waterway Managers are detailed in the introduction to each waterway and hold considerable autonomy. All craft using BW waterways must be licensed and charges are based on the length of the craft. This licence covers all navigable waterways under BW's control and in a few cases includes reciprocal agreements with other waterway authorities (as indicated in the text). Permits for permanent mooring on the canals are also issued by BW. Apply in each case to:

Customer Services
British Waterways
Willow Grange
Church Road
Watford WD1 3QA
Telephone: 01923 226422
Facsimile: 01923 226081

Since 1st January 1997 BW and the Environment Agency have introduced the Boat Safety Scheme, setting technical requirements for good and safe boat-building practice. A safety certificate will be necessary before applying for a craft licence.

Other navigational authorities relevant to this book are mentioned where appropriate.

LICENSING – CYCLISTS

Cyclists using BW towpaths are no longer required to purchase an annual licence. However they must apply for a free permit which in turn should be attached to their bicycle. Permits are obtainable from the address above; from Waterway Offices and, in many cases, from cycle shops near a waterway.

TOWPATHS

Few, if any, artificial cuts or canals in this country are without an intact towpath accessible to the walker at least. However, on river navigations towpaths have on occasion fallen into disuse or, sometimes, been lost to erosion. In today's leisure climate considerable efforts are being made to provide access to all towpaths with some available to the disabled. Notes on individual waterways in this book detail the supposed status of the path but the indication of a towpath does not necessarily imply a public right of way or mean that a right to cycle along it exists. If you are in any doubt, check with the latest published Ordnance Survey Map before you proceed. Motorcycling and horse riding are forbidden on all towpaths. Where bicycling is forbidden, exceptions may apply to boat crews 'lock-wheeling' to set locks ahead of their boats.

BW NAVIGATION GUIDE

Previously known as the Boaters Guide this publication has for many years set out the operating details of individual canals, listing everything from bridge and lock availability times through to telephone numbers for Regional and Waterway Offices. It is essential reading to accompany any guide to BW navigable rivers and canals of this country. It is regularly updated and a copy may be obtained, free of charge, from the address above. It should be read in conjunction with the General Canal Bye-laws, also free from BW.

INDIVIDUAL WATERWAY GUIDES

No national guide can cover the minutiae of the individual waterway and more recently Waterway Managers have been producing guides to specific navigations under their charge. Copies of individual guides (where they are available) can be obtained by phoning the Waterway Office detailed in the introduction. It should be noted that times – such as operating times of bridges and locks – do change year by year and from winter to summer.

STOPPAGES

British Waterways works hard to programme its major engineering works into the winter period when demand for cruising is low. To this end it publishes a National Stoppage Programme and Winter Opening Hours leaflet which is sent out to all licence holders, boatyards and hire companies. Inevitably emergencies occur necessitating the unexpected closure of a waterway, perhaps during the peak season. Water shortages – particularly prevalent during recent dry summers – lead to restrictions and occasionally closure. Details are published on lockside noticeboards or by telephoning Canalphone on 01923 201401 for North West, North East and Midlands & South West Regions; 01923 201402 for Midlands & South West and Southern Regions.

STARTING OUT

If you are hiring a boat for the first time, the boatyard will brief you thoroughly. Take notes, follow their instructions and *don't be afraid to ask* if there is anything you do not understand.

GENERAL CRUISING NOTES

Most canals are saucer-shaped in section so are deepest at the middle. Few have more than 3-4ft of water and many have much less. Keep to the middle of the channel except on bends, where the deepest water is on the outside of the bend. When you meet another boat, keep to the right, slow down and aim to miss the approaching craft by a couple of yards: do not steer right over to the bank or you are likely to run aground. If you meet a loaded commercial boat keep right out of the way and be prepared to follow his instructions. Do not assume that you should pass on the right. If you meet a boat being towed from the bank, pass it on the outside. When overtaking, keep the other boat on your right side.

Speed

There is a general speed limit of 4 mph on most BW canals. This is not just an arbitrary limit: there is no need to go any faster and in many cases it is impossible to cruise even at this speed: if the wash is 'breaking' against the bank or causing large waves, slow down.

Slow down also when passing moored craft, engineering works and anglers; when there is a lot of floating rubbish on the water (and try to drift over obvious obstructions in neutral); when approaching blind corners, narrow bridges and junctions.

Mooring

Generally speaking you may moor where you wish on BW property, as long as there is sufficient depth of water, and you are *not causing an obstruction*. Your boat should carry metal mooring stakes, and these should be driven firmly in with the mallet if there are no mooring rings. Do not stretch mooring lines across the towpath. Always consider the security of your boat when there is no one aboard. On tideways and commercial waterways it is advisable to moor only at recognised sites, and allow for any rise or fall of the tide.

Bridges

On narrow canals slow down and aim to miss one side (usually the towpath side) by about 9 inches. *Keep everyone inboard when passing through bridges*, and take special care with moveable structures – the crew member operating it should hold the bridge steady as the boat passes through.

Tunnels

Make sure the tunnel is clear before you enter, and use your headlight. Follow any instructions given on notice boards by the entrance.

Fuel

Hire craft usually carry fuel sufficient for your rental period.

Water

It is advisable to top up every day.

Lavatories

Hire craft usually have pump-out toilets. Have these emptied *before* things become critical. Keep the receipt and your boatyard will usually reimburse you for this expense.

Boatyards

Hire fleets are usually 'turned around' on a Saturday, making this a bad time to call in for services. Remember that moorings at popular destinations fill quickly during the summer months, so do not assume there will be room for your boat. Always ask.

LOCKS AND THEIR USE

A lock is a simple and ingenious device for transporting your craft from one water level to another. When both sets of gates are closed it may be filled or emptied using gate or ground paddles at the top or bottom of the lock. These are operated with a windlass.

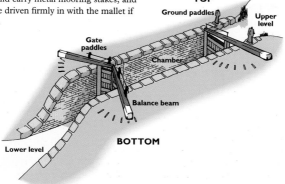

TOP

Ground paddles

Upper level

Gate paddles

Chamber

Balance beam

Lower level

BOTTOM

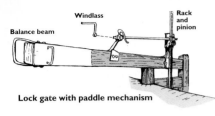

Lock gate with paddle mechanism

General tips:
- Make safety your prime concern. *Keep a close eye on young children.*
- Always take your time, and do not leap about.
- Never open the paddles at one end without ensuring those at the other are closed.
- Never drop the paddles – always wind them down.
- Keep to the landward side of the balance beam when opening and closing gates.
- Never leave your windlass slotted onto the paddle spindle – it will be dangerous should anything slip.
- Be wary of fierce *top gate* paddles, especially in wide locks. Operate them slowly, and close them if there is *any* adverse effect.
- If a lock keeper is present, always follow his/her instructions.

PLANNING A CRUISE

Many a waterways holiday has been spoiled by trying to go too far too fast. Go slowly, don't be too ambitious, and enjoy the experience.

A *rough* calculation of time taken to cover the ground is the 'lock-miles' system:

Add the number of *miles* to the number of *locks* on your proposed journey, and divide the resulting figure by three. This will give you a guide to the number of *hours* it will take. But don't forget your service stops (water, shopping, pump-out), and allow plenty of time to visit that special pub!

TIDAL WATERWAYS

The typical steel narrow boat found on the inland waterways system has the sea-going characteristics of a bathtub, which renders it totally unsuitable for all-weather cruising on tidal estuaries. However the more adventurous will inevitably wish to add additional 'ring' cruises to the more predictable circuits within the calm havens of inland Britain. Passage is possible in most estuaries if careful consideration is given to the key factors of weather conditions, crew experience, the condition of the boat and its equipment and, perhaps of overriding importance, the need to take expert advice. In many cases it will be prudent to employ the skilled services of a local pilot. Within the text, where inland navigations connect with a tidal waterway, details are given of sources of both advice and

pilotage. This guide is to the Inland Waterways of Britain and therefore recognizes that tideways – and especially estuaries – require a different skill and approach. We therefore do not hesitate to draw the boater's attention to the appropriate source material.

GENERAL

British Waterways manages and cares for more than 2000 miles of Britain's rivers and canals. Other substantial lengths of waterway are administered by the Environment Agency and by individual Canal Authorities and Trusts. Whilst BW strives for consistency in what they do and how they do it – their objectives are enshrined in the Citizen's Charter – other organisations work within differing sets of parameters. The boater, conditioned perhaps by the uniformity of our national road network, should therefore be sensitive to a need to observe different codes and operating practices. Similarly it is important to be aware that some waterways are only available for navigation today solely because of the care and dedication of a particular restoration body, often using volunteer labour and usually taking several decades to complete the project. This is the reason that, in cruising the national waterways network, additional licence charges are sometimes incurred. The introduction to each waterway gives its background history, details of recent restoration (where relevant) and also lists the operating authority.

British Waterways is a public body, responsible to the Department of the Environment and, as subscribers to the Citizen's Charter, they are linked with an ombudsman. Problems and complaints should, in the first instance, be addressed to the local Waterway Manager as listed in the introduction to individual waterways. The current management structure is well suited, in the majority of cases, to providing swift and effective remedy. If satisfaction cannot be gained at this level then the ombudsman can be contacted as follows:

Waterways Ombudsman
2 Paper Buildings
Temple
London EC4Y 7ET
Telephone: 0171 582 0377
Facsimile: 0171 820 9429

FREEPHONE CANALS

This is available if you need help from British Waterways outside normal office hours on weekdays and throughout weekends. Simply dial 100 and ask for Freephone Canals. This service is completely free of charge. You should give details and location of your problem so that you can receive help as soon as possible. If you have a mobile telephone dial 01384 240948.

BASINGSTOKE CANAL

MAXIMUM DIMENSIONS

Length: 72'
Beam: 13' 6"
Headroom: 5' 10"

MILEAGES

WOODHAM JUNCTION (River Wey) to:
Woodham Top Lock: 1 mile
Goldsworth Bottom Lock: 5 miles
Pirbright Bridge: 8 miles
Deepcut Top Lock: 10 miles
Mytchett: 13 miles
Ash Lock: 16 miles
Pondtail Bridges: 20 miles

Crookham Wharf: 23 miles
Barley Mow Bridge: 27 miles
Odiham Wharf: 29 miles
Limit of navigation: 30 miles
Greywell Tunnel: 31 miles

29 locks

LICENCES

Boat Licence Clerk
Basingstoke Canal Office
Mytchett Place Road
Mytchett
Surrey GU16 6DD
(01252) 370073

An Act of Parliament for the building of this canal was passed in 1778, and the navigation opened to Basingstoke in 1794. Intended as an artery to and from London for mainly agricultural produce – timber, grain, fertilizers, chalk and malt – it was never a financial success. Built by the great canal contractor, John Pinkerton (who issued his own tokens or coins as payment to his navvies), it was originally estimated to cost £86,000. By 1796 £153,463 had been spent. Tonnages of goods carried averaged about 20,000 per annum, 10,700 tons below what was anticipated, and profit forecasts of £7,783 8s 4d proved wildly optimistic, the best figure achieved being £3,038 4s 2d in 1800–1.

The Napoleonic Wars, and the danger they brought to coastal shipping, benefited the Basingstoke Canal, which could transport goods bound for Portsmouth and Southampton in safety. But with the advent of peace, trade slumped – the canal managers commenting that 'some considerable injury must be sustained by the Canal'.

There was a minor boom in goods carried in 1839 to build the London & South Western Railway, but when this opened it was clear that the navigation had been instrumental in its own demise. Trade flourished for a while in 1854 with the building of the barracks at Aldershot, but this was short-lived. Plans for a revival by building a link canal from Basingstoke to the Kennet & Avon Canal at Newbury came to nothing, and the company went into liquidation in 1866. A dissolution order followed in 1878. Purchased by new owners in 1896, and renamed the Woking, Aldershot & Basingstoke Canal, a considerable amount of money was spent on improvements, to link with the new brickworks at Up Nately, but all to no avail, and by 1904 it was once again offered for sale. It was in 1913 that the last barge reached Basingstoke. The canal was owned by A.J. Harmsworth between 1923 and 1947 (his grandson is now the manager) who did much to ensure its ultimate survival, despite the collapse of Greywell Tunnel in 1934. Munitions were transported on the canal during World War II, and the last commercial traffic, a load of coal to Woking Gasworks, came up the canal in 1950. In that same year it was auctioned and sold to the Inland Waterways Association but due to insufficient funds being raised the canal was sold on to what was to become the New Basingstoke Canal Company. Now owned by the County Councils of Hampshire and Surrey, its restoration represents a magnificent achievement by both councils, the Surrey and Hampshire Canal Society and the IWA.

Woking

The Basingstoke Canal leaves the River Wey Navigation at Woodham Junction, near a large electricity sub-station and overshadowed by the M25 motorway. Its course is immediately lined with a fine mixture of mature trees, a feature which is to persist throughout most of its route to Greywell Tunnel. The Woodham flight of six locks (apart from Lock 1) was the last on the canal to be restored, and the re-establishment of through navigation has disturbed the peaceful, and almost secret, houseboat world which exists between Locks 1 and 3. These floating homes were established here around 1950, on narrow boat hulls brought from the Midlands. Above Woodham Top Lock the waterway maintains its seclusion, with the large private gardens of an expensive residential area backing onto the canal. Horsell Common provides more open views before Woking is reached. The last commercial traffic on the canal brought coal to Woking Gasworks in 1950. There is easy access to shops, banks and pubs from Lock 2 – walk south west into West Byfleet;

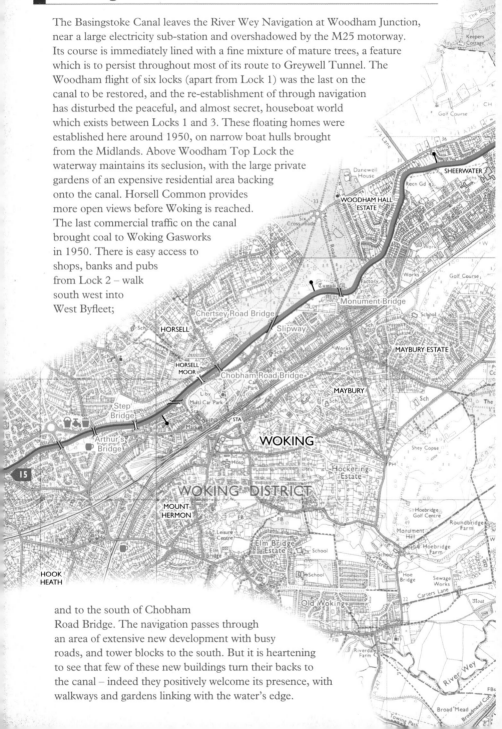

and to the south of Chobham Road Bridge. The navigation passes through an area of extensive new development with busy roads, and tower blocks to the south. But it is heartening to see that few of these new buildings turn their backs to the canal – indeed they positively welcome its presence, with walkways and gardens linking with the water's edge.

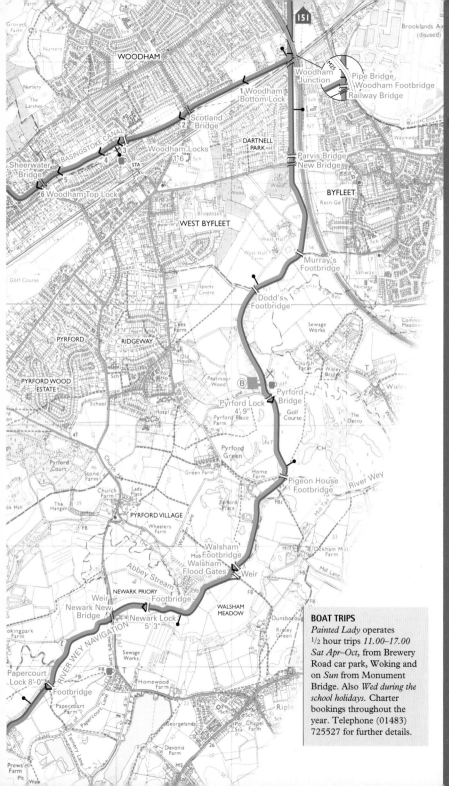

BOAT TRIPS

Painted Lady operates
1/2 hour trips *11.00–17.00
Sat Apr–Oct*, from Brewery
Road car park, Woking and
on *Sun* from Monument
Bridge. Also *Wed during the
school holidays*. Charter
bookings throughout the
year. Telephone (01483)
725527 for further details.

1 Facilities for boaters are at present fairly limited on the Basingstoke Canal. There is water available at Mytchett, Ash Lock, Fleet and Winchfield (BW key required for all 4 sites) together with pump-out facilities at Mytchett. There are, however, many garages close to the route.

2 Slipways are available at Chertsey Road Bridge, Woking; Potters Steak House, Mytchett; Farnborough Road, Aldershot and Barley Mow Bridge, Winchfield. A BW sanitary station key is required to unlock the barriers. To use the Woking slipway first contact the Leisure Services Officer on (01483) 755855.

● **Woking**

Surrey. MD Tue, Fri, Sat. All shops and services. Surrey's largest town, built around the railway, which came here in 1838. The original village, Old Woking, lies 2 miles to the south. Development carries on apace, making dormitory homes for the thousands of commuters who rush up to the city daily. It is, however, worth walking south from Monument Bridge, and taking the third turning on the right, Oriental Road, to see the Shah Jehan Mosque, built in 1889 and reminiscent of the Taj Mahal in India with its onion-shaped dome. Built by the enormously rich Begum Shah Jehan, ruler of Bhopal State in India, its design, by W.I. Chambers, is honest and dignified. A P&O captain was employed to take bearings to ensure an exact orientation towards Mecca. It is now the main centre for Muslims in England.

Brooklands Museum Weybridge (01932 857381). A museum assembled around what remains of the Brooklands race track, the world's first purpose-built circuit, constructed by wealthy landowner Hugh Locke King in 1907. Its heyday was in the 1920s and 30s, when records were being set by the likes of Malcolm Campbell and John Cobb, driving vehicles with wonderfully evocative names, such as the Napier, Delage, Bentley and Bugatti. It became very fashionable, and was known as The Ascot of Motorsport. It was also an aerodrome, and it was here that A.V. Roe made the first flight in a British aeroplane. The Sopwith Pup and Camel were developed here, and later the Hawker Hurricane and the Vickers Wellington were built here. The outbreak of war in 1939 brought an end to racing, and aircraft production ceased in 1987. Now you can walk on part of the legendary circuit, and see historic racing cars and aircraft in the museum. The Clubhouse is listed as an ancient monument. *Open 10.00–17.00 (16.00 winter) Tue–Sun & B Hols. Closed G Fri & Xmas.* Charge.

Elmbridge Museum Church Street, Weybridge (01932 843573). Above the public library.

Collection covering local and social history and featuring Cecil Hepworth, pioneering local film-maker, and Mary Bennet's early 19thC album of sketches and watercolours. *Open Mon, Tue, Wed & Fri 11.00–17.00; Sat 10.00–13.00 & 14.00–17.00.* Buses or train to Weybridge.

New Victoria Theatre Woking (01483 747422). Situated in the Peacocks Arts & Entertainments Centre and providing a 1300 seat venue for drama, musicals, opera and ballet. Also big screen cinemas, bars, cafés and restaurants. Disabled access. Buses.

Woking Leisure Centre Woking (01483 771122). Leisure lagoon with all the latest water based fun. State of the art children's play areas, 9 screen video wall, cafés, etc. Disabled access. Buses.

Planets Woking (01483 773313). Town centre, indoor theme park featuring tenpin bowling, games, a brewery, cafés and restaurants.

Woking Miniature Railway Society Mizens Farm, Woking (01483 720801). One mile north of Monument Bridge along A320. Ground level miniature steam railway in a scenic location on the banks of the River Bourne. Tearoom. *Open Easter–Oct, 1st & 3rd Sun in month.* Charge. Buses.

● **Woodham**

Surrey. EC Wed. All shops and services. A typical commuter conurbation of dull, closely packed houses, only pretty in the more expensive areas, where large, spacious houses and gardens nestle among trees. Definitely at its best and most characterful by the canal.

● **Horsell**

Surrey. Indistinguishable from Woking (see above), although if you look hard enough, you will find a few original cottages. St Mary's Church is unremarkable save for two interesting monuments – to Sir John Rose and his wife, on the west wall (1803), and to James Fenn and his wife, whom he faces across a jumble of books (1787).

UPS AND DOWNS ON THE BASINGSTOKE

The Basingstoke Canal is sometimes portrayed as a restoration failure but this is borne entirely out of a misconception. At the outset the objective of the two county councils involved was to create a 32 mile, linear country park for the benefit of a wide variety of potential users, of which boaters were to be but one (albeit significant) group.

Two barge movements a day was the average traffic when the waterway was opened and water supply was always constrained by an undertaking not to tap existing watercourses, jealously guarded by millers and landowners alike. More recently local water abstraction and, quite possibly, oil extraction in the Basingstoke area, have conspired to lower water tables and diminish further the water supply (reduced by a half since 1983) available to the navigation. Apart from springs and rainwater run-off – plentiful during the winter months – the only other water source is limited to two pumped supplies: one at Woking and a second at Frimley, lifting storm water from a drainage sump on the trackbed of the mainline railway. Back pumping is always a possibility but costly to install and operate. Current water losses are ultimately to the River Wey (its own water supply down by one third since 1983) and in the form of transpiration through the abundance of vegetation and trees lining the waterway. A mature oak consumes over 150 gallons on a hot day when the canal level can drop $1/8$th inch over a 24 hour period.

Springs work on more or less a six month cycle so the time to visit the canal is between February and mid-June and in the remaining winter months if there are no maintenance stoppages. The Canal Authority, who manage the navigation on behalf of the two county councils, are happy to accept booked passages within these periods and operate a well-tried procedure to ensure that boaters pass efficiently through the locks and are able to derive the maximum enjoyment from their visit.

It has aptly been described as a sleepy backwater of a canal and navigating it is more akin to 1950s boating: locks fill slowly, require care and caulking, and the waterway itself is not to be rushed along. Herein lies its real charm and to appreciate it – together with the abundant wildlife and SSSIs – the visitor must understand its constraints, together with the way in which it has successfully fulfilled all the aims of its restorers and delighted one and a half million diverse visitors annually.

The towpath

The towpath is in excellent condition throughout the entire length of the navigation including the disused section west of Greywell Tunnel as far as Penny Bridge. The short section across Greywell Hill, however, may be uneven and overgrown. The towpath is well used by walker and cyclist alike and in conjunction with the numerous British Rail stations, situated at regular intervals close to the canal, it is easy to plan excursions without having to double back.

Pubs and Restaurants

There are plenty of pubs and restaurants in Woking and West Byfleet but only one is adjacent to the canal.

Claremont West Byfleet (01932 345048). Opposite West Byfleet Station, south of Lock 3. Tetley's and Burton real ales in a large, lively pub. *Lunchtime food available Mon–Sat and snacks thereafter Mon–Thur.*

Bridge Barn Woking (01483 763642). By Arthur's Bridge. A tastefully converted 17thC timbered barn now housing a Beefeater Restaurant. Food is available *all day, 7 days a week* together with Boddingtons, Flowers and guest real ales. Canalside garden with children's play area. Moorings outside. Venue for the Basingstoke Canal Festival held *every May.*

Star Wych Hill, Hookheath (01483 760526). Tetley's, Friary Meux, Young's and guest real ales in a lively and very welcoming oasis in suburbia. Bar meals *lunchtimes and evenings Mon–Fri.* Strictly carnivorous fare. Garden with children's play area. Pool, and quiz *Sun.* Open all day.

Brookwood

Gradually Woking is left behind as the canal rises through the five Goldsworth Locks to Kiln Bridge. Here there is easy access to shops, Indian and Chinese restaurants, and a laundrette. The railway, which accompanies the canal to Frimley Green, comes very close at Knaphill, and is then replaced by the trees of Brookwood Lye. Houseboats moored here, by Hermitage Bridge, add a picturesque touch. A collection of used cars are parked almost at the edge of Brookwood Bottom Lock, but the remaining two locks are pleasantly situated and once again the trees reappear. An old overgrown pill box still guards Pirbright Bridge. Beyond the bridge is the first of the Deepcut, or Frimley, flight of locks.

The army now begins to make its presence felt, with distant pops and bangs from the rifle range. The Basingstoke Canal now climbs steadily up the Deepcut, or Frimley, flight of 14 locks, in a superb, tree-lined setting. Even the vast Pirbright Army Camp to the north hardly intrudes. Between many of the locks there are wide pools – check the depth of these carefully if you intend to stray off the direct course. Each of the locks has a footbridge, and a ladder in the chamber, but not all have an easy means of landing below the bottom gates, so it is a good idea for a member of the crew to walk ahead to open the gates while ascending. Above the top lock is a dry dock, rebuilt in 1984. The building here was once a workshop and forge.

● **St John's**
Surrey. PO, tel, stores, take aways, chemist, laundrette. Swallowed up by Woking, the area around Kiln Bridge somehow, against all odds, manages to retain the feel of a village centre. Notice the well-restored building topped by a clock tower, right by the bridge.

● **Knaphill**
Surrey. Basically a large Victorian village around the barracks and the site of the gaunt Brookwood Mental Hospital, a mid-19thC asylum which was once entirely self-sufficient, generating its own electricity and running its own farm in the grounds. To the west is

Bisley, famous for its annual rifle shooting competitions.
Brookwood Cemetery A superbly landscaped expanse of heathland covering 2400 acres, to the south of Brookwood Station, where mature trees and eccentric mausoleums coexist harmoniously. Founded by the London Necropolis Company in 1854, when the numbers of dead Londoners were becoming increasingly difficult to accommodate, it was once served by a railway – indeed one of the station buildings still survives. There is a military cemetery in the south-west corner where British and American soldiers are buried.

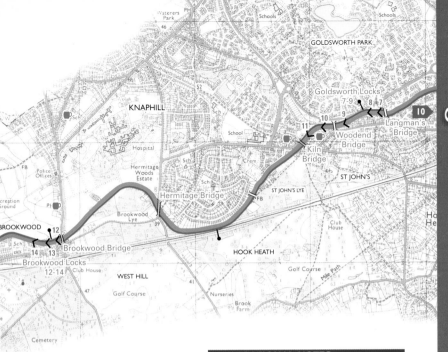

NAVIGATIONAL NOTES

Do not stray from the direct course of the canal without first checking the depth. Many of the wide pools are quite shallow.

Pubs and Restaurants

Rowbarge St John's, Woking (01483 761618). Tetley's and guest real ales and inexpensive bar food available *lunchtimes Mon–Fri.* Children and vegetarians catered for. Traditional pub games. *Open all day except Sun.*

Robin Hood 88 Robin Hood Road, St John's (01483 472173). A fine pub majoring on conversation and good beer, serving Courage and guest real ales together with food *lunchtimes Mon–Sat.* Children's area. Large garden and spontaneous summertime events. Traditional pub games.

Hunter's Lodge Knaphill (01483 797240). North of Brookwood Bridge. An attractive and welcoming pub offering Bass and Fuller's real ales, together with traditional English bar food *all day, 7 days a week.* Children and vegetarians catered for. Garden and children's play area. Free from loud music and fruit machines. *Open all day.*

Garibaldi 136 High Street, Knaphill (01483 473374). North east of Brookwood Bridge. Fuller's, Harveys and guest real ales in a traditional two bar pub offering bar meals *lunchtimes Mon–Sat.* Outside seating and inside peace and quiet.

Froggies 42–44 High Street, Knaphill (01483 480835). A restaurant/wine bar with a warm and cosy atmosphere. Good value at lunchtime. *L & D (Closed Sun & Mon D).*

The Brookwood Hotel Beside Brookwood Station (01483 472109). A well-preserved Victorian pub with an à la carte restaurant, Tetley's real ale and inexpensive bar meals *lunchtimes and evenings, 7 days a week.* Friendly atmosphere. Children and vegetarians catered for. Large beer garden and a children's play area. Traditional pub games. *Quiz Mon,* disco *Wed & Fri. Open all day.*

Mytchett

Having climbed 90 feet, the navigation now enters the dramatic Deepcut cutting, 1000yds long and up to 70ft deep. Lined with large, mature, deciduous trees, it is shady and remote. Beyond Wharfenden Lake, now part of a country club, and the supposedly lead-lined aqueduct over the railway, the canal turns sharply south towards Mytchett, with wood and heathland rising to the east. Mytchett Lake, owned by the army and renowned amongst anglers for the size of its pike, adjoins the canal, but is closed to navigation. The canal continues south, enclosed by the railway and thick woods on one side, and leafy gardens on the other. Just beyond the railway bridge at Ash Vale is the corrugated iron boathouse where 15 barges were built between 1918 and 1935. There is a post office here (by the station), an off-licence and easy access to shops. Greatbottom Flash is surrounded by trees, and signs indicate that this is a Danger Area, used by the army. The water is very clear, revealing just how shallow the canal is here. Large houses with gardens landscaped to the water's edge face a busy road at Ash Vale before the navigation resumes its general westerly course, passing handy shops, another post office and Chinese take away at Ash Wharf Bridge. It then crosses Spring Lake on an embankment and the Blackwater Valley Road on a new aqueduct, leaving Surrey and entering Hampshire. There are good moorings above Ash Lock, opposite the Canal Depot (slipway). The reappearance of army property – barrack blocks behind high wire fences – announces the approach to Aldershot; the canal having climbed 195ft since leaving Woodham Junction. Queen's Avenue Bridge is notable for its modestly ornate iron balustrades, bringing a little light relief from the army camps which now completely enclose the waterway. Do not be alarmed should you see soldiers wearing full combat gear – with helmets and gas masks, carrying rifles – trudging out of the woods, or above you guarding the bridges. For the uninitiated the distant gunfire and clatter of helicopters can be a little unnerving. Beyond Eelmoor Bridge, the canal widens at Eelmoor Flash, a Site of Special Scientific

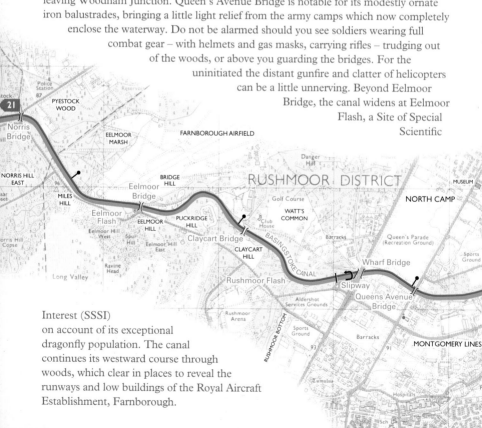

Interest (SSSI) on account of its exceptional dragonfly population. The canal continues its westward course through woods, which clear in places to reveal the runways and low buildings of the Royal Aircraft Establishment, Farnborough.

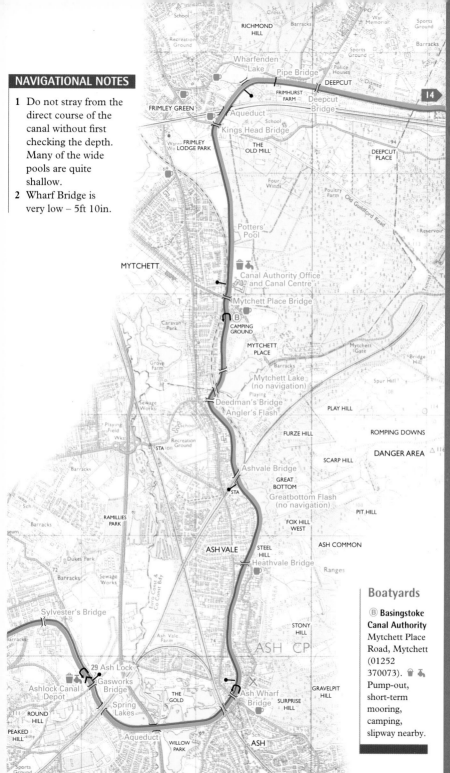

NAVIGATIONAL NOTES

1 Do not stray from the direct course of the canal without first checking the depth. Many of the wide pools are quite shallow.
2 Wharf Bridge is very low – 5ft 10in.

Boatyards

Ⓑ **Basingstoke Canal Authority** Mytchett Place Road, Mytchett (01252 370073). Pump-out, short-term mooring, camping, slipway nearby.

Royal Logistic Corps Museum Princess Royal Barracks, Deepcut, Camberley (01252 340871). Reconstructed as a museum depicting the history from 1414 to the present day of the Royal Corps of Transport, the Royal Pioneer Corps, the Army Catering Corps and the Postal and Courier Services of the Royal Engineers. *Open 10.00–16.00 Mon–Fri & 10.00–15.00 Sat. Closed Sun & B. Hols.* Free.

Basingstoke Canal Authority Mytchett Place Road, Mytchett (01252 370073). Visitor centre with an exhibition showing 200 years of canal history. Model of a barge cabin and a reconstruction of the Greywell tunnel. Shop. *Summer* boat trips, picnic facilities, camping, caravanning. Tearoom (*summer only*). Visitor Centre *open 10.30–17.00 Tue–Sun & B. Hols (10.30–16.30 Tue–Fri in winter).* Charge.

● **Ash and Ash Vale**
Surrey. EC Wed. PO, tel, stores. Villages now enclosed by the sprawl of Aldershot. St Peter's Church, Ash, is early medieval and retains a Norman window, a finely detailed south door, c1200, a 17thC wooden font and a Palladian memorial to John Harris, dated 1759.

Royal Army Medical Corps Museum Keogh Barracks, Ash Vale (01252 340212). East of Mytchett Lake. The achievements of the RAMC in war and peace – the Duke of Wellington's hearing aids, Napoleon's dental instruments, and branding and flogging equipment used on soldiers. Fine medal collection. Shop. *Open 08.30–16.00 Mon–Fri & evenings and weekends by appointment.* Free.

Queen Alexandra's Royal Army Nursing Corps Museum Keogh Barracks, Ash Vale (01252 340320). History of army nursing from Florence Nightingale to the Gulf War conflict. Photographs, diaries, albums and scrapbooks. Shop. *Opening details as per Royal Army Medical Corps Museum above.*

● **Farnborough**
Hants. MD Tue. All shops and services (but some distance north of the canal). A name synonymous with the famous biennial air show (see below), Farnborough is now just a northerly extension of Aldershot, the original village having been engulfed by light industry, housing and the military. Almost 2 miles north of Wharf Bridge is St Peter's Church, dating from around 1200, with a wooden porch and weatherboarded tower. A short walk further north of this is Farnborough Hill, the former home of the Empress Eugenie, wife of Napoleon III of France, from the time of her exile to England in 1871 until her death in 1920. The building is now a convent school but is occasionally open to the public (see below for details). The Empress built an extravagantly French mausoleum for her husband, her son and herself in 1871, as well as an abbey, known as St Michael's, now occupied by English Benedictine monks.

Farnborough Hill Farnborough (01252 545197). Mid-Victorian Gothic house, completed in 1863, home to Empress Eugenie. *Open Mon, Wed & Fri in Aug & Spring B. Hol Mon. Tours at 14.00, 15.00 & 16.00.* Charge.

Royal Aircraft Establishment Farnborough. This aerodrome was set up in 1905 as His Majesty's Balloon Factory. The American showman, Samuel Cody, and a Red Indian friend, made the first powered flight in Britain at Laffan's Plain, Farnborough, in 1908, when Cody was Chief Kiting Instructor at the Balloon School here. Cody died in an air crash in 1913. During the two World Wars extensive research into developing military aircraft was carried out at the airfield, and this continues today, although it has now broadened into the sphere of civil aviation. Much of the design and development work on Concorde was executed here. The world-famous Farnborough Air Show is held here biennially in *September,* and attracts over 200,000 visitors with its static exhibitions and dramatic flying displays. Considering the orientation of the main runway, you should get a good view from the canal.

● **Aldershot**
Hants. MD Thur. All shops and services, cinema and theatre (but some distance south of the canal). In 1854 the army bought 10,000 acres of heathland surrounding the rural hamlet of Aldershot, bringing building materials on the Basingstoke Canal and descending upon the area in force. It has never been the same since. In spite of a great deal of redevelopment it is still, for the most part, an uninspiring place, the military being all pervasive. What is left of the original village, and it is not much, is to the south east of the station. The spectacular biennial army display, held in *June,* attracts over 250,000 visitors.

Airborne Forces Museum Browning Barracks, Aldershot (01252 349619). Smaller exhibits include briefing models – outside there is a Dakota and various guns spanning Arnhem, Suez and the Falklands. *Open 10.00–16.30 daily.* Charge.

Aldershot Military Museum Queen's Avenue, Aldershot (01252 314598). North of Queen's Avenue Bridge. Military history spanning 130 years, including a Victorian barrack room, photographs, models and personal mementoes. Armoured vehicles and guns outside. *Open*

10.00–17.00 daily Mar–Oct & 10.00–16.30 Nov–Feb. Charge. Shop.

Army Physical Training Corps Museum Queens Avenue, Aldershot (01252 347168). Records, equipment, medals and history of the corps since its inaugural course held at Oxford University in 1860. *Open 08.30–12.30 & 14.00–16.30 Mon–Fri. Free.*

Princes Hall Barrack Road, Aldershot (01252 29155). One of two local arts centres. Telephone for details.

Royal Army Dental Corps Museum Next door to the Military Museum (01252 347782). Displays military dentistry from 1660 to the present day. *Open 10.00–12.00 & 14.00–16.30 Mon–Fri. Closed B. Hols. Telephone to confirm times before visiting. Free.*

West End Centre Queens Road, Aldershot (01252 330040). The other local arts centre. Telephone for details.

Tourist Information Centre Aldershot Military Museum, Queen's Avenue, Aldershot (01252 20968). *Open as per Military Museum.*

BOAT TRIPS

Lady of Camelot Gourmet cruises for parties up to 40, operating from the Canal Centre, Mytchett. Booking essential. For further details telephone (01252) 378779 or (0374) 649540.

Daydream provides either self-steered day boat hire or skippered cruises for small groups. Operates from the Canal Centre, Mytchett. For further details telephone (01252) 378779 or (0374) 649540.

Pubs and Restaurants

🍺 ✕ **King's Head Harvester** Old Guildford Road, Frimley Green, Camberley (01252 835431). By King's Head Bridge, Frimley Green. Harvester restaurant with large garden filled with children's play facilities. Food available *all day, every day (in summer)* together with Bass real ale. *Open all day Sat & Sun and every day in summer.*

🍺 **Rose & Thistle** 1 Sturt Road, Frimley Green (01252 835524). West of the King's Head. Friendly family pub, overlooking the village green, serving Tetley's, Friary Meux, Burton and guest real ales and meals *all day, 7 days a week.* Vegetarians and children catered for. Patio and children's play area. Darts. Quiz *Tue* and darts night *Thur.* Non-smoking area.

🍺 **Old Wheatsheaf** 205 Frimley Green Road (01252 835074). South of the Rose & Thistle along A321. Old village local with panelled alcoves, serving a range of Morland real ales together with *lunchtime bar food, Mon–Sat.* Outside seating. Skittle alley and traditional pub games. *Open all day Sat.*

🍺 ✕ **Potters Steak House** Mytchett Place Road, Camberley (01252 513934). Above Mytchett Place Bridge. A large pub and restaurant with children's park (and *summertime* bouncy castle) in the gardens. An extensive table d'hôte menu is served *L & D Mon–Fri* and an à la carte selection is available *L & D (reduced prices between 18.00 & 19.00), 7 days a week.* Courage, John Smith's and guest real ales. A public slipway in the garden and good off-line moorings. Bar snacks and restaurant overlooking the canal. *Slipway users must park their cars at the Canal Centre opposite.*

🍺 **Swan** Ash Vale (01252 28259). At Heathvale Bridge. Warm welcoming Victorian-style pub with a large canalside garden offering children's amusements. Courage real ale, and inexpensive food *all day.* Children welcome if eating. Quiz *Wed & Sun.* Traditional pub games. *Open all day.*

✕ ♀ **Ashram Tandoori** 2 Wharf Road, Ash Hill (01252 313638). By Ash Wharf Bridge. Indian restaurant. *L & D. Wed* Hundee night – eat as much as you can.

🍺 ✕ **Standard of England** 158 Ash Hill Road, Ash Hill (01252 25539). East of Ash Wharf Bridge. Ruddles, Fuller's, Courage and John Smith's real ales in a friendly local serving an extensive range of inexpensive food *lunchtimes and evenings, 7 days a week.* Children and vegetarians catered for. Garden and patio seating. Darts, dominoes and crib. Music and karaoke *Fri & Sat. Open all day.*

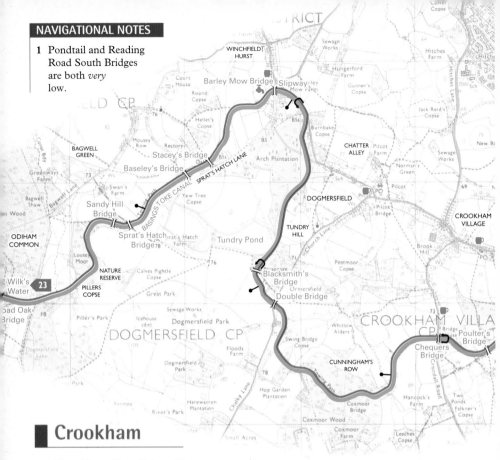

Crookham

Notwithstanding all the military presence, the
course of the navigation is very rural and isolated, and approaches Fleet in a richly
wooded cutting through Pyestock Hill. There is an excellent licensed supermarket at
Pondtail Bridges, selling fresh meat and vegetables as well as the usual things – this marks
the eastern extremity of Fleet. Houses and gardens back on to the canal and generally
seem to appreciate it being there. A canoe slalom course is marked and there are some
moored craft. Shops are close at hand to the north west of Reading Road South Bridge.

> **BOAT TRIPS**
> **Basingstoke Canal Canoe Club** Fleet (01276 476760). A useful contact for another type of boating
> very popular on this canal.
> **North East Hants Water Activity Centre** Fleet (01252 621381). Canoeing and rowing for the disabled
> with specially adapted boats and hoists as required.

● **Fleet**
Hants. EC Wed. All services. Useful for its shops
and services, but little else of interest.
Tourist Information Centre Harlington Centre,
Fleet Road, Fleet. (01252 811151). *Open
09.00–17.00 Mon–Sat.*

● **Crookham Village**
Hants. PO, stores.

● **Dogmersfield**
Hants. A well-preserved village with pretty
thatched and timbered houses.

● **Winchfield**
Hants. Walk north from Barley Mow Bridge to
see the Norman church of St Mary, dating from
c1170. There are three original windows in the
tower, and boldly decorated doorways. The
pulpit (1634) is prettily worked.

Pubs and Restaurants

🍴♟ **Sorrel's Brasserie** Fleet Road, Fleet (01252 613775). Immediately north of Reading Road South Bridge. Comfortable establishment specialising in European cuisine served *L Tue–Fri & D 7 days a week. Also Sun L.* Good value *lunchtime* specials and table d'hôte menu.

🍺 **Hogshead** Fleet Road, Fleet (01252 620198). A remarkable 14 real ales – including Boddingtons, Abroad Cooper, Marston's and Flowers – are available in this committed beer drinkers pub, together with Belgian bottled beers, bottle conditioned beers and real ciders. Bar food is available *daily 12.00–19.00* and there are regular events including beer festivals, music nights, games and tasting sessions. No children or dogs. *Open all day.*

🍺 **Old Emporium** Fleet Road, Fleet (01252 816797). Young persons pub, describing itself as an Ale Café, serving Greene King and guest real ales and an interesting selection of snacks and bar meals *all day.* Vegetarians and children catered for. Garden and patio seating. *Open all day.*

🍺 **Oatsheaf** Crookham Road, Fleet (01252 614700). At the Oatsheaf crossroads, north of Reading Road South Bridge. Tetley's, Burton, Friary Meux and guest real ales and food *lunchtimes* in a large main road pub. Children welcome when eating. Large garden. Quiz *Sun;* student prices *Tue* and bingo *Wed.* B & B. *Open all day.*

🍺 **Fox & Hounds** Crookham Road, Crookham (01252 615980). A friendly pub with a large canalside garden and landing stage. Courage and guest real ales, *lunchtime* snacks and family room. Darts, dominoes and cards. The Folk Club meets here *every Tue. Open all day Fri & Sat.* ♟

🍺🍴 **Chequers** Crookham (01252 615336). North of Crookham Wharf. Wide ranging menu includes an à la carte selection in the restaurant and a variety of snacks and meals (including a children's menu) in the bar *lunchtimes and evenings, 7 days a week.* Badgers, Fuller's, Hall & Woodhouse and guest real ales can be enjoyed in a quiet relaxed atmosphere. Garden and children's play area. Darts and dominoes. *Mon* informal singles club; *Thur* quiz and food theme nights *monthly, on Fri.*

🍺 **Black Horse** The Street, Crookham Village (01252 616434). A smart village local serving Courage, Hogs Back, Wadworth and guest real ales together with inexpensive *lunchtime* bar meals *Mon–Sat.* Garden with children's play area. Darts and dominoes. Quiz *winter Sun.*

🍺 **Queen's Head** Dogmersfield (01252 613531). A lovely sign announces the presence of this fine 17thC country pub, where Catherine of Aragon met Arthur, Henry VIII's brother. Courage and guest real ales and an extensive range of food *lunchtimes and evenings.* Children and vegetarians catered for. Small garden.

🍺🍴 **Barley Mow** The Hurst, Winchfield (01252 617490). Large country pub, with an intriguing central fireplace, serving Ushers and Courage real ales and meals *lunchtimes and evenings, 7 days a week.* Children and vegetarians catered for. Garden. Draughts, dominoes and darts, and the home of the local cricket team.

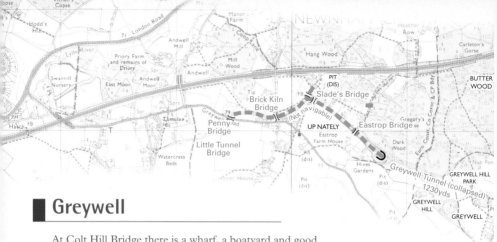

Greywell

At Colt Hill Bridge there is a wharf, a boatyard and good moorings. The course of the canal now becomes more open as it makes its approach to Greywell Tunnel. The few houses and gardens of North Warnborough are followed by a lift bridge, beyond which is the limit of navigation for cruisers, by Odiham Castle. It is then just a short walk to the eastern portal of the collapsed Greywell Tunnel (1230yds), passing the remains of Lock 30. This was built to raise the water level above here by 12ins, to give increased draft and aid navigation. A footpath leads over the tunnel portal to Greywell village, and the Fox & Goose pub. It is possible to follow paths over Greywell Hill to see what remains of the western entrance to the tunnel and a short isolated stretch of the canal passing the village of Up Nately. Greywell Tunnel is, of course, famous for its colony of some 12,500 bats, including the largest known colony of the Natterer's bat.

NAVIGATIONAL NOTES

1 The lift bridge at North Warnborough is operated with a BW sanitary station key.
2 The limit of navigation is a few yards beyond Odiham Castle. Do not attempt to take your boat any further than this. *Turn here.*

TRIP BOATS

John Pinkerton This is a 50-seater boat operated by the S & HCS for public trips and private charter *Easter–Oct.* Telephone (01962) 713564 for details.
Mildred Stocks is a 12-seater dayboat, able to take up to five wheelchairs, designed for the disabled and based at Odiham. Bookings and further details on (01252) 621501/622520.
Madame Butterfly is a 7 berth, 63ft long, broad beam holiday boat fitted with wheelchair lifts fore and aft. Based at Odiham. Bookings and further details on (01252) 621501/622520.

Boatyards

Ⓑ **Galleon Marine** Colt Hill Bridge, Odiham (01256 703691). ⛽ 🛒 D E Pump-out, gas, narrow boat hire, day hire craft, overnight mooring (by arrangement), winter storage, slipway, chandlery, books, maps and gifts, boat sales and repairs, engine sales and repairs (especially outboards), telephone, DIY facilities, solid fuel (by arrangement).

Ⓑ **Wendy's Pleasure Boats** Colt Hill Bridge, Odiham (01256 703691). Hire of rowing boats, canoes and punts by the hour, or longer. Tea, coffee and refreshments.

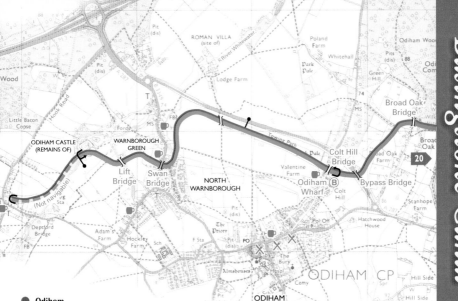

● **Odiham**
*Hants. PO, tel, stores, butcher, off-licence, take
aways, chemist, bakery.* It's a pleasant walk up
the road from Colt Hill Bridge, past May's
Model Cottages (1862) to the broad High
Street, rich with 17th and 18thC buildings.

● **North Warnborough**
Hants. PO, tel, stores. A group of attractive
houses, some thatched and dating from the
15th century. There is no church, the village
being virtually an extension of Odiham.

Odiham (King John's) Castle
Dating from 1207, this picturesque pile of
flint is all that remains of the only octagonal
keep in England, a three-storeyed building used
by King John as a stopping place between
Windsor and Winchester.

● **Greywell**
Hants. A village of charming red-brick houses
around the pub and tunnel entrance.

Pubs and Restaurants

🍴 ✕ **Water Witch** Colt Hill Bridge, Odiham
(01256 702778). A comfortable beamed pub
decorated with canal artefacts and with a vast
waterside garden with animals for children.
Excellent food *lunchtimes and evenings.* Family
room and good moorings. *Open all day Sat & Sun.*

✕ ♟ **Kings** 65 High Street, Odiham (01256
702559/703811). Smart restaurant in a
converted pub, serving Peking and Szechuan
cuisine – not cheap, but good value. *Closed Sun
and Mon L.* Take away service.

✕ ♟ **La Forêt** High Street, Odiham (01256
702697). Family run restaurant specialising in
French and modern European cuisine using only
fresh produce, bought in daily. *Open L Sun–Fri
& D Mon–Sat.* Children's menu and crèche
available *Sun L.*

🍴 ✕ **George Hotel** High Street, Odiham (01256
702081). A handsome 16thC hotel with a
Georgian façade. Inside are beams and an
Elizabethan fireplace taken from Old Basing
House. Bar food and real ales. Restaurant special-
ising in seafood. *Open L Mon–Fri & D Tue–Sat.*

✕ ♟ **Grapevine Bistro & Restaurant** 121 High

Street, Odiham (01256 701122). *Open L
Mon–Fri & D Mon–Sat.* Welcoming establishment with an interesting menu. Bargain meals
available 18.00–19.30. Vegetarian dishes and
children's portions. Non-smoking.

🍴 ✕ **Swan** At Swan Bridge, North
Warnborough (01256 702727). A dark, cosy
local dating from the 16thC with a log fire,
serving Courage, Ushers and guest real ales and
a varied menu (including vegetarian) of home-
made food *lunchtimes and evenings.* Garden with
children's play area. *Open all day.*

🍴 **Anchor** The Street, North Warnborough.
(01256 702740). A cheerful 18thC village
pub offering Courage and guest real ales and
inexpensive food *lunchtimes and evenings. Open
all day Fri & Sat.*

🍴 **Fox & Goose** Greywell Street, Greywell
(01256 702062). Comfortable beamed pub
with a log fire, serving Ushers and Courage real
ales together with traditional bar food *lunchtimes
and evenings.* Large garden with children's play
area. Regular venue for hot air balloon launch-
ing. No children in the bar.

KENNET & AVON CANAL

MAXIMUM DIMENSIONS	MILEAGE
Bath to Hanham Lock	*READING to*
Length: 75'	Aldermaston Wharf: 10 miles
Beam: 16'	Tile Mill Lock: 8 miles
Headroom: 8' 9"	Newbury Lock: 18^1/$_2$ miles
Reading to Newbury	Kintbury: 24^1/$_2$ miles
Length: 70'	Hungerford: 27^1/$_2$ miles
Beam: 14'	Crofton Top Lock: 35 miles
Headroom: 7' 9"	Pewsey Wharf: 41^1/$_2$ miles
Newbury to Bath	Devizes Top Lock: 53^1/$_2$ miles
Length: 70'	Bradford-on-Avon: 65^1/$_2$ miles
Beam: 12'	Dundas Aqueduct: 70 miles
Headroom: 7'	Bath, junction with River Avon: 75^1/$_4$ miles
or	*HANHAM* Lock (start of tidal section): 86^1/$_2$ miles
Length: 72'	Bristol Docks: 93 miles
Beam: 7'	*AVONMOUTH* entrance to Severn
Headroom: 7'	Estuary: 100^3/$_4$ miles
MANAGER	Locks: 104
(01380) 722859	

The Kennet & Avon Canal is one of the most splendid lengths of artificial waterway in Britain, a fitting memorial to the canal age as a whole. It is a broad canal, cutting across southern England from Reading to Bristol. Its generous dimensions and handsome architecture blend well with the rolling downs and open plains that it passes through, and are a good reminder of the instinctive feeling for scale that characterised most 18th and early 19thC civil engineering.

The canal was built in three sections. The first two were river navigations, the Kennet from Reading to Newbury, and the Avon from Bath to Bristol, both being canalised. Among early 18thC river navigations the Kennet was one of the most ambitious, owing to the steep fall of the river. Between Reading and Newbury 20 locks were necessary in almost as many miles, as the difference in level is 138ft. John Hore was the engineer for the Kennet Navigation, which was built between 1718 and 1723 and included 11 miles of new cut. Subsequently Hore was in charge of the Bristol Avon Navigation, carried out between 1725 and 1727. These river navigations were interesting in many ways, often because of the varied nature of the country they passed through. The steep-sided Avon Gorge meant that a fast-flowing river had to be brought under control. Elsewhere the engineering was unusual: for example the turf-sided locks on the Kennet, now partially replaced with brick structures.

For the third stage, a canal from Newbury to Bath was authorised in 1794. Rennie was appointed engineer, and after a long struggle the canal was opened in 1810, completing a through route from London to Bristol. The canal is 57 miles long, and included 79 broad locks, a summit level at Savernake 452ft above sea level and one short tunnel, also at Savernake. Rennie was both engineer and architect, anticipating the role played by Brunel in the creation of the Great Western Railway; in some ways his architecture is the more noteworthy aspect of his work. The architectural quality of the whole canal is exceptional, from the straightforward stone bridges to the magnificent neo-classical aqueducts at Avoncliffe and Limpley Stoke. Rennie's solution to the anticipated water supply problems on the top pound was to build a 4312yd tunnel, thereby providing a reservoir 15 miles long. The company called in William Jessop to offer a second – and hopefully cheaper solution – and it was he who suggested a shorter tunnel in conjunction with a steam pumping engine. This resulted in a saving of £41,000 and a completion date 2 years earlier. In some places the canal bed was built over porous rock, and so leaked constantly, necessitating further regular pumping.

Nevertheless, the canal as a whole was a striking achievement. West of Devizes the waterway descends Caen Hill in a straight flight of 16 locks. In total 29 locks are navigated within two miles of Devizes. The many swing bridges were designed to run on ball bearings, one of the first applications of the principle. The bold entry of the canal into Bath, a sweeping descent round the south of the city, is a firm expression of the belief that major engineering works should contribute to the landscape, whether urban or rural, instead of imposing themselves upon it as so often happens nowadays. Later the Kennet & Avon Canal Company took over the two river navigations, thus gaining control of the whole through route. However traffic was never as heavy as the promoters had expected, and so the canal declined steadily throughout the 19thC. It suffered from early railway competition as the Great Western Railway duplicated its route, and was eventually bought by that railway company. Maintenance standards slipped, and this, combined with a rapidly declining traffic, meant that navigation was difficult in places by the end of the 1914–18 war. The last regular traffic left the canal in the 1930s, but still it remained open, and the last through passage was made in 1951 by *nb. Queen*, with the West Country artist P. Ballance on board. Subsequently the canal was closed, and for a long time its future was in jeopardy. However, great interest in the canal had resulted in the formation of a Canal Association shortly after the 1939–45 war, to fight for restoration. In 1962 the Kennet & Avon Canal Trust was formed out of the Association, and practical steps towards restoration were under way. Using volunteers to raise funds from all sources, and with steadily increasing inputs from BW, the trust has catalysed the reopening of the entire navigation as a through route from Reading to Bristol. This achievement was commemorated on 8th August 1990, with HM The Queen navigating through Lock 43, at the summit of the Caen Hill flight, which now bears her name. However, this must be seen as very much a beginning and not an end. Water supplies to the long pounds and the summit level have still to be secured by a combination of back pumping on several lock flights and the sealing of the remaining areas of porous canal bed. This will require substantial capital expenditure by BW and the trust, while the waterway will always incur considerable ongoing running costs. Basic facilities, such as water and pump-outs, are becoming much more readily available in response to a steadily increasing demand. The Caen Hill back pumping scheme was completed in 1996 and, despite the dry summer, it not only kept pace with demand but also managed to raise the level in the Long Pound above the flight. It is anticipated that the necessary resources will be found to upgrade pumps at Bath and install a new system at Wootton Rivers. This will support a strategy of moving water from the west end of the navigation through to the top pound, thereby taking the pressure off Crofton and the Wilton Water supply. These funds will also be deployed towards bed sealing measures – in the Bath area and in the Long Pound above Devizes – and in a wide range of upgraded facilities throughout the waterway, for the benefit of all users.

Today the Kennet & Avon Canal benefits from a unique funding regime sharing contributions from a partnership made up of BW, the Canal Trust and a consortium of local authorities. The pattern of capital expenditure therefore differs markedly from that incurred on other inland waterways in the sole control of BW. Priorities reflect, perhaps, broader needs. Yet undoubtedly this partnership is an outstanding success, well on the way to providing a superb amenity unfettered by previous water supply problems aided by a successful Heritage Lottery Fund bid.

Reading

The River Kennet leaves the Thames east of Reading. The mouth of the river is marked by a gasometer and the main railway, which runs parallel to the south bank of the Thames. The Kennet leads south west towards the centre of Reading, passing Blake's Lock (0118 957 2251), the only lock maintained by the Thames Conservancy that is not actually on the Thames. A variety of new developments complement the river's passage through this section of the town. The Kennet through Reading is narrow, shallow and fast flowing, being a river navigation; also there are several sharp blind bends in the town, so great care in navigation is needed. This section is controlled by traffic lights – boaters should not proceed until a green light is displayed. Keep a sharp lookout for other boats and remember to allow for the flow of the river. The river cuts across the middle of the town, and so access to all facilities is easy. Rows of riverside cottages and a surprising variety of bridges decorate the Kennet in Reading, High Bridge being the most central access point. The Kennet passes over a weir with County Lock adjoining. The weirs are a feature of river navigation that should be treated with respect, as the current

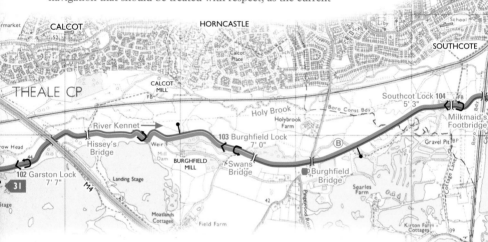

they create can often affect the course of a boat, especially when making a slow approach to a lock. The river gradually leaves the town, passing through Fobney Meadow to Fobney Lock. Continuing west, the navigation passes Burghfield Bridge, a handsome stone arch. The Kennet winds through water meadows, the straight stretches marking the canal sections. The M4 motorway and the railway inevitably affect the peace and quiet of this section, although the country to the south of the Kennet improves steadily as it progresses westwards. Berkshire is well known as orchard country.

Boatyards

There are currently no boatyards on the Kennet & Avon in Reading. For details of boatyards on the River Thames see page 144. **Reading Marine Co,** previously based in the town and now relocated at Aldermaston Wharf, retain some long-term moorings in

Reading. Telephone (0118) 971 3666 for further details.
Ⓑ **Kennet Cruises** 14 Beech Lane, Earley, Reading (0118 987 1115). 🚽 🚾 ⛽ Pump-out, narrow boat hire, day hire craft, overnight mooring, long-term mooring.

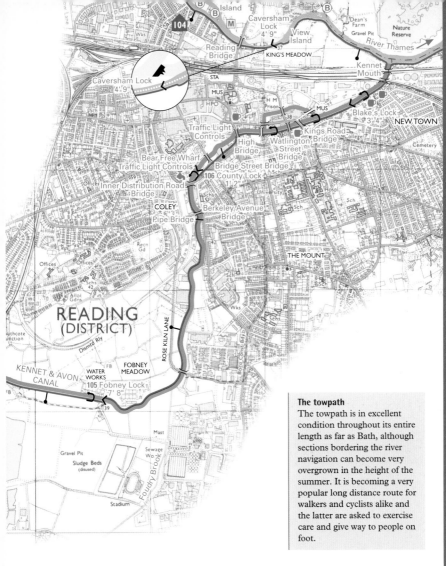

The towpath
The towpath is in excellent condition throughout its entire length as far as Bath, although sections bordering the river navigation can become very overgrown in the height of the summer. It is becoming a very popular long distance route for walkers and cyclists alike and the latter are asked to exercise care and give way to people on foot.

NAVIGATIONAL NOTES

1 The Kennet & Avon Canal locks require windlasses of an intermediate gauge – $1^1/8$ in instead of the normal 1in or $1^1/4$ in.
2 **Fobney Lock** – care should be taken when using the landing stage below the lock as a strong weir stream flows at right angles.
3 Certain locks need to be left empty. Observe instructions on lock beams.
4 Good overnight moorings can be found in Reading on the backwater along Chestnut Walk and the prison.
5 River Thames licences are obtainable from: Environment Agency, Kings Meadow House, Kings Meadow Road, Reading, RG1 8DQ.
6 Short-term BW and Thames licences can be obtained from Blake's Lock *Apr–Oct.*

Aldermaston Swing bridge (see page 30)

BOAT TRIPS

Kennet Cruises operate *Sun* boat trips *Easter–mid Sep* from The Cunning Man, Burghfield Bridge to Garston and back. Also *Wed mid Jul–Aug* and special, longer cruises, during summer months. Telephone (0118) 987 1115 for further details.

● Reading

Berks. MD Wed, Thur, Fri & Sat. All services.
The town lies at the extremity of the Berkshire Downs and the Chiltern Hills, where the Thames becomes a major river. It is the Victorian architecture that makes this town interesting, as the university buildings are not to everyone's taste. Canal walkers in Reading will find there is no towing path in the centre of town; however, west of Reading the whole canal is a public right of way.

Abbey Ruins Fragmentary remains of this 12thC abbey built by Henry I lie on the edge of Forbury Park. The 13thC gatehouse, altered by Scott in 1869, still stands.

Blake's Lock Museum Gas Works Road, off Kenavon Drive, Reading (0118 939 0918). Beside Blake's Lock. Housed in a handsome pumping station built in the 1870s, the museum depicts all aspects of navigation in and around

Reading. There are also reconstructions of a printer's workshop, a bakery and a barber's shop, and displays of local industry. Shop. *Open Tue–Fri 10.00–17.00; Sat, Sun & B. Hol Mon 14.00–17.00.* Free. Temporary mooring for visitors. Disabled access.

Film Theatre PO Box 217, Palmer Building, Whiteknights, Reading (0118 986 8497). Imaginative programme of non-mainstream cinema, showing approximately 4 times a week. Visit Tourist Information for up-to-date details.

Foxhill World of Carriages Visitor Centre, Spencers Wood, Basingstoke Road, Reading (0118 988 3334). Large collection of horse drawn carriages, horses and ponies, many of which have featured in films and popular television series. Also a dairy display, wheel-wright's shop and sleigh collection. *Open daily 10.00–17.00.* Charge. Buses from the centre of Reading.

The Gaol Forbury Road. Designed by Scott and Moffatt in 1842–4 in the Scottish Baronial style. Oscar Wilde wrote his *Ballad of Reading Gaol* while imprisoned here.

Hexagon Queen's Walk, Reading (0118 959 1591). Mainstream theatre, pantomime, films, shows and art exhibitions.
Encore Café Bar *open Mon–Sat 10.00–17.00 & 1¹/2 hours before evening shows.* Inexpensive, home-made food.

Museum of English Rural Life University of Reading, White Knights, Reading (0118 931 8663). A fascinating collection of relics of old English agriculture, and a small display of painted canal ware with a set of tools used for making narrow boats. *Open Tue–Sat 10.00–13.00 & 14.00–16.30. Closed Sun, Mon & B.Hols.* Charge.

Museum of Reading The Town Hall, Blagrave Street, Reading (0118 939 9800). Victorian replica of the Bayeux Tapestry, an exceptional natural history and local archaeology collection, together with the history of Reading's development through the ages. Also prehistoric collection. All set in the magnificent red and grey brick Town Hall. Shop and excellent meals and refreshments in the 3Bs Café Bar *Mon–Sat. Opening as per Blake's Lock Museum.* Free. Disabled access.

21 South Street The Hexagon, Queen's Walk, Reading (0118 950 4911). A wide-ranging programme of music (all types), workshops and drama in a lively arts centre which also incorporates:
Macdevitt's Bar (0118 956 8155). *Open for drinks and home-cooked food Mon–Sat, lunchtimes and evenings.* Disabled access.

Reading Buses (0118 959 4000). Information on urban and rural services.

Tourist Information Centre The Town Hall, Blagrave Street, Reading (0118 956 6226). *Open Mon–Fri 10.00–17.00 & Sat 10.00–16.00.*

Pubs and Restaurants

🍺 **Jolly Angler** Kennetside, Reading (0118 926 1666). East of Blake's Lock. There is a quaint façade to this pub which marks the last refreshment point before the Thames. Ruddles and guest real ales, *lunchtime* bar snacks, riverside patio, children welcome. Quiz *Sun*. Darts, dominoes and pool. No dogs. *Open all day.*

🍺 **Fisherman's Cottage** Kennetside, Reading (0118 957 1553). A pretty 18thC canalside pub, west of Blake's Lock, serving Fuller's real ale. Food *lunchtimes and evenings.* Garden. Children welcome. Open fires. *Open all day Fri & Sat.*

🍺 **Lyndhurst Ale House** Queen's Road, Reading (0118 957 4615). South of Watlington Street Bridge. Whitbread, Flowers, Boddingtons and guest real ales, inexpensive food *lunchtimes Mon–Sat.* Patio seating. Quiz *Wed. Open all day.*

🍺 ✗ **Ben's Bar & Thai Restaurant** King's Bridge, Reading (0118 959 6169). A modern canalside establishment serving Fuller's real ale and an enticing range of inexpensive Thai cooking *L (12.00–14.30) & D (18.00–22.00).* Take away service. *Open all day.*

🍺 **Dove** 119 Orts Road, Reading (0118 935 2556). Behind Reading College. Friendly, welcoming pub serving Brakspear real ale and *weekday lunchtime food.* Pub games. Irish folk music *Wed* and blues *Thurs. Open all day Sat.*

🍺 **Hobgoblin** 2 Broad Street, Reading (0118 950 8119). Constantly changing range of real ales including a selection from Wychwood. Real cider. No children. Non-smoking area. *Open all day except Sun Nov–Easter.*

🍺 **Hop Leaf** 163–165 Southampton Street, Reading (0118 931 4700). Hop Back Real ales and snacks *Mon–Fri until 19.00* together with a brewhouse at the rear (resurrected from a derelict Courage house) and now a thriving town local. Children's room and traditional pub games. *Open all day.* .

🍺 **Horn** St Mary's Butts, Reading (0118 957 4794). North of Bridge Street Bridge. Listed 16thC timber-framed pub serving Courage, Theakston and John Smith's real ales together with home-made bar food *lunchtimes, evenings and all day Sat & Sun.* Patio, darts and crib. No children. *Open all day.*

🍺 **Sweeney & Todd** 10 Castle Street (off St Mary's Butts), Reading (0118 958 6466). Something of a local institution – a pub integrated with a pie shop and dispensing Wadworth, Adnams, Eldridge Pope and guest real ales. Excellent, inexpensive food *lunchtimes and evenings. Open all day, closed Sun evening.*

🍺 ✗ **Cunning Man** Burghfield Bridge, near Reading (0118 959 0771). A Harvester pub with large canalside garden and children's play area. Bass real ale. Food *lunchtimes and evenings.* Children and vegetarians catered for.

✗ **Bridge Café** Burghfield, near Reading. Opposite the Cunning Man. *Open all day* for breakfast, snacks, meals and take aways.

Aldermaston

At Theale there is the first of the swing bridges that occur along the Kennet & Avon Canal. Fortunately, since the completion of the M4, this bridge has reverted to carrying relatively infrequent road vehicles, so the passage of a boat no longer causes a major traffic hold-up. Make sure that you close the traffic barriers first of all and open them behind you. Theale village is 3/4 mile north of the bridge. After Theale, the Kennet flows steadily through wooded fields towards Sulhamstead and reaches Tyle Mill after a pleasant tree-lined straight cut. The nature reserves of Cumber Lake to the north and Woolwich Green Lake to the south can be reached by a short walk from Sulhamstead Lock. Originally gravel pits excavated since 1960, the lakes offer an undisturbed habitat for all forms of wildlife. The moorings at Tyle Mill are administered by BW. Telephone (01380) 722859 for further details. Leaving Tyle Mill the canal continues south west, constantly joining and leaving the River Kennet. Swing bridges are common, often carrying busy roads. The A4 runs parallel for many miles, but always keeps its distance; the Great Western Railway also runs parallel but much closer.

Boatyards

ⓑ **Reading Marine Co.** Aldermaston Wharf, Padworth, Reading (0118 971 3666). 🛢 🚽 ♿ D Gas, pump-out, narrow boat hire, overnight mooring, long-term mooring (also available in Reading), winter storage, boat sales and repairs, engine sales and repairs, boat building and fitting out, books, maps and gifts, telephone, toilets, RYA international helmsman's certificate courses. *24 hour* emergency call out.

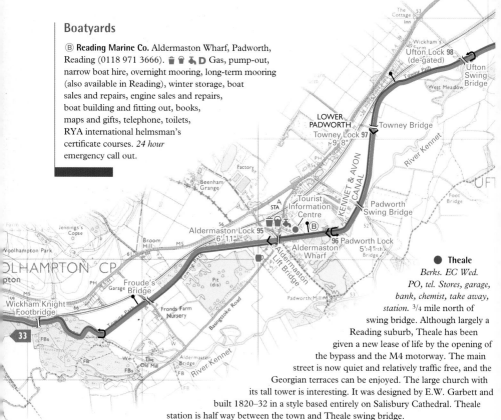

● **Theale**
Berks. EC Wed. PO, tel. Stores, garage, bank, chemist, take away, station. 3/4 mile north of swing bridge. Although largely a Reading suburb, Theale has been given a new lease of life by the opening of the bypass and the M4 motorway. The main street is now quiet and relatively traffic free, and the Georgian terraces can be enjoyed. The large church with its tall tower is interesting. It was designed by E.W. Garbett and built 1820–32 in a style based entirely on Salisbury Cathedral. Theale station is half way between the town and Theale swing bridge.

● **Sulhamstead**
Berks. A scattered village 1/4 mile south east of Tyle Mill, but with no real centre. There are several large houses standing in their own grounds; the most impressive is Folly Farm, built by Lutyens in 1906 in a William and Mary style. In 1912 Lutyens extended the house, this time using a Tudor style. The mixture of the two periods is most successful. The house is *private*.

Ufton Green

Berks. A lush, peaceful hamlet built round a small triangular green. All that remains of the church is one flint wall, standing proudly in the middle of a field,

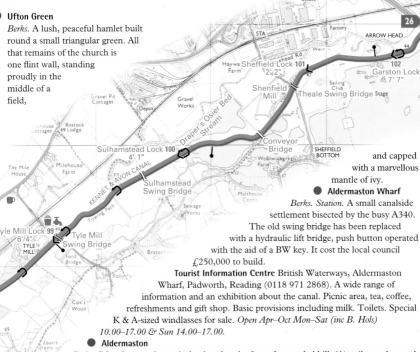

and capped with a marvellous mantle of ivy.

Aldermaston Wharf

Berks. Station. A small canalside settlement bisected by the busy A340. The old swing bridge has been replaced with a hydraulic lift bridge, push button operated with the aid of a BW key. It cost the local council £250,000 to build.

Tourist Information Centre British Waterways, Aldermaston Wharf, Padworth, Reading (0118 971 2868). A wide range of information and an exhibition about the canal. Picnic area, tea, coffee, refreshments and gift shop. Basic provisions including milk. Toilets. Special K & A-sized windlasses for sale. *Open Apr–Oct Mon–Sat (inc B. Hols) 10.00–17.00 & Sun 14.00–17.00.*

Aldermaston

Berks. PO, tel, stores. Attractively placed at the foot of a wooded hill, 1½ miles to the south of Aldermaston Wharf (along a minor road), the village is particularly fine. Mellow brick houses of all periods face each other across the sloping main street, which has survived the inroads of traffic. At the top of the street is the pebble dashed church, and Aldermaston Court, a private house containing magnificent 17thC woodwork.

Pubs and Restaurants

The Gathering 41 High Street, Theale (0118 930 3478). Downstairs bar serving real ales and a restaurant above serving *L & D 7 days a week.* Children and vegetarians catered for. Patio seating. *Open all day.*

Falcon High Street, Theale (0118 930 2523). An 18thC pub serving Courage, Archers and Young's real ales. *Lunchtime* bar food. Traditional pub games and garden. *Open all day.*

Red Lion 5 Church Street, Theale (0118 930 2394). Flowers and guest real ales together with inexpensive bar food *lunchtimes and evenings, 7 days a week (not Mon evening).* Children and vegetarians welcome. Patio seating. Darts, skittle alley, dominoes, crib and shove ha'penny. *Open all day.*

Crown Inn Church Street, Theale (0118 930 2310). Wethered and Flowers real ales and *lunchtime food (not Sun).* Children and vegetarians catered for. Garden and children's play area. Skittle alley, darts, dominoes and pool. *Open all day.*

Mulligan's Fish and Chips Restaurant and

Oyster Bar Bath Road, Sulhamstead (0118 930 2310). Half mile north of Tyle Mill. Unusual establishment serving a fish-based menu in comfortable, old world surroundings, *L & D.*

Butt Inn Aldermaston Wharf (0118 971 2129). Boddingtons, Butts and Flowers real ales together with a full menu served *lunchtimes and evenings, 7 days a week.* Children and vegetarians catered for. Garden with animals including goats, chickens and rabbits. Pool, dominoes and crib. Quiz *winter Thur* and music *winter weekends. Open all day in summer.*

Hind's Head Aldermaston (0118 971 2194). An imposing building which faces up the main street. Formerly The Congreve Arms, until it changed hands following the devastation of a great fire. The Hind's Head once brewed its own beer, selling at 2d a pint; now Fuller's, Courage and guest real ales are served from the bar. The pub also offers good food in both bar and attractive dining room, catering for children and vegetarians. Garden, children welcome. B & B.

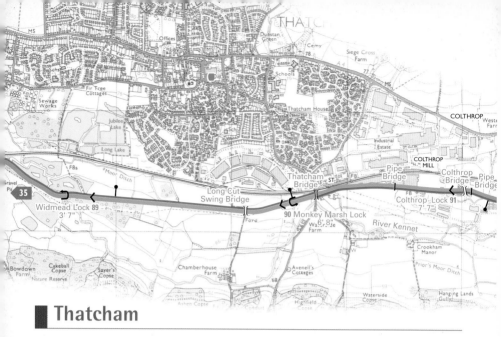

Thatcham

Thatcham station is conveniently beside the canal; a hotel is nearby. The village itself is a mile to the north west. The canal now flows very straight through isolated water meadows under a railway bridge to Bull's Lock. This section of canal probably best serves to illustrate the wide variety of work jointly undertaken by a consortium made up of County and District Councils, Manpower Services job creation programmes, British Waterways and the Kennet & Avon Canal Trust, who have been at the forefront of fund raising for more than 30 years. For example, Heale's Lock to the east and Bull's Lock to the west have both been rebuilt with consortium labour, while Widmead Lock has been reconstructed to a very high standard by outside contractors at a cost in excess of £385,000. The many swing bridges have either been totally rebuilt or, in some cases, replaced by a high level structure: Colthrop Bridge being privately funded. Old Monkey Marsh Lock, one of only two remaining examples of a turf-sided lock, has been listed as an ancient monument by English Heritage. It is now restored with iron piling to two feet above low water level, turf-lined banks sloping to the top of the lock, together with a timber framework to delineate the actual lock chamber when full. The lock should be left *empty* after use.

NAVIGATIONAL NOTES

Woolhampton Lock The current below the lock can cause problems, therefore, when approaching **upstream** set the lock before swinging the bridge, head into the current, turning into the lock at the last moment. When coming **downstream** swing the bridge before leaving the tail of the lock and aim straight for the skewed bridge. **Ensure that the bridge is fully open.**

● **Woolhampton**
Berks. PO, tel, stores, garage, station. A village on the A4 that owes its existence to the days of mail coaches on the old Bath road. There is a good mixture of buildings in the main street, several pubs and hotels. Up on the hill to the north of the village are the Victorian church, the Georgian buildings of Woolhampton Park and Douai Abbey and School, the latter a fine group of 19thC buildings with more recent additions.

● **Thatcham**
Berks. EC Wed. All services. The main square of this rapidly expanding village, now almost a suburb of Newbury, is all but dominated by sprawling housing development. Set back from the A4, it manages to retain some peace which carries over into the nearby cluster of older buildings grouped at the east end of the pretty Victorian church and churchyard.

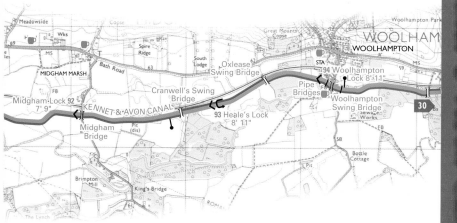

Nature Discovery Centre Muddy Lane, Lower Way, Thatcham (01635 874381). North of Widmead Lock. A centre for the study of the unique lake and reed bed habitats of the area; rare butterflies and large Reed and Sedge Warbler populations. A multi-activity base where children (and adults) can make their own discoveries and the chance to get a bird's eye view of the world. *Open in term time Tue–Fri 12.00–15.00 (10.00–16.00 during school holidays except Xmas) & weekends 12.00–17.00. Seasonal adjustments – telephone for details.*

Pubs and Restaurants

🍺✕ **Row Barge** Station Road, Woolhampton. Popular canalside pub offering both restaurant and bar food, *lunchtimes and evenings, 7 days a week.* Vegetarians and children catered for. Real ales include John Smith's, Fuller's, Brakspear, Greene King and Courage. Large garden.

🍺 **Falmouth Arms** Bath Road, Woolhampton (0118 971 3202). Eldridge Pope real ale and bar food *lunchtimes and evenings, 7 days a week.* Vegetarians and children catered for. Darts. Garden.

🍺✕ **Angel Inn** Bath Road, Woolhampton (0118 971 3307). An imposing ivy-clad building in the centre of the village. The pub serves a variety of guest beers along with Boddingtons, Flowers and Marston's real ales. There is a wide range of food, including vegetarian, served *lunchtimes and evenings,* in both the bar and restaurant, including Sunday lunch. Garden, children welcome. Pool, scrabble, dominoes and backgammon. Quiz *last Sun in month. Open all day.*

🍺 **Old Chequers** Thatcham (01635 861233).

Comfortable old pub, popular with young people, serving Tetley's and Burton real ales. *Open all day.*

🍺 **Kings Head** Thatcham (01635 862145). Courage and Theakston real ales and *lunchtime* bar snacks *Mon–Sat.* Garden and children's play area. Darts, crib and dominoes. Music *Sat & Sun.* B & B. *Open all day Thur–Sat.*

🍺 **White Hart** High Street, Thatcham. A choice of real ales including Courage and Wadworth in this old coaching inn, dating back more than 350 years. Excellent home-cooked food served *lunchtimes and evenings,* all reasonably priced. Vegetarians catered for and children welcome if eating. Patio. *Open all day Mon–Fri.*

🍺 **Crickets** High Street, Thatcham (01635 862113). Ushers, Courage, John Smith's and Fuller's real ales in a pub that takes sport very seriously: three rugby teams, a cricket and a football team are all based at this establishment. For the more sedentary there are darts, dominoes, pool and crib. *Open all day.*

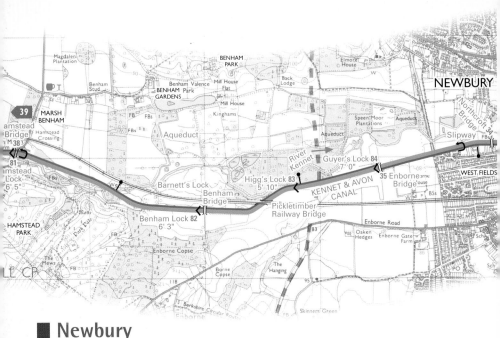

Newbury

The navigation enters Newbury under a handsome new road bridge. Just beside this bridge is Newbury Wharf, where there is a stone building used by the K & A Canal Trust as an information centre and shop, and old warehouses, which have been ingeniously converted into bus station buildings. This large wharf used to be the terminus of the Kennet Navigation from Reading, before the Kennet & Avon Canal Company extended it to link up with the Avon at Bath. There are plans to recreate a basin in this area. West of the wharf the channel gets narrower and faster until it reaches a splendid stone balustraded bridge. Just beyond is Newbury Lock. The river cuts right through the town, and the town makes the most of it. West of the lock is the delightful, quiet West Mills area, where rows of terraced houses face the navigation, where there are extensive moorings. West of Newbury, the navigation again passes through extensive water meadows before the wooded hills of Hamstead Park close in from the south.

NAVIGATIONAL NOTES

The lower cill at Bull's Lock is shallow. Take care through bottom gates.

Boatyards

ⓑ **Newbury Boat Co.** Greenham Lock Cottage, Newbury (01635 42884). 🛥 🛢 🔧 D E Pump-out, gas, overnight mooring, long-term mooring, slipway, books and maps, boat and engine repairs (including outboards), dry dock, wet dock, DIY facilities, toilet, telephone. *24 hour* emergency call out. The boatyard is divided between three sites:

Greenham Island to the west; Ham Lock to the east and the main office and workshop on the central site at Greenham Lock cottage. For basic services – diesel, pump-out, etc – boaters should go to Greenham Island. Long-term moorings are located at Ham Lock.

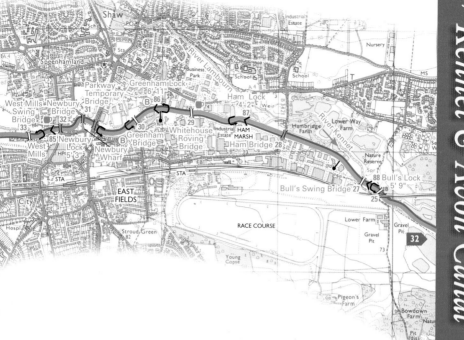

BOAT TRIPS

Kennet Horse Boat Co. 32 West Mills, Newbury, Berks (01635 44154). Horse drawn and motor barge. 2 hour public trips *Mid Apr–Sep* on the motor barge *Avon* from Newbury Wharf. Also 1½ hour trips on the horse drawn boat *Kennet Valley* operating from Kintbury. Telephone for further details. Booking essential.

● **Newbury**

Berks. MD Tue Thur Sat. All services.
Newbury developed in the Middle Ages as a cloth town of considerable wealth, its stature indicated by the size of the church. Although the cloth trade has long vanished, the town has managed to retain much of its period charm. It is a busy shopping centre, and the shop fronts in the main streets have buried many 17th and 18thC houses. Elsewhere in the town the 18thC is well in evidence, especially in the West Mills area. There are fine almshouses, and a pretty ornamental stone bridge over the navigation. There are also signs of the agricultural importance of Newbury: the 19thC Italianate Corn Exchange, for example (see below).
1st Battle of Newbury, 20 Sep 1643 Site of Wash Farm off A343. 1¾ miles south of Guyer's Lock. The Royalists were defeated by the Parliamentarians in one of the

bloodiest onslaughts of the Civil War. Guyer's and Higg's Locks are named after troop commanders in the battle.
2nd Battle of Newbury, 28 Oct 1644
Donnington Castle, Donnington. 1½ miles north of Newbury Lock off the A34. The Royalists were in possession of Donnington Castle when the Parliamentarians attacked. Charles' army withdrew to Oxford, but a week later they returned and relieved the castle. There is a reconstruction model of the battle in Newbury Museum.
Corn Exchange Market Place, Newbury (01635 522733). Now sensitively restored, the Corn Exchange offers an extensive range of arts activities – film, theatre, dance, music, comedy and children's events. *Open daily throughout the year.*
District Museum The Wharf, Newbury (01635 30511). Originally built in 1626 as a cloth-weaving workshop to give employment to the

poor, this is one of the most interesting buildings in Newbury. Adjoining is the corn store, once on the edge of the Kennet Wharf. The museum collection illustrates the prehistoric and Saxon history of the region, as well as the medieval and modern. Also a natural history section with an excellent display of moths and butterflies. An audio-visual presentation tells the story of the Battle of Newbury and hot air ballooning. *Open Apr–Sep Mon–Sat 10.00–17.00 & Sun & B. Hols; 13.00–17.00 Oct–Mar Mon–Sat 10.00–16.00. Closed Wed throughout year except during school holidays.* Free.

Kennet & Avon Canal Trust The Wharf, Newbury (01635 30495). Shop and canal information – a place for a chat and the opportunity to find out more about the waterway over a cup of tea. Souvenirs, gifts, ices and refreshments. *Open Easter–Sep daily 10.00–17.00.*

Newbury Fair Northcroft Lane, Northcroft, Newbury. Leave canal at Kennet Bridge. Annual Michaelmas fair held since 1215. *Wed following 11 Oct.*

Newbury Buses (01635 40743). Network of local urban and rural services.

Newbury Racecourse Newbury (01635 40015). *Midweek and weekend racing.* Flat Racing *Apr–Sep* & National Hunt Racing *Oct–Mar.* Charge.

Round Barrow Cemetery Wash Common, near the site of the 1st Battle of Newbury in 1643. Memorial stones to the victims surmount the two smaller mounds.

St Nicholas Church West Mills, Newbury. Borders the canal on the south bank. A large Perpendicular church, built c1500 at the height of Newbury's prosperity as a wool town. Its 17thC pulpit is most unusual.

St Nicholas School Enborne Road, Newbury. By Butterfield, 1859.

Watermill Theatre & Restaurant Bagnor, near Newbury (01635 46044/45834). Enterprising theatre, set in an idyllic location, staging a variety of drama, music and musicals, including world premieres. Also licensed restaurant serving snacks and meals *lunchtimes and evenings.* Telephone for programme. Although 2¹/₂ miles north of the town this makes a rewarding walk or taxi ride.

Wyld Court Rainforest Hampstead Norreys, Thatcham, near Newbury (01635 200221/202444). The opportunity to experience the beauty of rainforest plant life under glass. Three climates featuring different plant species and rainforest creatures. *Open daily (except Xmas Day & Box. Day) Mar–Oct 10.00–17.00 & Nov–Feb 10.00–16.30.* Charge. Bus (Newbury–Reading route) or taxi from Newbury.

Hamstead Park A very fine park bordered by the canal. There used to be a castle here and several interesting buildings adjoin the church on the side of the hill. There is an old watermill by the lock. The hamlet of Hamstead Marshall lies to the south, 1¹/₂ miles from Hamstead Lock.

Tourist Information Centre The Wharf, Newbury (01635 519562). *Open Apr–Sep Mon–Sat 10.00–17.30 (Sat 17.00) & Sun 13.00–17.00; Oct–Mar Mon–Sat 10.00–17.00 (Sat 16.00).*

Woolhampton (see page 32)

Pubs and Restaurants

White House Riverside, Newbury (01635 42614). North east of Whitehouse Bridge. John Smith's, Theakston and guest real ales together with traditional, home-cooked pub food *lunchtimes and evenings, 7 days a week.* Bar snacks *available all day.* Children and vegetarians catered for. Karaoke *Thur* and disco/live bands *Fri & Sat.* Moorings and garden. *Open all day except Sat.*

Old Waggon & Horses Market Place, Newbury (01635 46368). 100yds east of Newbury Bridge. This comfortable pub has a pleasant terrace (with moorings) overlooking the river. Courage real ale and inexpensive *lunchtime* food served *7 days a week.* Pool and darts. Quiz *alternate Thur. Open all day (not Sun).*

Rat & Parrot 137 Bartholomew Street, Newbury (01635 43254). 200yds south of Newbury Bridge. Once the Bricklayers Arms and now more a continental-style café bar than a pub. *Open 09.00–22.00* and serving breakfast *until 11.30.* There is also an interesting and extensive range of snacks and meals served *all day, 7 days a week.* Vegetarian choices. John Smith's, Wadworth and Theakston real ales. Outside patio seating. No children.

Lock Stock & Barrel 104 Northbrook Street, Newbury (01635 42730). Fuller's real ales served in a spacious, riverside pub with an attractive terrace. Food available *lunchtimes and evenings* and coffee served *from 10.00.* Non-smoking area and disabled access. *Open all day.*

Lion West Street (off Northbrook Street), Newbury (01635 528468). Alcoved areas in the bar and jazz memorabilia give this pub a cosy atmosphere set off by the wooden floor. A range of Wadworth real ales together with Hall & Woodhouse and a guest beer are served *lunchtimes, evenings and all day Fri.* Inexpensive, home-cooked food also available. Disabled access.

Catherine Wheel 35 Cheap Street, Newbury (01635 47471). South of Newbury Bridge. A small, town pub offering Courage and Marston's real ales. *All day* bar snacks. Garden, children welcome. *Open all day.*

Hobgoblin Cheap Street, Newbury (01635 47336). 50 yards south of Newbury Bridge. Wychwood real ales; for other details see entry for the Reading Hobgoblin on page 29.

Water Rat Marsh Benham. 1/4 mile north east of Hamstead Lock. Charming pub-cum-restaurant in a thatched estate village near Benham Park. Once the local bakery it now dispenses Brakspear, Wadworth and two guest real ales. An expensive, though appetising menu is served in the bar and restaurant *lunchtimes and evenings, 7 days a week.* Vegetarians and vegans catered for. Emphasis is on the excellent quality food. Attractive garden. Vies with the White Hart, Hamstead Marshall in the standards of excellence of its cuisine.

A horse drawn boat at Kintbury (see page 38)

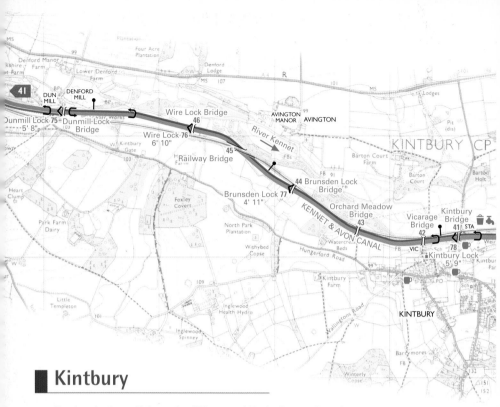

Kintbury

Passing the beautiful woods of Hamstead Park, the canal reaches
Hamstead, Copse, Drewett's and Kintbury Locks. Wooded, rolling hills flank the canal
to the south as it climbs up the locks towards Kintbury, making this a particularly
attractive stretch. The canal enters the village beside the railway, and the Dundas
Arms, which overlooks the lock. The centre of Kintbury is up on the hill to the south of
the lock. Leaving the wharf, the waterway follows the railway, passing the Victorian
Gothic vicarage, and then continues westwards through pleasing open countryside.
The railway and the River Kennet are constantly present, the navigation leaving the
river bed for the last time west of Kintbury. Locks 77 and 76 carry the canal past
Avington, with its Norman church visible among the trees. Pretty woods keep company
with the waterway to the south as it approaches Hungerford, while to the north river
and canal run side by side through water meadows, separated only by a narrow ridge
carrying the towpath. As the diminutive River Kennet accompanies the canal past
Dunmill lock, the towpath turns over to the south bank. From the bridge there is a
good view of Denford Mill.

● **Kintbury**
Berks. PO, tel, stores, station. A quiet village with
attractive buildings by the canal, including a
watermill and canalside pub. The church is originally 13thC, but was restored in 1859; the railway lends excitement, and noise, to the situation.
● **Avington**
Berks. The village is best approached along the

track that runs east from Wire Lock, although
the more adventurous can go directly across the
water meadows, crossing the Kennet on a small
footbridge. The little church is still wholly
Norman, and contains a variety of original work;
the chancel arch, the corbels and the font are
particularly interesting.

NAVIGATIONAL NOTES

Allow for river current when winding and when approaching Copse Lock.

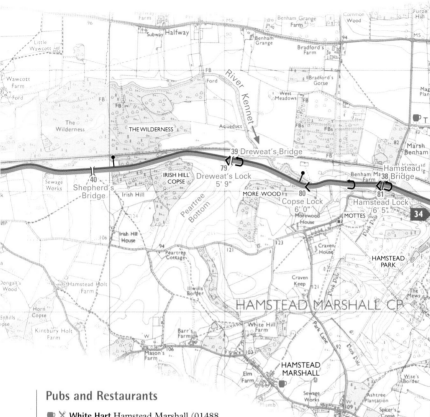

Pubs and Restaurants

🍺 ✗ **White Hart** Hamstead Marshall (01488 658201). 1 mile south of Hamstead Lock – there is a footpath avoiding the road. For superb, classical Italian cuisine from the dedicated owner/chef and a warm welcome this pub is really worth the walk. Not cheap but excellent value for money. Food is available in both the bar and restaurant *L & D, Mon–Sat.* Children and vegetarians catered for. Real ales include Hall & Woodhouse and Wadworth. Log fires in a heavily beamed building, dating from 1684, where tenants once paid their annual dues to the estate. Friendly female ghost. Attractive B & B in converted stables.

🍺 ✗ **Dundas Arms** Kintbury (01488 658263/658559). The River Kennet and the canal flow on either side of this pub, which was named after the Lord Dundas who opened the canal in 1810. Real ales include Bass, Morland and Wells. The restaurant has an interesting French menu and a good wine cellar. Food

available *lunchtimes and evenings except Sun & Mon evening.* Children welcome, canalside garden, B & B.

🍺 **Prince of Wales** Kintbury (01488 658269). 300yds south east of Kintbury Bridge. Courage and guest real ales in a traditional village local with a friendly, welcoming landlord. Inexpensive home-made bar food – *lunchtimes and evenings, 7 days a week* – with tasty pies a speciality – at least three to choose from. Children welcome, garden with play area. Darts, pool and crib. Quiz *Tue.* Open all day Sat.

🍺 **Blue Ball** Kintbury (01488 608126). 500yds south of Kintbury Bridge. Courage and guest real ales. Bar food *lunchtimes and evenings except Tue.* Children's menu. Darts and pool. *Open all day Fri & Sat.*

As the canal enters Hungerford, the Kennet swings away to the north, feeding the trout farm that lies between canal and river. Gardens flank the canal as it comes into the centre of the town and access is easy via the handsome bridge, which leads directly to the wide main street. Leaving Hungerford, the canal passes the old wharf. An original stone warehouse survives, but much of the wharf area has now been built on. West of the wooded 19thC church, the navigation suddenly enters an open landscape.

FROXFIELD

Froxfield Bridge
55

Froxfield Bottom Lock 70
7' 0"

WATERCRESS BEDS

Froxfield Middle Lock 69
6' 11"

FRITH COPSE

Oakhill Down Lock 68
5' 11"

56 Oakhill Down Bridge

OAK HILL

TRINDLEDOWN COPSE

JUGG'S WOOD

57 Fore Bridge

CHISBURY

Little Bedwyn Lock 67
6' 11"

Little Bedwyn Footbridge
LITTLE BEDWYN

58 Little Bedwyn Bridge

HILL FORT

CHISBURY

LITTLE BONNING'S COPSE

CHISBURY WOOD

Potters Lock 66
7' 6"

River Dun

PARLOW BOTTOM

SPAINES

Burnt Mill Lock 65
7' 9"

59 Burnt Mill Footbridge

STROCKERIDGE COPSE

JOCKEY COPSE

GREAT BEDWYN

60 Bedwyn Wharf Bridge

Great Bedwyn Wharf

Bedwyn Church Lock 64
7' 11"

61 Bedwyn Church Bridge

JOCKEY GREEN

62 Mill Bridge

CASTLE COPSE

Beech Grove Lock 63

63 Beech Tree Walk Bridge

103 New Bridge

62

45

NAVIGATIONAL NOTES

Hungerford Marsh Swing Bridge is over Hungerford Marsh Lock. Boats over 30ft long (approx) will have to swing it clear before using the lock.

Water meadows and pasture, rich in buttercups, flank the waterway, which seems to be more river than canal. The railway is in a cutting to the south, and the quiet browsing cattle give a feeling of 18thC rural serenity. The canal is then carried on to an embankment as the wooded hills reappear on both banks, crossing the River Dun on a small brick aqueduct. The railway crosses the waterway west of the aqueduct, and now hugs the north bank for several miles. The roar of the frequent high speed trains to and from the West Country is the only interruption to the natural peace and solitude of the canal. Froxfield lies to the north, flanking the A4; the best access is from the new bridge. This was rebuilt in 1972 during a road improvement scheme using traditional methods and materials, even to the correct colour of brick. Three locks carry the canal past Froxfield, and then the spire of Little Bedwyn Church comes into view, half hidden by trees on the north bank. The village is cut in half by the navigation and the railway. In the centre the lock continues the climb towards the summit. Leaving Little Bedwyn, the waterway continues through a rolling landscape towards its summit, closely accompanied by the railway. To the north is a hill fort, overlooking ridges that break up the farmland. The canal stays on the south side of the valley, a shallow side-cutting carrying it into Great Bedwyn. The village is ranged over the hillside to the north of the waterway, newer houses spilling downwards towards the canal and railway station.

Boatyards

Ⓑ **Bedwyn Boat Services** 6 Church Street, Little Bedwyn (01672 870158). 🛉 Long-term mooring, pump-out – only by arrangement on *Sat morning*.

BOAT TRIPS

Kennet & Avon Canal Trust 1¹/₂ hour trips to Dunmill Lock from Hungerford on *Rose of Hungerford*, *Apr–Oct at weekends, Weds and on B. Hol afternoons*. Also longer *4-hour* trips to Froxfield on *summer evenings*. Available for private charter, up to 50 persons. Details on (01488) 683389.

Hungerford

Berks. EC Thur. MD Tue & Wed. PO, tel, stores, garage, bank, station. Hungerford is built along the A338, which runs through the town southwards from the junction with the A4. The pleasant 18th and 19thC buildings are set back from the road, giving the spacious feeling of a traditional market town. None of the buildings are remarkable, but many are individually pretty. Note the decorative ironwork of the house by the canal bridge. The manor was given to John of Gaunt in 1366, and any monarch passing through the town is given a red rose, the Lancastrian emblem, as a token rent.

Hocktide Ceremonies On the *second Tuesday after Easter*, 99 commoners (those living within the original borough who have the rights of the common and the fishing) are called to the Town Hall by the blowing of a horn. Two Tuttimen are appointed, who have to visit the houses of the commoners to collect a 'head penny' from the men and a kiss from the women: they give oranges in return. All new commoners are then shod by having a nail driven into their shoes. This ceremony dates from medieval times.

Froxfield

Wilts. Tel. The village is ranged along the A4, which has obviously affected its development. The main feature of the village is the Somerset Hospital, a range of almshouses founded by the Duchess of Somerset in 1694, extended in 1775 and again in 1813. Facing onto the road, the hospital is built round a courtyard, which is entered by a Gothic-style gateway, part of the 1813 extension.

Littlecote 1½ miles north of Froxfield. A Tudor building of the 16thC. Littlecote is the most important brick mansion in Wiltshire. The formal front overlooks the gardens that run down to the Kennet. Inside, the Great Hall, the armoury and the Long Gallery are particularly notable.

Little Bedwyn

Wilts. Tel. Divided by the canal, the village falls into two distinct parts. North is the estate village, pretty 19thC terraces of patterned brick running eastwards to the church, half hidden among ancient yew trees. To the south is the older farming village, handsome 18thC buildings climbing the hill away from the canal.

Great Bedwyn

Wilts. PO, tel, stores, garage, station. The main street climbs gently away from the canal and the railway. It is wide, with generous grass verges; attractive houses of all periods line the street. At the top are the pubs. The large church, with its well-balanced crossing tower, is mostly 12th and 13thC; inside are some interesting monuments. The road running westwards to the church passes the Bedwyn Stone Museum, an amazing establishment (see below).

Bedwyn Stone Museum A collection of stone work of all types, showing the work of seven generations of stonemasons. There are statues, tombstones, casts, even the fossilised footprint of a dinosaur. *Open daily.*

Hungerford Marsh

Pubs and Restaurants

Downgate Down View 13 Park Street, Hungerford (01488 682708). 1/4 mile south east of Station Road Footbridge. A full range of Arkell's real ales in a charming little pub overlooking the common. Food available *lunchtimes and evenings (not Sun or Mon evening)*. Garden, open fires *in winter* and traditional pub games.

Railway Tavern Hungerford (01488 683100). 200yds south of Station Road Footbridge. Hall & Woodhouse and Wells real ales together with inexpensive bar meals available *all day, 7 days a week. Sunday* roasts. Garden, children welcome. Darts and pool. Live music on *Fri.*

✕ Three Swans Hotel Hungerford (01488 682721). Resort hotel, south of the canal. Butts and Bass real ales together with restaurant meals *L & D, 7 days a week* and *lunchtime* bar snacks. Afternoon tea. Children and vegetarians catered for. B & B. *Open all day.*

Plume Hungerford (01488 682154). South of the canal. Morland real ale and inexpensive *lunchtime bar food, 7 days a week.* Children and vegetarians catered for. Garden, darts and pool. Music *Fri–Sun. Open all day Sat & Sun.*

John of Gaunt Hungerford (01488 683535). 16thC pub north of the canal, serving Morland and guest real ales. Bar meals available *all day, 7 days a week.* Vegetarians catered for and children's menu. Garden. Dominoes and Jenga, game involving the removal of building blocks from a stack. *Sun* raffle for a gallon of beer. B & B. *Open all day.*

Bear Charnham St, Hungerford (01488 682512). North of canal. Resort hotel with 13thC restaurant serving cordon bleu menu *L & D.* Also *morning* coffee, packed lunches, afternoon tea and bar meals *lunchtimes and evenings.* Visited by several illustrious visitors over the centuries – including Elizabeth I, Henry VIII and Samuel Pepys – this hotel has, today, a very relaxed atmosphere together with charming courtyard and riverside seating. Also an original Parliamentary clock used to time the mail coaches. Bass and guest real ales.

Monthly jazz sessions and a dinner dance in the restaurant on *last Fri in month in winter.* B & B. *Open all day.*

Lamb Charnham St, Hungerford (01488 686390). North of canal. Old Georgian coaching house that now dispenses Ushers real ales and bar food *lunchtimes and evenings, 7 days a week except Mon evening. All day Sun* roasts. Patio seating, darts, pool, cards, crib, dominoes and shove ha'penny. *Regular Fri music.* B & B. *Open all day Sat.*

✕ Pelican Froxfield (01488 682479). On A4, 1/4 mile north west of Froxfield Bridge. Fuller's and guest real ales. A la carte restaurant menu served *L & D* together with bar snacks and meals available *all day, 7 days a week.* Children's menu and outdoor play area. Garden. Pool. Jazz *Sun lunchtime; monthly* music nights and a band/DJ *Fri & Sat until 02.00.* B & B. *Open all day.* Booking advisable *at weekends.*

✕ Harrow Little Bedwyn (01672 870871). In the southern half of the village, serving Hook Norton and guest real ales. This attractively compact pub is owned by the local community and offers an enticing range of English country cooking on separate à la carte and bar menus *L & D (except Sun evening and Mon lunchtime).* Expensive but good value. Vegetarians and children catered for. Attractive garden. *Closed Mon lunchtime. Booking advisable.*

Three Tuns Great Bedwyn (01672 870280). Wadworth and Flowers real ales and real cider. Home-made bar meals available *lunchtimes and evenings except Sun evening.* Children and vegetarians catered for. Garden, darts, crib, dominoes and pool. *Fortnightly* entertainment *Fri/Sat. Open all day Sat & Sun.*

Cross Keys Great Bedwyn (01672 870678). Friendly village centre pub in a terrace dating back to the 18thC serving Bass and Fuller's real ales and bar meals *lunchtimes and evenings, 7 days a week in summer (closed Wed & Thur lunchtime in winter).* Children and vegetarians catered for. Crib, cards and children's games. B & B.

CLOSE(ISH) ENCOUNTERS

Hungerford commoners, anxious to exercise their piscatorial rights (see Hocktide Ceremonies, page 42), should be grateful to have been spared the experience of one Alfred Burtoo. This 78 year old fisherman, whilst casually casting into the nearby Basingstoke Canal one night, was disturbed by the arrival of two figures in green overalls, 4 feet tall, wearing helmets with smoked visors. After pausing for several seconds they beckoned him to follow them, which he did. 'I was curious,' explained Alfred, 'They showed no sign of hostility and at 78, what had I to lose?' He was led along the towpath to a large oval object – 40-50 feet wide – and upon ascending some steps found himself inside an octagonal room. Here he stood until a voice instructed him to stand under an amber light fixed to the cabin wall. He was asked his age and, after a further pause, the voice bade him depart, stating: 'You are too old and infirm for our purpose'.

Burbage Wharf

The canal leaves the village of Great Bedwyn past the church, and enters a wooded stretch that takes it up towards Crofton. The hills encroach more sharply as the summit draws nearer. Crofton appears as the canal starts a wide swing to the north west. The engine house stands on a rise above the canal, its iron-bound chimney making its purpose unmistakable. To the south lies the long expanse of Wilton Water, a dammed valley fed by springs, from which the Crofton pumps draw their supplies. After Crofton the country opens out for a while as the flight of locks continues the final climb to the summit. Then, as the land rises steeply on both banks, it prepares itself for the short Bruce Tunnel. A wooded cutting leads towards the tunnel, taking the canal through the fringes of the Old Savernake Forest. To the north are the extensive parklands of Tottenham House, and Savernake Forest itself. The towpath climbs over the top of the tunnel and, passing under the railway, descends steeply to the navigation.

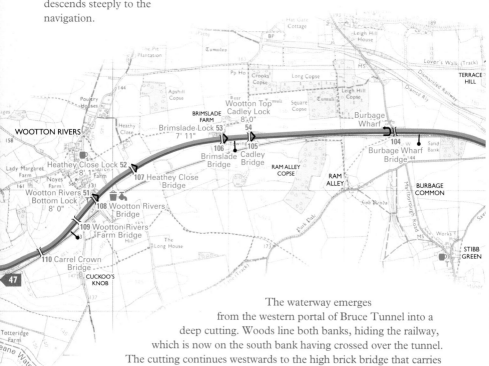

The waterway emerges from the western portal of Bruce Tunnel into a deep cutting. Woods line both banks, hiding the railway, which is now on the south bank having crossed over the tunnel. The cutting continues westwards to the high brick bridge that carries the A346, and then the landscape opens out: the rolling hills still follow the canal, but recede slightly. Immediately after the bridge is Burbage Wharf; several of the original brick canal buildings still stand, attractively converted to domestic use, and a restored wooden wharf crane hangs, a little insecurely, beside the water. Pasture and arable land flank the navigation on its course to the first of the four Wootton Rivers Locks. This flight ends the short summit pound, and starts the long descent towards Bath. By the first lock there is a pretty cottage and garden, while the second is in the middle of Brimslade Farm, whose attractive tile-hung buildings date from the 17thC. The last two locks take the canal to Wootton Rivers; the houses stretch northwards away from the canal, which is overlooked by the church.

● **Wilton**
Wilts. Tel. A compact village at the southern end of Wilton Water, with a pretty duck pond in the centre.
Wilton Windmill Wilton (01672 870427). 1 mile south of the canal, along the footpath at lock 60.

● **Crofton**
Wilts. The scattered village is dominated by the brick pumping station with its separate chimney. It houses two 19thC steam engines, one built in 1812 by Boulton and Watt, the oldest original working beam engine in the world, the other in 1845 by Harvey's of Hayle, Cornwall. Both have been restored to working order, and are steamed on several weekends in the year. The pumping station and the engines are open for viewing *daily Easter–Oct 10.30– 17.00.* For details of

'steaming' weekends – which are *approximately once a month Easter–Aug* – telephone (01672) 870300.
Bruce Tunnel Named in honour of Thomas Bruce, Earl of Ailesbury. 502yds with the remains of the chains on the walls, which were used to pull boats through.

● **Wootton Rivers**
Wilts. Tel. A particularly pretty village composed almost entirely of timber-framed, thatched houses, climbing gently up the hill away from the waterway. The church has a most unusual clock, its face having letters in place of numbers. Inside, its mechanism is equally eccentric, being assembled from a bizarre collection of cast-off agricultural implements.

Pubs and Restaurants

● **Swan Inn** Wilton (01672 870274). ½ mile south east of lock 60, along a footpath running beside Wilton Water, serving Wadworth, Fuller's and Hook Norton real ales together with home-made bar meals (curries a speciality) *lunchtimes and evenings, 7 days a week. Sunday* roasts *in winter.* Children's menu and vegetarians catered for. A very friendly establishment in a 1920s building that replaces the original pub, which is now a private dwelling. Darts, crib, pool and dominoes. *Open all day Sat.*

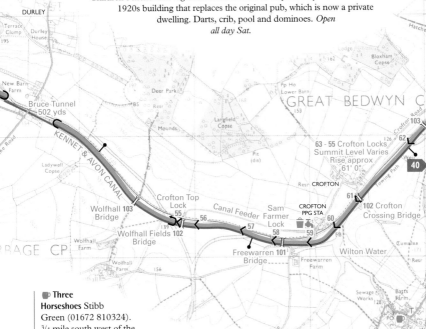

● **Three Horseshoes** Stibb Green (01672 810324). ³/4 mile south west of the Savernake Forest Hotel. Well kept Wadworth and guest real ales served in a traditional country pub where conversation and good beer predominate. Home-made bar meals are available *lunchtimes and evenings (except Sun evening)* and children are welcome *at lunchtimes only.* Good selection of vegetarian dishes. Patio.
● ✗ **Royal Oak** Wootton Rivers (01672 810322). North of the canal. A very attractive 16thC pub in the main street, serving Wadworth, Ushers and guest real ales and a good choice of wines. A very extensive range of home-cooked meals are available *lunchtimes and evenings, 7 days a week.* Children and vegetarians catered for. Garden. Darts, dominoes, pool and board games. B & B. *Open all day Sat & Sun.*

Pewsey

The 15 mile long pound continues westwards towards Devizes through rolling hills. To the north, hills descend to the water's edge, and to the south the land opens out, giving fine views over the Vale of Pewsey. New Mill is a small hamlet south of the canal where there is still evidence of a small wharf. The waterway turns towards Pewsey, but still passes well outside the town, which fills the Vale to the south. Pewsey Wharf is 1/2 mile from the town centre, and so has developed as a separate canalside settlement, with a pub, cottages, and warehouse buildings.

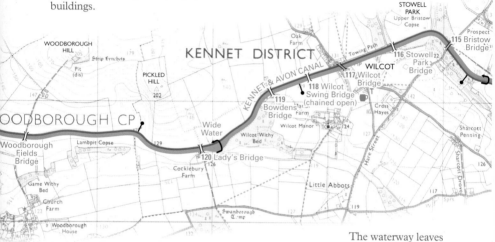

The waterway leaves Pewsey in a low wooded cutting, swinging back to its usual westerly course. The woods continue past Stowell Park, whose landscaped grounds extend to the north. The house, built early in the 19thC, can be seen clearly from the canal. A miniature suspension bridge, the only surviving example of its kind, carries a private footpath from the park across the canal. A straight stretch leads to the first cottages of Wilcot; the rest of the village is to the south. The steep bare mound of Picked Hill dominates the canal as it passes Wilcot and enters the wooded Wide Water. In 1793 this stretch was owned by Lady Susannah Wroughton who objected to the canal cutting through her land. She was appeased by £500, the building of an elaborately decorated bridge (dated 1808 and attributed to Rennie) and the landscaping of the marshy area around it. This area is now a haven for wildlife. The canal skirts Picked Hill, giving a good view of the field terracing that is a relic of Celtic and medieval cultivation. The equally dominant Woodborough Hill now fills the north bank, while to the south open country leads to the village of Woodborough.

- ● **New Mills**
Wilts. Tel. A pretty hamlet scattered below the canal. The mill that gave it its name is now a house, with a fine garden.
- ● **Pewsey**
Wilts. EC Wed. PO, tel, stores, garage, bank, station (but very few trains stop). The little town is set compactly in the Vale of Pewsey. At its centre, overlooking the young River Avon, is a fine statue of King Alfred, erected in 1911. From this all the roads radiate. There is the usual mixture of

buildings; but while many are attractive, none are noteworthy. The church is mostly 13th and 15thC, but parts of the nave are late Norman: the altar rails were made from timbers of the *San Josef*, captured by Nelson in 1797.

Pewsey Wharf – Kennet & Avon Canal Trust (01380 721279). Canal information, shop and tearoom, souvenirs, gifts, ices and refreshments. *Open Easter-Oct, daily 10.00–17.00.*

Pewsey White Horse 1 1/2 miles south of the town. Dating from the 18thC, the horse was re-cut in

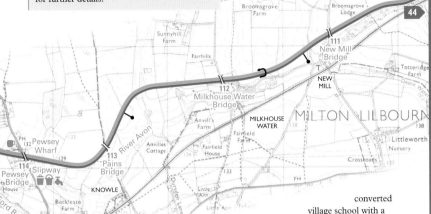

converted
village school with a
prominent bell. Parts of the church
date from the 12thC, but it was mostly rebuilt
in 1876 after a fire. An important event in the
village is the annual carnival dating back to
1898. Lasting for 2 weeks it *commences on the
3rd Sat in Sep* – drawing large crowds – and
there is at least one event every evening thereafter. The centenary promises to be a special
cause for celebration.

1937 by members of the
Pewsey Fire Brigade, to celebrate the
coronation of George VI. It is 66ft long.
- **Wilcot**
Wilts. Tel. A pretty village scattered round the
green; there are several thatched houses, and a

Pubs and Restaurants

French Horn Pewsey (01672 562443).
Just north of Pewsey Wharf, on the A345. A
friendly pub serving Wadworth and guest real
ales together with bar meals and snacks
lunchtimes and evenings, 7 days a week. An
interesting à la carte menu is served *D* and both
vegetarian and children's dishes are available
in the bar and restaurant. The emphasis is very
much on family eating. Garden.

Royal Oak North Street, Pewsey (01672
563426). In the town centre – a family pub
with a warm welcome. Wadworth real ale and
an appetising range of inexpensive, home-
made food (including vegetarian and vegan
dishes) available *lunchtimes and evenings.*
Garden and children's play area. Darts, pool,
crib and dominoes. *Winter* events. B & B.

The Crown Wilcot Road, Pewsey (01672
562653). Wadworth and John Smith's real ales
together with inexpensive, home-made bar
meals *lunchtimes and evenings, 7 days a week.*
Children and vegetarians catered for. Garden

and play area. Skittle alley, darts, dominoes,
pool and cards. B & B.

Greyhound North Street, Pewsey (01672
562439). Lively, welcoming pub serving
Wadworth, Flowers and guest real ales. Home-
made bar food available *all day, every day.*
Vegetarian menu and children welcome.
Garden and tree house. Crib, darts, pool,
cards and children's games. Night club
Thur–Sat 21.00–01.00. Open all day. The very
active Pewsey Vale Railway Society meet here
on *1st Wed in the month at 20.00.*

Golden Swan Wilcot. A one-handed ghost is
said to haunt this pub, which stands beyond
the green at the far end of the village. A very
affable landlord and friendly locals, together
with Wadworth real ale and home-made bar
meals *lunchtimes and evenings (except Sun &
Mon evening and Mon lunchtime).* Bar billiards,
darts and crib. Random folk nights. Two
cricket teams are based at the pub. Camping
and B & B.

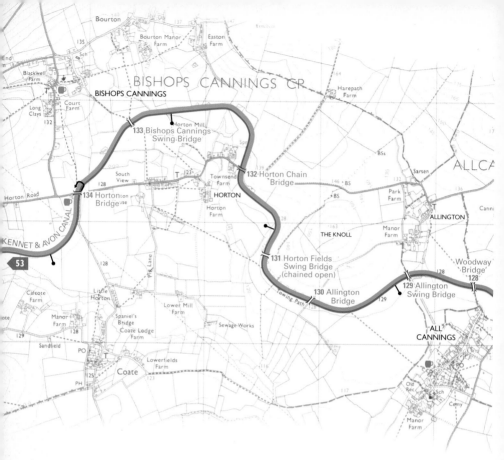

All Cannings

Leaving Woodborough Hill behind, the long pound continues westwards towards Devizes. To the south the land falls away, while to the north the tower of Alton Priors Church comes into view. Beyond the village can be seen the white horse, cut into the hill in 1812, a copy of the one at Cherhill. The canal passes Honey Street Wharf with its boatyard and canalside pub. The waterway now begins to meander through the open countryside, roughly following a contour line to maintain its level. Its progress is marked by a succession of shallow cuttings and low embankments. Several villages are near the navigation, all visible and easily accessible from the many bridges, but none actually approach the waterside. Their interests lie rather in the rich agricultural lands that flank the canal. Beyond Allington the canal curves round the Knoll, a major feature of the landscape to the north. Leaving Horton, the lock-free pound extends westwards towards Devizes. Following the contour of the land, it swings in a wide arc towards Bishops Cannings. The rolling hills climb fairly steeply to the north, while the pasture falls away to the south. After a low cutting, the tower of Bishops Cannings church comes into view, half hidden by trees: a footpath from the swing bridge is the quickest way to the village. At Horton Bridge, where there is a convenient canalside pub, the waterway enters another short cutting.

Boatyards

Ⓑ **Gibson Boat Services** Old Builders Wharf, Honey Street (01672 851232). 🚿 🛠 D E Pump-out, gas, overnight mooring, long-term mooring, winter storage, chandlery, solid fuel, boat surveys, toilet.

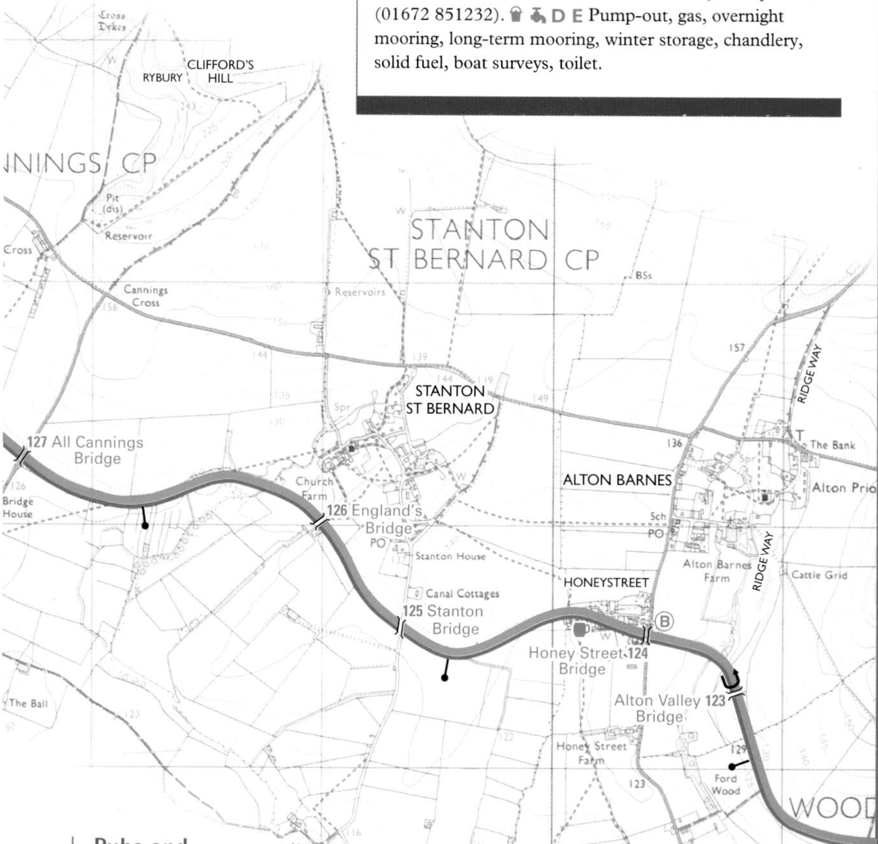

[Map of the Kennet & Avon Canal area showing Stanton St Bernard, All Cannings, Alton Barnes, Honeystreet, with bridges numbered 123–127]

Pubs and Restaurants

🍺 **Barge Inn** Honey Street, Pewsey (01672 851705). An imposing canalside pub which was once a slaughterhouse, a bakehouse, a brewery and a grocers. Ushers real ale and bar meals *lunchtimes and evenings.* Canalside beer garden. Dinghy hire and temporary moorings. Camping, toilets and showers.

🍺 **Kings Arms** All Cannings (01380 860328). 1/4 mile south of Woodway Bridge. A very comfortable and charming village pub, serving Wadworth real ale, and inexpensive bar snacks *lunchtimes and evenings.* Vegetarians and children catered for. Darts, pool, dominoes and crib. Garden. *Closed Mon lunchtime.*

🍺 **Crown Inn** Bishops Cannings (01380 860218). A friendly village pub, serving locally brewed Wadworth real ale and Flowers. Food served *lunchtimes and evenings.* Vegetarians catered for. Children welcome. Large garden with crazy golf and swings. Barbecues *in summer.* Skittles.

🍺 ✕ **Bridge Inn** (01380 860273). At Horton Bridge. An attractively refurbished pub with a mellow brick interior. Well kept real ales include Flowers, Wadworth and Hall & Woodhouse. Food is available in the bar and restaurant *lunchtimes and evenings 7 days a week.* Vegetarian dishes. Barbecues *in summer.* Children welcome. Disabled facilities. Garden.

Honey Street

Wilts. A traditional canalside village, complete with sawmills, incorporating some new development and, arguably, one of the most attractively landscaped and charming boatyards on the waterways.

Alton Barnes

Wilts. Tel, stores. The village runs along the road northwards from Honey Street. The best part is clustered around the church. Fine farm buildings and an 18thC rectory are half hidden among the trees. The church is essentially Anglo Saxon, but has been heavily restored; everything is in miniature, the tiny gallery, pulpit and pews emphasising the compact scale of the whole building.

Alton Priors

Wilts. Tel. Approached along a footpath from Alton Barnes churchyard, the isolated church is the best feature of this scattered hamlet. This pretty Perpendicular building with its wide, well lit nave contains a most interesting monument: a big box tomb is surmounted with a large engraved Dutch brass plate, dated 1590, rich in extravagant symbolism. To the east of the village the Ridgeway runs southwards towards Salisbury; this Bronze Age drover's road swings north east along the downs for 50 miles, finally joining the Thames valley at Streatley.

Stanton St Bernard

Wilts. Tel. Built in a curve of the hills, the village has one main street, flanked by pretty gardens. The best building is the 19thC manor, which incorporates relics of an earlier house. The battlemented church is Victorian.

All Cannings

Wilts. PO, tel, stores open 08.00–18.00 Mon–Sat, 09.30–12.00 Sun. An attractive village built around a square, with houses of all periods. To the south there is a large green, overlooked by the church with its tall central tower. Although the church is mainly 14thC, its most interesting feature is the ornamental High Victorian chancel, added in 1867.

Allington

Wilts. Tel. A small agricultural village with picturesque cottages scattered around a Victorian church. East of the village is All Cannings Cross, a large Iron Age settlement.

Bishops Cannings

Wilts. PO, tel, stores. Apart from one or two old cottages, the main feature of this village is the very grand church. This cruciform building, with its central tower and spire, is almost entirely Early English in style; its magnificence is unexpected in so small a village. Traces of the earlier Norman building survive. Inside is a 17thC penitential seat, surmounted by a giant hand painted on the wall with suitable inscriptions about sin and death.

Pultney Bridge, Bath (see page 63)

Devizes

Passing the new marina the canal enters the long wooded cutting that carries it through Devizes. Houses appear, their gardens overlooking the cutting, and the traffic noise on the busy A361 marks the return to civilisation. Several very elegant large stone bridges (some listed as ancient monuments) span the cutting. Access to the town is easy at all the bridges. At Cemetery Road Bridge the towpath turns over to the north bank for a short stretch, returning to the south at the next bridge. Between these two bridges is Devizes Wharf, where the Kennet & Avon Canal Trust has a museum and shop in a converted warehouse. The wharf is also the home of the Wharf Theatre. Beyond the wharf, the long pound ends at the first lock (lock 50) of the famous Devizes flight, preceded by the generous stone bridge with its separate towpath archway. Locks now occur at regular intervals, each separated by a long, wide pound. These were designed to hold sufficient water while permitting the locks to be close together to follow the slope. The towpath is in very good condition and the whole area is obviously used for recreation by the people of Devizes. To the south the busy A361 accompanies the canal down the hill, but it is out of sight for most of the way. At lock 44 the Caen Hill section of the 16 lock flight starts; wide lock follows wide lock down the hill, each with an enormous side pound. The scale of the whole flight is most impressive. At lock 29 the Caen Hill section ends, but another 7 locks continue the descent, now separated once again by longer pounds. The canal passes under the B3101 road bridge, and then at lock 22 reaches the end of the long fall – 29 locks in $2^1/4$ miles. At Lower Foxhangers Bridge the towpath turns over to the north bank.

● **Devizes**
Wilts. EC Wed. MD Thur, Sat. PO, tel, stores, garage, bank, cinema. Despite the effects of traffic, Devizes still retains the atmosphere of an old country market town. Originally the town grew up around the castle, but as this lost its significance the large marketplace became the focal point. In the early 19thC Devizes held the largest corn market in the west of England and was also a centre for the selling of hops, cattle, horses and cloth, there being many manufacturers of wool and silk in the area. The lower floor of the town hall was the site of the cheese market. Handsome 18thC buildings now command the square, while the market cross records the sad story of Ruth Pierce. Elsewhere there are timbered buildings from the 16thC. The two fine churches, one built for the castle and the other for the parish, tend to dominate the town, and hold it well together. Only the mount and related earthworks survive of the original Norman castle; the present building is an extravagant Victorian folly. The town's own brewery, Wadworth, in Northgate Street, fills the air with the aroma of malt and hops. Wadworth still deliver their beer around the town by horse and dray.

Battle of Roundway Down, 13 July 1643
Devizes was held by a Royalist army that had already tested the Roundhead forces, who were tired, dispirited and short of supplies after their defeat at Lansdown Hill, near Bath. A Royalist cavalry charge took the Roundheads by surprise, and most of the confused and battle-weary Roundheads were killed or captured. The battlefield, off the A361 north east of Devizes, is still largely intact, and can easily be explored on foot. Mock battles are re-enacted here.
Devizes Bikes Cycle Hire (01380 721433).
Devizes to Westminster Canoe Race The toughest and longest canoe race in the world takes place *every Easter*. The course, from Park Road Bridge, Devizes, to County Hall Steps, Westminster, includes 54 miles of the Kennet & Avon, and 71 miles of the Thames, the last 17 of which are tidal. There are 77 locks. The race grew from a background of local rivalry in Pewsey and Devizes to find the quickest way to the sea by boat; in 1948 the target was 100 hours. In 1950 the first regular annual race over the course took place; three years later the junior class was introduced. Anyone may enter the race, but they would have difficulty in beating the highly-trained army and navy teams from Britain and Europe.

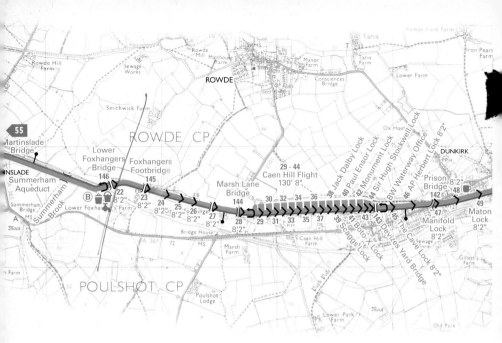

Devizes Museum 41 Long Street (01380 727369). One of the finest prehistoric collections in Europe including finds from the Neolithic, Bronze and Iron Age sites in Wiltshire, the most famous being the Stourhead collection of relics excavated from burial mounds on Salisbury Plain. There are also Roman exhibits. *Open Mon–Sat 10.00–17.00. Closed Sun & B. Hols.* Charge.

Kennet & Avon Canal Trust The Wharf, Devizes (01380 721279). The Trust's central office, canal shop and museum. Books, gifts, souvenirs, maps, videos and information. *Open daily mid-Feb–Xmas 10.00–17.00. Museum open Mar–Xmas 10.00–16.30.*

St John's Church Built by Bishop Roger of Sarum, who was also responsible for the castle, this 12thC church with its massive crossing tower is still largely original. There are 15thC and 19thC additions, but they do not affect the Norman feeling of the whole.

St Mary's Church Dating from the same time as St John's, this church was more extensively rebuilt in the 15thC; plenty of Norman work still survives, however.

Wharf Theatre The Wharf, Devizes (01380 725944).

Wiltshire Bus Line (0345 090899).

Tourist Information Centre St John's Street, Devizes (01380 729408). *Open daily. Closed Sun Nov–Mar.*

Boatyards

ⓑ **Devizes Marina** Horton Avenue, Devizes (01380 725300). 🚽 🛒 D E Pump-out, gas, overnight mooring, long-term mooring, full size slipway, boat sales and repairs, engine sales and repairs (including outboards), boat building and fitting out, dry dock, wet dock, DIY facilities, solid fuel, chandlery, books, maps and gifts, telephone, solid fuel, toilets. *24hr* emergency call out.

ⓑ **White Horse Boats** 8 Southgate Close, Pans Lane, Devizes (01380 728504 or 0374 732338). Hire boats – short and long term – and boat building.

ⓑ **Wharfside Chandlery** Couch Lane, Devizes

(01380 725007/723250). Extensive range of chandlery, waterproofs and marine paint.

ⓑ **BW Waterway Office** Bath Road, Devizes (01380 722859).

ⓑ **Foxhanger Wharf** Lower Foxhangers, Devizes (01380 828254). 🚽 🛒 Gas, day hire craft, overnight moorings, long-term moorings, slipway, toilets, showers, telephone, camping, B & B, self-catering holidays.

ⓑ **Nelcris Marine** Foxhanger Wharf, Devizes (01380 828807/0589 844984). Boat and engine sales, boat and engine repairs (including outboards), engine surveys, engine spares.

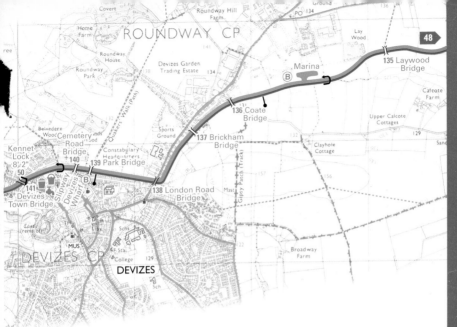

Pubs and Restaurants

There are many good pubs and restaurants in Devizes. The following are simply a convenient selection.

✕ ♀ **Wharfside Restaurant** The Wharf, Devizes (01380 726051). Farmhouse cooking in a canalside restaurant *open daily 09.00–16.30. Closed Sun afternoons in winter.* Also morning coffee, afternoon teas and home-made snacks.

Artichoke Bath Road, Devizes (01380 723400). 100yds north west of Devizes Town Bridge. Known locally as the Vegetable, it is not far from Wadworth's Brewery, and serves their beers, delivered by a dray and horses. Bar food *lunchtimes and evenings.* Garden and traditional pub games.

Bell by the Green Estcourt Street, Devizes (01380 723746). Wadworth and guest real ales together with bar meals *lunchtimes and evenings.* Garden with children's swings and animals. Traditional pub games. B & B.

British Lion 9 Estcourt Street, Devizes (01380 720665). A continually changing selection of real ales (often including their own house beer) and real cider. Traditional pub games. *Open all day.*

Hare & Hounds Hare & Hounds Street, Devizes (01380 723231). The full range of Wadworth real ales served in traditional pub surroundings. *Lunchtime food (not Sun),* a garden, open fires and pub games. Disabled access.

Lamb 20 St John's Street, Devizes (01380 725426). Basic town pub serving Wadworth real ale, with small rooms surrounding the bar area. Traditional pub games.

Black Horse Devizes (01380 723930). By lock 48, on the Caen Hill section. Well placed to refresh those exhausted by the locks. Wadworth real ale, and food *lunchtimes and evenings (not Mon).* Canalside garden.

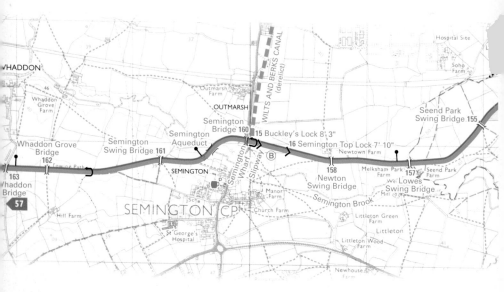

Seend Cleeve

The canal turns past Sells Green in a low cutting that hides most of the village, and then strides along the valley. The hills to the south climb steeply up to the village of Seend, and to the north flat pasture land stretches away. After two swing bridges the waterway reaches the first of the five Seend Locks; this is the best point for access to the village. By the third lock there is a pub, and a lane leading to Seend Cleeve village. Leaving Seend Locks behind, the navigation continues its western course, maintaining a fairly straight line through open country. The two Semington Locks continue the descent towards Bath with an attractive lock house by lock 15. Just beyond the lock the canal is crossed by the A350; this is the best access point for Semington. A close examination of the north bank just before the bridge will reveal a bricked-up side bridge; this marks the site of the junction with the long abandoned Wiltshire & Berkshire Canal, which used to go to Abingdon.

Boatyards

ⓑ **Tranquil Boats** Lock House, Semington, Trowbridge (01380 870654). Electric day boat for hire, covered dry dock, slipway, DIY.

● **Sells Green**
Wilts. Tel, garage. A scattered main road village, the houses doing their best to hide from the traffic behind decorative gardens.

● **Seend**
Wilts. PO, tel, stores, garage. Although the main road cuts the village in half, Seend is still attractive. Elegant 18thC houses flank the road, and

conceal the lane that leads to the battlemented Perpendicular church.

● **Seend Cleeve**
Wilts. Tel. An agricultural village built on the steep slopes of the hills that overlook the canal.

● **The Wiltshire & Berkshire Canal**
Opened in 1810, the canal wound in a meandering course for 51 miles between Semington on

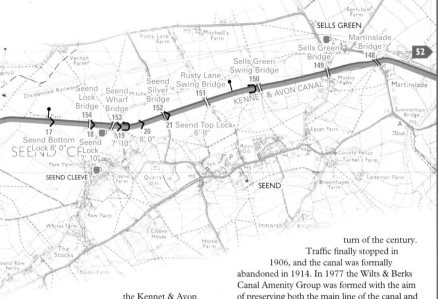

the Kennet & Avon Canal and Abingdon on the River Thames. A branch was opened in 1819 from Swindon to connect with Latton on the Thames & Severn Canal. Although the carriage of Somerset coal was the inspiration for the canal, its eventual role was agricultural. Profits were never high, partly because the wandering line of the canal and its 45 locks made travel very slow, and so it suffered early from railway competition. By the 1870s, moves were afoot to close the canal, and, despite various efforts to give it a new lease of life, the situation had become hopeless by the turn of the century. Traffic finally stopped in 1906, and the canal was formally abandoned in 1914. In 1977 the Wilts & Berks Canal Amenity Group was formed with the aim of preserving both the main line of the canal and the northern branch to Latton. Twenty years later its avowed aim is to restore the waterway to form a navigable link between the K & A; the Thames at Abingdon and either the Thames or the Thames & Severn Canal at Cricklade.

● **Semington**
Wilts. PO, tel, stores (open until 21.00 daily), garage. Despite the main road, Semington is a pretty village. There are several large, handsome houses with fine gardens, some dating from the 18thC. The little stone church, crowned with a bellcote, is at the end of a lane to the west of the village.

Pubs and Restaurants

● **Three Magpies** Sells Green (01380 828389). 200yds south of Sells Green Bridge. A comfortable pub, with converted stables, offering Wadworth and Courage real ales. An imaginative menu is served *lunchtimes and evenings every day.* Garden. Barbecues *Sun in summer.*

● ✕ **Bell Inn** Seend (01380 828338). ½ mile south of lock 21. An exciting conversion of an old brewhouse once patronised by Cromwell and his troops when they breakfasted here on their way to attack Devizes Castle in 1645. Wadworth real ales and food in the bar and restaurant *lunchtimes and evenings. Booking advisable at weekends.* Vegetarian dishes. Children welcome. Outside terrace with panoramic views over Salisbury Plain.

● ✕ **Barge Inn** Seend (01380 828230). By lock 19. An extensive and extremely popular pub occupying the former wharf house and stables, dating back to 1805. The house was once the home of the Wiltshire Giant, Fred Kempster, who reached the inconvenient height of 8ft 2ins. An interesting collection of canalware adorns the walls. Wadworth, Courage, Hall & Woodhouse and guest real ales. Meals available in the bar and restaurant *lunchtimes and evenings every day.* Children welcome. Canalside garden. Barbecues *in summer.*

● **Brewery Inn** Seend Cleeve (01380 828463). 200yds south of lock 19. A genuine, unadulterated village local. Courage and Ruddles real ales and food *lunchtimes and evenings (not Tue eve).*

● ✕ **Somerset Arms** Semington (01380 870067). ¼ mile south of Semington Bridge. Ushers, Smiles and Wadworth real ales in a traditional, 400-year-old pub. Meals available in the bar and restaurant *lunchtimes and evenings, 7 days a week.* Vegetarian dishes. Children welcome. Garden. B & B.

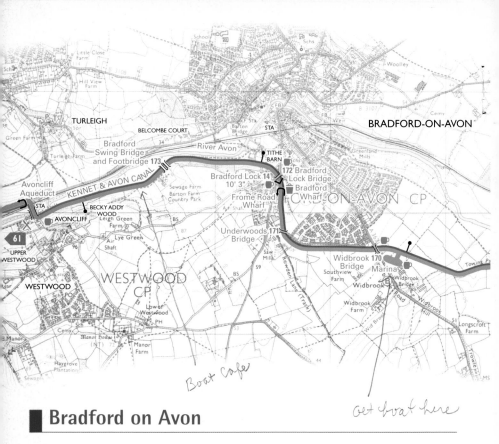

Boat Cafe

Get boat here

Bradford on Avon

Continuing its westerly course, the canal passes through open countryside: the wide Avon valley, which the canal now follows, begins gradually to narrow as the hills encroach to the north and the south. The navigation curves round below Hilperton; although the main village is a mile to the south, there is a convenient pub, post office and stores by the road bridge and wharf where a large new marina has been built. West of Hilperton, the waterway passes the grounds of Wyke House, whose Jacobean-style towers stand among the trees; then the land to the north falls away as the navigation returns to its original course on a sweeping curve. Canal and river now converge as the waterway swings on a huge embankment towards the Avon, crossing the railway and the River Biss on two stone aqueducts. The classical arch over the river is particularly handsome; it is necessary to walk down the side of the embankment in order to see it properly. The view northwards across the Avon valley is very fine. For a while river and canal run side by side, the river down in the valley, the canal high above in a side cutting, shielded by trees, and then they part again to make their separate entries into Bradford. There is a useful stores 1/4 mile north of Widbrook Bridge. The waterway stays high above the town, which fills the steep-sided valley, while the river cuts the town in two. Bradford basin appears suddenly, followed by the lock, and then the canal turns to pass to the south of the town. It rejoins the course of the river, and now the two run closely together all the way to Bath. West of Bradford the navigation passes through beautiful woods on the steep southern slope of the valley. From this point

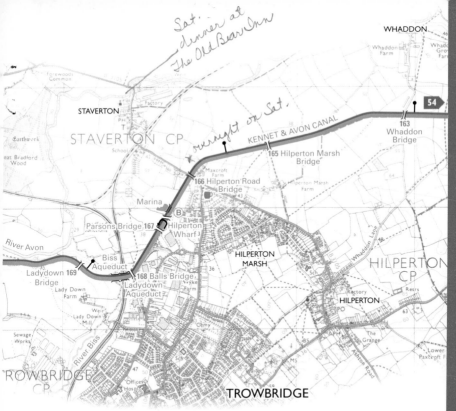

Sat.
dinner at
The Old Bear Inn

overnight on Sat.

WHADDON

STAVERTON

STAVERTON CP

KENNET & AVON CANAL

165 Hilperton Marsh Bridge

166 Hilperton Road Bridge

Marina

Parsons Bridge 167

Hilperton Wharf

River Avon

Ladydown 169 Bridge

Biss Aqueduct

168 Balls Bridge

Ladydown Aqueduct

HILPERTON MARSH

HILPERTON CP

HILPERTON

TROWBRIDGE

ROWBRIDGE CP

54

163 Whaddon Bridge

there are fine views of the town, spread out beyond the Tithe Barn, which is right beside the canal. Cyclists appear on the towpath, since this is part of the Wiltshire Cycleway route. The Avon rushes along the valley and beyond it the railway appears and disappears among the trees on the far side, while the canal pursues its more sedate course towards Bath. The thick woods often give the canal user a feeling of total seclusion. The elegant stone arches of the Avoncliff Aqueduct carry the canal high above the fast flowing river and the railway. A tea shop (*open daily in summer 10.00–17.30*), a canal bookshop (01225 723812) (*open Easter–Oct*) and a fine pub make this a worthwhile stop. The canal then turns west again to continue its wooded course. The towpath crosses back to the south side by the aqueduct.

BOAT TRIPS
Nb. Ladywood operated by the Kennet & Avon Canal Trust from Upper Bradford Wharf. Public trips through Bradford on Avon lock to the Avoncliff aqueduct and return *Easter–Oct Sun & B. Hols.* Additional trips *Jul–Aug Wed & Jun–Aug Sat.* Private charter available. Also rowing boats for hire. Telephone (01225) 864378 for further details.

Boatyards

(B) **Hilperton Marina** Hilperton Wharf, Hammond Way, Trowbridge (01225 765243). 🚽 ⛽ �’ D E Pump-out, gas, slipway, overnight mooring, long-term mooring, winter storage, chandlery, books, maps and gifts, boat sales and repairs, engine repairs (including outboards), boat building and fitting out, wet dock, DIY facilities, solid fuel, toilets. *24hr* emergency call out.

(B) **Wessex Narrowboats** Wessex Wharf, Hilperton Marina, Trowbridge (01225 769847). Narrow boat hire, day hire craft, books and maps.

(B) **Bradford on Avon Marina** Trowbridge Road, Bradford on Avon (01225 864562). 🚽 ⛽ �’ D E Pump-out, gas, overnight mooring, long-term mooring, winter storage, boat sales and

repairs, engine sales and repairs, chandlery, dry dock, books, maps and gifts, toilets, showers, telephone.

(B) **Sally Boats** Bradford on Avon Marina (01225 864923). Narrow boat hire.

(B) **Chris Halliwell** Widbrook Dry Dock, Bradford on Avon Marina (01225 863535/01749 850766). Surveys and valuations, dock services, modifications and maintenance, solid fuel.

(B) **Kennet & Avon Canal Trust** Upper Bradford Wharf, Bradford on Avon (01380 721279). Overnight moorings, long-term moorings, slipway, winter storage, DIY facilities, dry dock. books, maps and gifts. *Open Easter-Oct 10.00-17.00 every day.*

● **Hilperton**

Wilts. PO, tel, stores (open Mon–Sat 07.00–21.00 & Sun 08.00–20.00), garage. A scattered village that stretches away from the settlement by the canal wharf. Wyke House stands to the west of the village. This very ornate Jacobean mansion was in fact built in 1865, a replica of the original house. House *not open to the public.*

● **Staverton**

Wilts. Tel. The village lies to the north of the canal, spreading down to the bank of the Avon. A small isolated part of the Avon is navigable here, and is used by a few pleasure boats. In the village are terraces of weavers' cottages, a sign of what was once the staple trade of the area.

● **Bradford on Avon**

Wilts. EC Wed. PO, tel, stores, garage, bank, station. Set in the steeply wooded Avon valley, Bradford is one of the beauty spots of Wiltshire, and one of the highlights of the canal. Rather like a miniature Bath, the town is composed of fine stone terraces rising sharply away from the river, which cuts through the centre of the town. Until the 19thC it was a prosperous centre for weaving, but a depression killed the industry and drove most of the workers away. At the time that the canal was built Bradford had no less than thirty water-powered cloth factories and some of these buildings still survive. Bradford is rich in architectural treasures from the Saxon period to the 19thC, while the abundance of fine 18thC houses make the exploration of the town a positive pleasure. The centre is very compact, and so the walk down the hill from the canal wharf lays most of it open to inspection, including the town bridge, Holy Trinity Church, the Victorian town hall and the fine Gothic revival factory that dominates the riverside. There is also a swimming pool near the canal.

Bradford Upper Wharf The canal wharf is particularly attractive. There is a small dock with some of the original buildings still standing, plenty of mooring space, and an old canal·pub beside the lock. The lock here was built to raise the canal to the same level as the Wilts and Berks Canal which joins the canal at Semington.

Kennet & Avon Canal Trust Upper Bradford Wharf, Bradford on Avon (01380 721279). Canal shop and tearoom selling a range of souvenirs, gifts, ices and refreshments. *Open Easter-Oct 10.00-17.00 every day.*

Great Tithe Barn Bradford on Avon (01225 865797). Standing below the canal embankment, this great stone building is one of the finest tithe barns in England. It was built in the 14thC by the Abbess of Shaftesbury. Its cathedral-like structure (168ft long) is broken by two porches, with massive doors that open to réveal the beamed roof. The barn is part of Barton Farm, a medieval farm which was part of the monastic estate of Shaftesbury Abbey. The Granary and Cow Byres now house craft shops and galleries.

Holy Trinity Church Basically a 12thC building with additions dating over the next three centuries. Inside are some medieval wall paintings, and fine 18thC monuments. Many of the names that appear relate to the woollen industry.

Lock Inn Cottage 48 Frome Road, Bradford on Avon (01225 868068). Canalside café serving death-defying boatmen's breakfasts, light lunches and cream teas. *Open summer Mon–Sat 09.00–18.00 & Sun 09.00–19.00. Winter: week-ends only.* Canoe hire. Also bicycle sales, repairs and hire. All hire bikes can be used in conjunction with trailers for children, trailer bikes and child seats. Also tandems. Every permutation catered for! *Open daily 09.00–18.00, all year, except Xmas Day.*

Saxon Church of St Lawrence Founded in AD705, this tiny church was enlarged in the 10thC. Since then it has survived essentially unchanged, having been at various times a school, a cottage and a slaughterhouse. The true origins and purpose of the building were only rediscovered in the 19thC, and so it remains one of the best-preserved Saxon churches in England.

Town Bridge The nine-arched bridge is unusual in having a chapel in the middle, one of only four still surviving in Britain. Parts of the bridge, including the chapel, are medieval, but much dates from a 17thC rebuilding. During the 17th and 18thC the chapel fell out of use, and was turned into a small prison, serving as the town lock up.

Westwood Manor One mile south west of Bradford. This 15thC stone manor house contains original Jacobean plaster and woodwork, although much was lost when the manor became a farm in the 18thC. Skilful restoration by the National Trust has returned the manor to its former glory. *Open Wed afternoons Apr–Sep.* Charge.

Tourist Information Centre The Library, Bridge Street, Bradford on Avon (01225 865797).

● **Avoncliff**

Wilts. Station. A hamlet clustered in the woods beside the canal. Originally it was a centre of weaving, and many traces of the old industry can be seen: weavers' cottages, and the old mills on the Avon, which falls noisily over a weir at this point. At one time the mills were used for flocking, a process which involved the breaking up of old woollen material to make stuffing for mattresses and chairs. The hamlet is dominated by Rennie's aqueduct, built in 1804 to take the canal across the valley to the north side. A classical stone structure, the aqueduct suffered from casual repair work and patching in brick when owned by the Great Western Railways, due mainly to the inferior nature of the stone from which it was constructed.

Pubs and Restaurants

🍺 **Kings Arms** Hilperton Wharf (01225 755168). A Chef and Brewer pub serving Courage real ale. Bar food, including take aways, *lunchtimes and evenings (not Sun eve)*. Children welcome. Garden with play area.

🍺 ✕ **Old Bear Inn** Staverton (01225 782487). 1/3 mile north west of Hilperton Bridge. Nicely kept 300-year-old inn serving Bass, Ushers and Wadworth real ales. An extensive menu is available in the bar and restaurant *lunchtimes and evenings*. Vegetarians catered for. Children welcome. Garden.

🍺 **Beehive** Widbrook Bridge, Bradford on Avon (01225 863620). Unadulterated local with a selection of six guest real ales. Bar food served *lunchtimes and evenings (not Sun eve)*. Children welcome in the garden. Barbecues *weekends during summer*.

✕ 🍷 **Gongoozler** Bradford on Avon Marina (01225 862004). Smart new restaurant at the marina serving light snacks and à la carte menu *L & D*. Children welcome. Balcony overlooking the marina.

🍺 **Barge Inn** Bradford Wharf (01225 863403). Comfortable one bar pub with a good choice of real ales including Wadworth, Boddingtons, Flowers and Bass. Also a good wine list. Attractive eating area, decorated with canalware, where food is served *Mon–Sat lunchtimes and evenings & Sun 12.00–15.00.* Children welcome. Canalside garden. Moorings for patrons. B & B.

✕ **Curry Inn** Bradford on Avon (01225 866424). Across the road from the Canal Tavern. Tandoori restaurant and take away. *Open daily 12.00–14.00 & 17.30–24.00.*

🍺 **Canal Tavern** Lower Wharf, Bradford on Avon (01225 865232). It was outside the back door of this friendly pub that the first sod for the commencement of the canal was cut. The pub continues to benefit from its trade with an attractive terrace overlooking the navigation. Wadworth and Bass real ales and food (including an extensive vegetarian selection) *lunchtimes and evenings*. Barbecues and music in the garden *in summer*. Children welcome. Moorings for patrons.

🍺 **Cross Guns** Avoncliff Aqueduct (01225 862335). One of the most attractive pubs on the navigation with its low ceilings, stone walls and flagged floors. The terraced gardens are busy in summer with people enjoying this beautiful setting in a wooded valley. A good selection of real ales including Ushers, Courage and John Smith's plus own brew. An imaginative and well priced menu is served *lunchtimes and evenings*. Children welcome. Booking advisable.

Claverton

Leaving the Avoncliff Aqueduct, the canal continues westwards through the woods above the River Avon. The valley gets steeper and narrower as it approaches Bath and thick woods cover both sides as the river and navigation run side by side. The canal passes Limpley Stoke, scattered over the southern valley side. The country opens out slightly to allow views across the valley as the waterway approaches the Dundas Aqueduct, perhaps the best known feature of the Kennet & Avon Canal. Emerging from the woods, the canal turns suddenly onto the aqueduct, which carries it across the Avon valley and the railway to the south side. At the southern end of the aqueduct is a small wharf and basin, with an old crane standing over the water. Here is the junction with the Somersetshire Coal Canal, which, until its closure in 1904, ran south from the Kennet & Avon Canal towards Paulton. Beyond the basin the towpath turns over to the north bank, where it remains until Bath is reached. The waterway enters another thickly wooded stretch, a side cutting taking it towards Claverton. The woods soon give way to allow fine views to the north, across rolling country and the River Avon in the valley below. Claverton flanks the canal, but it is hidden by the folds of the land to the south. Access is easy, and both the village and Claverton Manor are worth a visit. Claverton Pumping Station houses a water-powered pump which lifts water up from the Avon to feed the canal. The pump has been restored by the Kennet & Avon Canal Trust, with help from engineering students from Bath University. Open country continues, allowing views across the valley to Warleigh Manor, now a college, and to Bathford church. The navigation follows the contours of the land as it turns towards Bath, maintaining the level of the 9 mile pound that runs from Bradford to Bath Top Lock.

Boatyards

ⓑ **Bath & Dundas Canal Co**. The Boatyard, Monkton Combe (01225 722292). At the end of the Somersetshire Coal Canal, where boats up to 62ft can turn, BUT do not bring your boat in without first walking along the main road to the office to check if space is available. ☏ D E Pump-out – *24hrs notice required*, gas, day hire craft (including canoes), overnight mooring, long-term mooring, slipway, dry dock, books and maps, boat sales and repairs, outboard engine sales and repairs, dry dock, wet dock, books, gifts and maps, telephone, café, toilets, B & B. *24hr* emergency call out on (01225) 722226 or 0860 821357. Provisions are available at the garage above Dundas Wharf.

● **Freshford**
Somerset. PO, tel. Although not on the canal, Freshford is well worth the 1/2 mile walk south from Limpley Stoke. It is a particularly attractive village, set on the side of the steep hill that flanks the confluence of the rivers Avon and Frome. At the top of the hill is the church, and terraces of handsome stone houses fall away in both directions, filling the valley below, and crowding the narrow streets. At the bottom of the hill is the river, crossed by the medieval bridge. The hills around were a rich source of Bath stone, limestone and fuller's earth and in the early 19thC the village was involved with the production of broad cloth in its extensive factory. Ruins of an old hermitage and friary, possibly connected with Hinton Abbey, were excavated locally, as were the remains of a Roman encampment.

● **Limpley Stoke**
Avon. PO, tel, stores. Built on the side of the valley overlooking the river, Limpley Stoke is a quiet village, a residential outpost of Bath. The little church includes work of all periods, from Norman to the 20thC: inside is a collection of carved coffin lids.
Dundas Aqueduct Built in 1804, this three-arch classical stone aqueduct is justifiably one of the most well-known features of the canal, and stands as a fitting monument to the architectural and engineering skill of John Rennie. It is necessary to leave the canal and walk down into the valley below to appreciate the beauty of the aqueduct, and to see it in the context of the narrow Avon valley into which it fits so well. The aqueduct was named in honour of the first chairman of the Kennet and Avon Canal

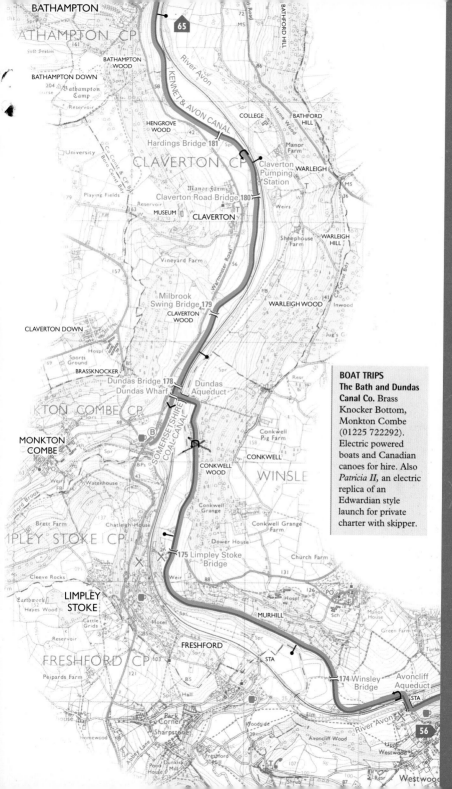

BATHAMPTON

BATHAMPTON CP

BATHAMPTON WOOD

BATHAMPTON DOWN

Bathampton Camp

River Avon

KENNET & AVON CANAL

BATHFORD HILL

65

HENGROVE WOOD

Hardings Bridge 181

CLAVERTON CP

COLLEGE

BATHFORD HILL

Manor Farm

Claverton Pumping Station

WARLEIGH

Manor Farm

Claverton Road Bridge 180

MUSEUM

CLAVERTON

Warminster Road

Sheephouse Farm

WARLEIGH HILL

Vineyard Farm

Milbrook Swing Bridge 179

CLAVERTON WOOD

WARLEIGH WOOD

Inwood

CLAVERTON DOWN

Sports Ground

BRASSKNOCKER

Dundas Bridge 178

Dundas Wharf

Dundas Aqueduct

KTON COMBE CP

SOMERSETSHIRE COAL CANAL

Conkwell Pig Farm

MONKTON COMBE

B

CONKWELL WOOD

CONKWELL

WINSLE

Conkwell Grange

Conkwell Grange Farm

Dower House

Brett Farm

Chatleigh House

IMPLEY STOKE CP

175 Limpley Stoke Bridge

Church Farm

Cleeve Rocks

LIMPLEY STOKE

MURHILL

FRESHFORD

FRESHFORD CP

STA

Peipards Farm

174 Winsley Bridge

Avoncliff Aqueduct

STA

River Avon

56

Park Corner

Sharpstone

Avoncliff Wood

Upper Westwood

Westwoo

BOAT TRIPS
The Bath and Dundas Canal Co. Brass Knocker Bottom, Monkton Combe (01225 722292). Electric powered boats and Canadian canoes for hire. Also *Patricia II,* an electric replica of an Edwardian style launch for private charter with skipper.

Company and is widely regarded as Rennie's finest architectural work. Urgent repair work had to be carried out in the early 1980s involving relining the structure with reinforced concrete.

Somersetshire Coal Canal Opened in 1805, this narrow canal was sponsored by the Somerset Coal owners, who wanted a more efficient means of moving their coal to Bath, Bristol and the rest of England. Originally surveyed by Rennie in 1793, the canal was to run from Limpley Stoke to Paulton, with a branch to Radstock. There were steep gradients to overcome at Midford and Combe Hay, and these plagued the canal throughout its life. The Radstock Arm was never completed and tramroads were built over the difficult stretches. The canal was never profitable, and was sold to the Somerset & Dorset Railway in 1871. The main line was completed throughout, but not before some remarkable solutions to the problems of the Combe Hay gradient had been tried out. First there was Robert Weldon's caisson lock; a watertight caisson, large enough to hold a narrow boat and crew, was pulled up and down an 88ft-deep water-filled cistern by means of a rack and pinion. This terrifying device was soon replaced by an inclined plane, which in turn was replaced by a conventional flight of locks. Once open, the canal carried a large tonnage of coal throughout the 19thC: it served 30 collieries more directly than the railway. However, by the end of the century the inevitable competition was taking away the traffic, which finally stopped in 1898. The canal was officially abandoned in 1904. The first ¼

mile has now been restored and is used by a boatyard, and for moorings. A stop lock at the entrance restricts its use to craft of 7ft beam only.

● **Claverton**

Somerset. Tel. Although devoid of all facilities, Claverton is well worth a visit. It is a manorial village of stone houses, surrounding the 17thC farm, and in early days was clearly dependent upon Claverton Manor. The main road misses the village, increasing the peace and seclusion.

The American Museum in Britain Claverton Manor, Bath (01225 460503). The manor was built in 1820 by Sir Jeffry Wyatville in the Greek revival style. It now houses a museum of American decorative arts from the late 17thC to the mid 19thC. Teas. *Open Apr–Oct 14.00–17.00. Closed Mon except during Aug & B. Hols.* Charge.

Claverton Pumping Station Ferry Lane, Claverton. Enquiries on (0117) 986 7536. The waterwheel pump at Claverton is the only one of its kind on British canals. Designed by John Rennie, the pump was built to feed the 9 mile Bradford—Bath pound, and started operating in 1813. The two undershot breast wheels, each 15ft in diameter and 11ft wide, then powered the pumping machinery until a major breakdown in 1952 prompted its closure, and replacement by a temporary diesel pump. The original machinery has now been restored, and pumping weekends are organised. New electric pumps now do the day-to-day work, raising water from the Avon 47ft below. The Pumping Station is run by the Kennet & Avon Canal Trust. *Open Sun Easter–Oct 10.30–16.30.* Pumps fully working *on 4th Sun in month.* Charge.

Pubs and Restaurants

🍺 **The Inn** Freshford (01225 722250). It is well worth the walk to this splendid, traditional pub overlooking the river. A good choice of real ales include Ushers, Bass, Courage and Ruddles. Bar food available *lunchtimes and evenings.* Garden, children welcome.

✕ **Fordside Tea Garden** Limpley Stoke (01225 722115). 100yds south of Limpley Stoke Bridge. An attractive private garden and tearoom, accessed through a hole in the hedge, serving tea, coffee, snacks, home-made cakes and refreshments. *Open weekends and most weekdays 11.00–18.00.* Large parties please give prior notice.

🍺 ✕ **Hop Pole** Limpley Stoke (01225 723134). Moor at Limpley Stoke Bridge, walk down to the railway bridge and turn left to find this popular oak-panelled pub. Courage, Bass and Butcombe real ales. Meals are served in the bar

and restaurant *lunchtimes and evenings 7 days a week.* Children welcome. Garden.

🍺 **Rose and Crown** Limpley Stoke (01225 722237). A Brewer's Fare establishment serving Wadworth real ale and bar food *all day 7 days a week.*

✕ 🍷 **Nightingale's** Limpley Stoke (01225 723150). An attractive restaurant in the centre of the village specialising in new Italian cuisine *open for D Tue–Sat 19.00–22.00 & L Sun 12.30–14.00. Booking advisable.*

🍺 ✕ **Viaduct Hotel** Brassknocker Hill, Monkton Combe (01225 723187). Moor south of Dundas Aqueduct, the pub is 400 yds south of the A36. Ushers real ale and food available in the bar and restaurant *lunchtimes and evenings 7 days a week.* Children welcome, large garden. Regular music nights. B & B.

Bath

Following the course of the River Avon, the canal turns west towards Bath, leaving behind Bathford church on the opposite side of the valley. Groups of houses appear more frequently scattered among the trees of the Avon valley; these form the outposts of Bath, whose suburbs are now visible to the west. The canal passes through Bathampton, on a low embankment above the school and church, and then continues on a straight course, closely flanked by the railway, which is in a cutting below. The railway is now accompanied by the new stretch of the A4 whose traffic drones continuously. On the south bank there are gardens running down to the water, which accompany the canal into Bath. The entry into Bath is magnificent. The canal sweeps round the south of the city, cut into the side of the hill, and so there are extensive views across Bath. From this point it is possible to pick out many of the features of the city, and the Georgian terraces can be seen spread out over the far side of the valley. As the buildings fill the valley, the canal and River Avon part, to make their separate entries into Bath. The first Georgian buildings flank the canal as it reaches Sydney Gardens. A short tunnel with a fine Adamesque portal takes the canal under a road, and then it passes two pretty cast iron bridges, both dated 1800. A cutting carries the canal through this attractive part of Bath, and so the houses seem to hang over the water. Another ornamental tunnel actually carries houses over the canal, among them Cleveland House, the old canal company's headquarters. The towpath turns over briefly to the south side, returning to the north at the next bridge. The cutting then ends, once more allowing magnificent views of the lock of the Widcombe flight. This flight of six locks takes the canal down to join the Avon. Locks 8 and 9 were merged together as part of a road building scheme, making one new lock with a fall of over 19ft. The canal joins the Avon immediately beyond Bath Lower Lock (number 7) in the middle of the industrial quarter of Bath. The railway station is opposite the junction of canal and river, and factories and warehouses flank the Avon as it leaves Bath. The fine Georgian city surrounds the unnavigable Avon to the east. The junction is the best point of access for Bath as a whole. A long belt of industry accompanies the river out of Bath but access to the towpath is always easy. There are several footbridges across the river, some of them private, and a disused railway (now a cycleway and footpath) crosses twice as the river meanders in long, gentle curves. As the industry gradually falls away, the navigation divides; the right fork leads to Weston Lock, the left to a weir. The River Avon at last leaves behind the industries of Bath, and enters a wooded stretch. The railway closely follows the south bank, vanishing at one point into a tunnel. As the river continues its wide, wandering course westwards, the valley opens out, and rolling hills and pasture flank both banks. A disused rail bridge is followed by the elegant single stone arch of New Bridge, carrying the A4. At this point the towpath crosses to the south bank, although, as on all river navigations, its position is never well defined. After New Bridge there is a small boatyard, and a line of moored craft along the north bank.

The towpath
West of Bath walkers and cyclists may find it easier to make use of the cycleway, along the old railway track, as far as the river bridge west of Swineford. The towpath can be somewhat indeterminate on parts of this section and rough for cycling.

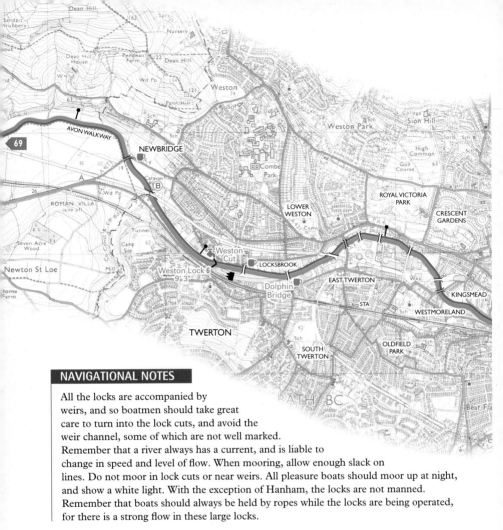

NAVIGATIONAL NOTES

All the locks are accompanied by
weirs, and so boatmen should take great
care to turn into the lock cuts, and avoid the
weir channel, some of which are not well marked.
Remember that a river always has a current, and is liable to
change in speed and level of flow. When mooring, allow enough slack on
lines. Do not moor in lock cuts or near weirs. All pleasure boats should moor up at night,
and show a white light. With the exception of Hanham, the locks are not manned.
Remember that boats should always be held by ropes while the locks are being operated,
for there is a strong flow in these large locks.

BOAT TRIPS

Bath Boating Station Forester Road, Bathwick, Bath (01225 466407). A unique surviving Victorian
boating station with tea gardens and a licensed restaurant. Traditional boats from skiffs, punts and
canoes for hire by the hour or the day. Free instruction for those new to punting. *Open daily
Apr–Sep 10.00–18.00* for boating. Restaurant *open for lunches and teas in summer. Evenings
19.00–22.30.* B & B.
John Rennie Sydney Wharf, Bath (01225 447276). Well-equipped 60-seater restaurant boat
available for private charter. Also cycle hire.
Pride of Bath North Parade Bridge, Bath (01225 333769). Large, 120 passenger cruise boat
available for charter. Bar, servery, dance floor. Also public lunch and afternoon tea cruises.
Telephone for further details.
Bath Hotelboat Company 2 Sydney Wharf, Bath (01225 448846). Nine passenger wide beam hotel
boat available for short break or weekly holiday cruises.
Kennet & Avon Canal Trust's *nb Jubilee* operates public and private charter cruises through Bath to
Bathampton *Sat & Sun Apr–Oct.* Also special cruises to Claverton and Dundas Aqueduct on *some
Sun & B. Hols.* Telephone (01225) 462313 for further details.

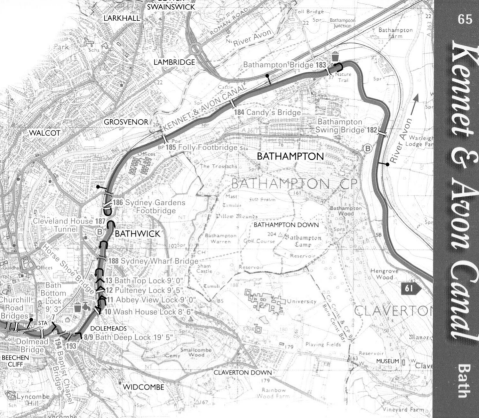

Pubs and Restaurants

Bath is well-endowed with distinguished restaurants, lively wine bars and excellent pubs. The following is a selection of pubs close to the canal.

George Inn Bathampton, Bath (01225 425079). Family pub with a canalside garden and children's play area, serving Courage and guest real ales. An extensive and enticing range of freshly prepared food is available in the bar *lunchtimes and evenings, 7 days a week.* Vegetarian menu. Moorings outside. *Open all day Sat & Sun in summer.*

Bathampton Mill Mill Lane, Bathampton (01225 469758). 400yds north of Bathampton Bridge. A Beefeater restaurant serving Flowers, Whitbread and Boddingtons real ale. Food is available in the bar and restaurant *all day.* Garden with play area and attractive riverside terrace.

Golden Fleece 1–3 Avon Buildings, Lower Bristol Road, Bath (01225 429572). One bar local 50yds south of the river, serving Courage and regular guest real ales and *lunchtime bar food, Mon–Fri.* Traditional pub games.

Dolphin Locksbrook Road, Bath (01225 445048). On the Weston Cut. Flowers, Boddington's and Marston's real ale. Bar meals available *lunchtimes and evenings* with seperate menus for each. Vegetarian menu. Garden and moorings. Children welcome. Darts, dominoes and crib. *Open all day Sat & Sun in summer.*

The Boathouse Brass Mill Lane, Bath (01225 482584). Just west of New Bridge. Brains, Wadworth and guest real ales in a pub and restaurant developed beside the marina. Bar meals available *lunchtimes* and an à la carte restaurant menu is served *D, 7 days a week.* This family orientated establishment has a huge riverside garden and moorings for patrons. *Open all day Sat & Sun. Booking essential for the restaurant.*

Boatyards

Ⓑ **John Knill & Sons** Longhope, Packhorse Lane, South Stoke, Bath (01225 463603). Long-term mooring.
Ⓑ **John Rennie Canal Cruises** Sydney Wharf, Bath (01225 447276). 🚻 ⚓ D Pump-out, narrow boat hire.

Ⓑ **Bath Marina** Brass Mill Lane, Bath (01225 424301). 🚿 🚻 ⚓ D Pump-out, gas, overnight mooring, long-term mooring, boat sales and repairs, engine repairs, chandlery, books, maps and gifts, DIY facilities, toilets, showers, groceries, laundrette, telephone.

● **Bathampton**

Avon. PO, tel, stores, garage. The centre of the village surrounds the canal and is still compact and undeveloped, but new housing around the village has turned it into a suburb of Bath. The church is mostly 19thC.

● **Bath**

Avon. MD Wed. All services. Bath was first developed by the Romans as a spa town and resort because of its natural warm springs. They started the trend of bathing and taking the waters which survives today. There are extensive Roman remains to be seen in the city, not least the baths themselves. The city grew further during the medieval period, when it was a centre of the wool trade; the fine abbey dates from this time. But the true splendour of Bath is the 18thC development, when the city grew as a resort and watering place that was frequented by all levels of English society, from royalty downwards. Despite heavy bombing in the 1939–45 war, Bath is still a magnificent memorial to the 18thC and Neo-classicism generally. The terraces that adorn the steep northern slope of the Avon valley contain some of the best Georgian architecture in Britain. Much of the city was designed by John Wood the Younger, who was responsible for the great sweeping Royal Crescent. Other architects include Thomas Baldwin, who built the Guildhall, 1766–75, and the Pump Room, 1789–99, and Robert Adam, whose Pulteney Bridge carries terraces of shops across the Avon. Bath is best seen on foot, for its glories and riches are far too numerous to list. Visitors should not fail to try the waters, which gush continuously from a fountain outside the Pump Room.

Bath Abbey Set in an attractive piazza, the abbey is a pleasingly uniform Perpendicular building, founded in 1499. Twin towers crown the west front, decorated with carved angels ascending and descending ladders. Inside, the abbey is justly famous for its fan vaulting, which covers the whole roof of the building but is not all of the same date. Inside also is a wealth of memorials of all periods, an interesting indication of the vast range of people who, over the ages, have come to die in Bath.

Holburne Museum and Crafts Study Centre Great Pulteney Street, Bath (01225 4666690). Housed in an 18thC Palladian building that was designed as part of the Sydney pleasure gardens, it contains collections of silver, ceramics, 18thC paintings and furniture, 20thC art and craft work. Teahouse. *Open daily.* Charge.

Museum of Costume Assembly Rooms, Bath (01225 477000). Display of fashion from the 17thC to the present day; one of the largest collections of costume in the world. *Open Mon–Sat 10.00–17.00 & Sun 11.00–17.00.* Charge.

Postal Museum 8 Broad Street, Bath (01225 460333). The place from which the first postage stamp was sent on 2nd May 1840. The history of the postal service and the development of the written word. *Open Mon–Sat 11.00–17.00 & Sun 14.00–17.00.* Charge.

Roman Baths Museum Stall Street, Bath (01225 477000). The great bath buildings with their dependent temple were the centre of Roman Bath. Much of these survive, incorporated into the 18thC Pump Room. The museum, attached to the bath buildings, contains finds excavated from the site. *Open daily all year 09.00–18.00.* Charge.

1 Royal Crescent Bath (01225 428126). The first house of this magnificent crescent built by John Wood the Younger between 1767–74. Complete with original furniture and fittings. *Open Mar–Oct weekdays and Sun afternoons.* Charge.

Royal Photographic Society Milsom Street, Bath (01225 462841). Five exhibition galleries and a display which traces the development of photography. *Open daily 09.30–17.30.* Charge.

Victoria Art Gallery Bridge Street, Bath (01225 477000). Collection of 18thC and modern paintings, prints and ceramics. Visiting exhibitions. *Open Mon–Sat.*

Tourist Information Centre Abbey Churchyard, Bath (01225 477000).

Keynsham

The river passes Kelston Park in a series of gentle bends, against a background of wooded hills to the north. The river straightens as it approaches Kelston Lock, where the stream again divides. Navigators should take the right fork to the lock, and avoid the weir on the left. Mooring is possible by the lock, and this is the best access point for boaters visiting Saltford. The towpath continues along the north bank, as the river curves towards Saltford Lock where there is an attractive riverside pub. The river then turns past Saltford Mead towards Swineford, passing a large factory on the low-lying land to the south. At Swineford the river again divides, the left fork leading to the particularly attractive lock, which is set against a background of trees and old mill buildings. After passing a vast brick and stone factory complex, dated 1881, which dominates the south bank, the river starts a long horseshoe bend that leads to Keynsham. The river divides, the right fork leading to the lock where there is a small settlement. As the valley narrows, steep wooded hills return to follow the north bank of the river as it twists and turns. After a particularly sharp bend Hanham Lock appears. Again the river divides, the left fork leading to the lock. This is lock 1, the last lock between Reading and Bristol, the end of BW's jurisdiction, and the beginning of the Port of Bristol Authority area. Note that the River Avon is tidal west of Hanham Lock. There is a small hamlet on the north bank, overlooking the weir, and two pubs, side by side. From here the river Avon continues through a steeply wooded valley to Bristol; a canal takes boats through Bristol harbour and then the navigation rejoins the river which flows down to join the Severn estuary at Avonmouth, having passed the Clifton Suspension Bridge and the Avon Gorge.

NAVIGATIONAL NOTES

Do not navigate in tidal waters without charts, tide tables, anchor, etc. Ensure your craft is suitable. Seek expert advice if in any doubt (the lock keepers are extremely helpful). Inland waterways craft do navigate the Severn Estuary to Sharpness *but this is a foolish practice without suitable weather conditions and the services of a river pilot*. For further details about pilotage telephone Amalgamated Gloucester Pilots on (01374) 226143.

Boatyards

ⓑ ⬤ ✕ **Saltford Marina** The Shallows, Saltford (01225 872226). Beside Kelston Lock. 🛉 🎣 D Overnight mooring, engine repairs, slipway, crane. Restaurant and bar.

ⓑ **Bristol Boats** Mead Lane, Saltford (01225 872032). Near Saltford Lock. Gas, overnight mooring, long-term mooring, slipway, gantry, boat sales and repairs, outboard engine sales and repairs, chandlery, toilets. *Closed Sun in winter.*

ⓑ **Port Avon Marina** Bitton Road, Keynsham. (0117 986 1626). 🛉 🛉 🎣 D Gas, overnight mooring, long-term mooring, winter storage, slipway, crane, chandlery, books, maps and gifts, boat sales and repairs, engine sales and repairs (including outboards), toilets, showers. *24hr emergency call out.*

BW Hanham Lock Toll office (0117 986 2550). K & A windlasses.

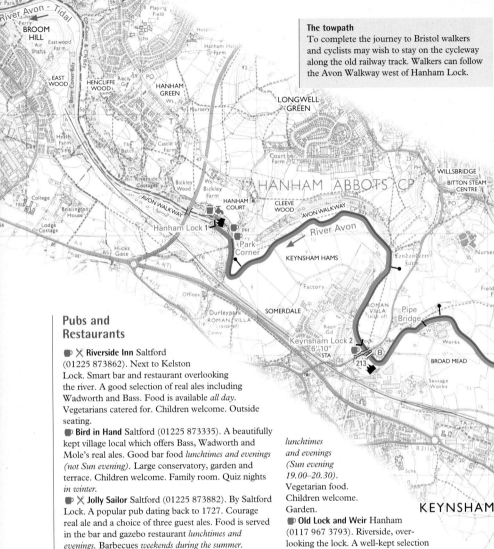

The towpath
To complete the journey to Bristol walkers
and cyclists may wish to stay on the cycleway
along the old railway track. Walkers can follow
the Avon Walkway west of Hanham Lock.

Pubs and Restaurants

🍺 ✕ **Riverside Inn** Saltford
(01225 873862). Next to Kelston
Lock. Smart bar and restaurant overlooking
the river. A good selection of real ales including
Wadworth and Bass. Food is available *all day*.
Vegetarians catered for. Children welcome. Outside
seating.

🍺 **Bird in Hand** Saltford (01225 873335). A beautifully
kept village local which offers Bass, Wadworth and
Mole's real ales. Good bar food *lunchtimes and evenings
(not Sun evening)*. Large conservatory, garden and
terrace. Children welcome. Family room. Quiz nights
in winter.

🍺 ✕ **Jolly Sailor** Saltford (01225 873882). By Saltford
Lock. A popular pub dating back to 1727. Courage
real ale and a choice of three guest ales. Food is served
in the bar and gazebo restaurant *lunchtimes and
evenings*. Barbecues *weekends during the summer*.
Children welcome.

🍺 ✕ **Swan** Swineford (0117 932 3101). Near
Swineford Lock. 200-year-old stone built cottage pub
with a good choice of real ales on offer including
Butcombe, Bass and Courage. Food served in the bar
and restaurant *lunchtimes and evenings*. Vegetarians
catered for. Children's garden.

🍺 **White Hart** Bitton (0117 932 2231). Wadworth,
Otter, Pedigree and Bass real ales and bar food
lunchtimes and evenings (not Mon). Garden, children
welcome. Quiz *Sun*.

🍺 **Lock Keeper** Keynsham Lock (01272 862383).
Unpredictable flood waters forced many a crew to stay
the night at the Lock Keeper. Smiles, Bass and guest
real ales are served at the bar with food available

*lunchtimes
and evenings
(Sun evening
19.00–20.30)*.
Vegetarian food.
Children welcome.
Garden.

🍺 **Old Lock and Weir** Hanham
(0117 967 3793). Riverside, overlooking the lock. A well-kept selection
of real ale includes Marston's, Bass,
Exmoor and Morland. Meals are available
lunchtimes and evenings, (not Sun evening).
Booking advisable Fri & Sat. Fresh fish nights,
Sunday roasts and special rates for children and
senior citizens. Cream teas and barbecues *in summer*.
Overnight moorings available for boaters eating at the
pub.

🍺 ✕ **Chequers** Hanham (0117 967 4242). Riverside.
Marston's and guest real ales are served in very plush
surroundings. Food is available *all day* in the bar and
in the restaurant *L (12.00–14.00) & D (19.00–21.00)*;
Wed, Fri & Sat until 21.30). Cream teas *in summer*.
Riverside garden. Children welcome. Moorings for
patrons.

● **Saltford**
Avon. EC Wed. PO, tel, stores, garage. Although Saltford has been developed as a large-scale dormitory suburb, the older parts by the river are still pretty and secluded.

● **Swineford**
Avon. Tel, farm shop. Although bisected by the A431, the settlement by the river is still attractive. The old mill buildings constructed in 1840 overlook the long weir. There is a farm shop next to the pub, *open daily 08.00–18.00 except Wed & Sun 14.00–18.00.*

People and Planet Swineford Mill, Swineford (0117 932 3505). An attractive shop and tea garden promoting products from the Third World. Open *Wed–Sat 10.30–17.00.* Gifts, foods, jewellery, textiles, books, clothes and environmentally friendly products. Home-made teas and light lunches. Mooring for patrons.

● **Bitton**
Avon. PO, tel, stores, garage. Although a main road village, Bitton's heart survives intact south of the road. Here is a fine group formed by the church, the grange, and the 18thC vicarage, all built around the churchyard. The church has a long Saxon nave with Norman details, a 14thC chancel, and a magnificently decorative late 14thC tower. There is also an embryonic preserved steam railway undergoing restoration.

● **Keynsham**
Avon. All services. Keynsham has grown steadily along the Bristol road, and so is now a vast shapeless suburb. However, the centre still retains a feeling of independence, and has many traces of Keynsham's past.

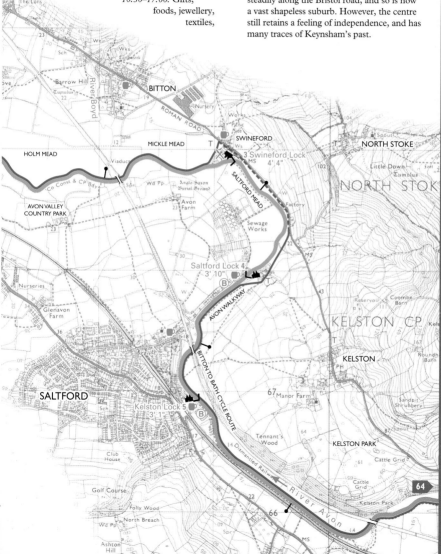

RIVER THAMES

FROM INGLESHAM TO TEDDINGTON:

The Environment Agency
Thames Region
Kings Meadow House
Kings Meadow Road
Reading
Berks RG1 8DQ
(0118) 953 5525

Those on the river are urged to obtain a copy of **A User's Guide to the River Thames**, published by the Agency, which details all navigational requirements.

All vessels must be registered with the Agency *before* using the non-tidal river – apply to the Craft Registration Dept at the above address. Vessels joining the river for short periods from connecting waterways can obtain short period registration from Thames locks adjacent to those waterways.

Boats must be constructed and equipped in accordance with the Boat Safety Requirements.

Pollution If you notice any pollution, notify the relevant Navigation Office (below), a lock keeper, or ring Freefone (0800) 807060.
Navigation Offices:
Oxford: (01865) 721271
Reading: (0118) 953 5533
Maidenhead: (01628) 22491
Sunbury: (01932) 781946

Speed Limit The maximum is 5 mph, in practice about 3 mph (the same as a brisk walking pace), and slower if your wash may cause damage to the river bank or small craft.

BELOW TEDDINGTON:

Port of London Authority
Devon House
58–60 St Katharine's Way
London E1 9LB.
0171 265 2656

The Port of London Authority (PLA) issues a selection of useful free **Information for**

Pleasure Boaters obtainable from the office above.

All river users are governed by the Port of London River Bye-laws, a copy of which can be obtained from (charge):
The Chief Harbour Master
London River House
Royal Pier Road
Gravesend
Kent DA12 2BG

All river movements on the tidal section of the river covered by this guide are under the control of **Woolwich Radio** who can be contacted by telephone on 0181 855 0315 and VHF channel 14.

All vessels over 20 metres must carry VHF radio and boat owners are reminded that they should hold an appropriate licence to operate such equipment.

MILEAGES:

INGLESHAM Junction with the Thames & Severn Canal to:
Lechlade: $1/2$ mile
Newbridge: $17^1/2$ miles
Kings Lock *Junction with Duke's Cut, Oxford Canal*: $27^1/2$ miles
Oxford *Junction with Oxford Canal (Isis Lock)*: $30^1/2$ miles
Abingdon Lock: $39^1/2$ miles
Wallingford Bridge: $53^1/2$ miles
Reading *Junction with Kennet & Avon Canal*: $70^1/2$ miles
Marlow Lock: $87^1/2$ miles
Windsor Bridge: $100^1/2$ miles
Shepperton *Junction with River Wey*: 114 miles
Teddington Lock: $125^1/2$ miles
Brentford *Junction with Grand Union Canal*: $130^1/2$ miles
Limehouse Basin *Junction with Regent's Canal and River Lee*: $146^1/2$ miles

As a river the Thames enjoys a special place in the hearts and minds of the British population, metamorphosed as a great patriarchal figure reaching back into the beginnings of time. It links the rural idyll of the Cotswolds, in the centre of the country, with the nation's bustling capital city, flowing past the seat of government. Stretching for 215 miles across country from west to east, its importance was recognised by the Romans, who built Watling Street, the Fosse Way, Ermine Street and the Icknield Way to cross the river. These crossings were usually fords, traces of which remain, but bridges were built at London and Staines. Many of the earliest settlements were close to the river. London grew into a great trading centre and port, and by the 19thC it was the largest port in the world.

Goods were shipped inland from the capital – carried upriver by horse drawn or sailing barges – and by the start of the 19thC the Thames had been linked to the main canal network, thereby affording access to many other parts of Britain. However, the importance of the river as a transport artery was short-lived and began to diminish with the expansion of the railways.

The economical and geographical importance of the river led to a growth of fortified buildings along its banks. The Romans had a vast military fortification on the site of the Tower of London. The Angles and Saxons, entering the country through the mouth of the Thames, built their fortified settlements on the Kent and Essex banks. The Norman plan to build castles at strategic points throughout England included Windsor and the Tower of London. The Tudors later extended the line of fortresses, under the threat of invasion from France and Spain.

During the Middle Ages the river was a source of livelihood for many people. Great monasteries were established, and mills were built using river power. From earliest times the Thames held an abundance of fish, and trout and salmon could be caught readily. The latter were once so common that they were eaten by the poor. The river was also thick with eels. The eels would swim up the river in such numbers that they could be caught with sieves and buckets, and were made into a form of cake. From the early 19thC increasing pollution drove all the salmon and eels from the lower river, but a vigorous clean-up campaign has now secured their return, and amateur fishermen are a common sight right through central London.

To catch the fish and power the mills, weirs were built, often in places where they hindered navigation. From earliest times there was constant dispute between the fishermen and millers, and the barge men. Some weirs, known as flash locks, had movable sections to allow barges to pass through. But even then the barge man would have to wait for the fierce rush of water to subside before passing the weir, or be pulled through by winch. Then he would have to wait on the far side for the depth of water to build up again. Legislation tried unsuccessfully to control the building of weirs, and so allow the river to fulfil its important role as a highway. Navigation did not improve until pound locks were introduced on the Thames, one of the first being built at Swift Ditch, near Abingdon, about 1620.

The Thames has often been the scene of festivity. In the 17th and 18thC Frost Fairs were held in London whenever the river froze. There were stalls, performing bears, fairground amusements and ox roasting on the ice. The last Frost Fair was held in 1814. The removal of the old London Bridge, which had the effect of a dam, and the building of the embankments in the 19thC, narrowed the river, and deepened and speeded the flow of water, so that it is now no longer possible for the tidal river to freeze over. However in 1963, the non-tidal Thames froze as far as Teddington.

Since the early 19thC the river has become the scene of regattas in summer, that at Henley being an international event.

Of particular significance to Londoners is the fact that their city is sinking at the rate of about twelve inches every 100 years. As long ago as 1236 the river flooded the Palace of Westminster; in 1928 central London was flooded with the loss of 14 lives; and the disastrous surge tide of 1953 left 300 dead along the east coast and Thames estuary. To counter this threat the magnificent Thames Flood Barrier has been built at Woolwich. Movable barriers can be raised from the river bed to hold back the tide – the four main gates having a span of 200ft and the strength to withstand a load of more than 9000 tonnes. The stainless steel shells housing the machinery are built on hardwood ribs, their design reminiscent of the Sydney Opera House.

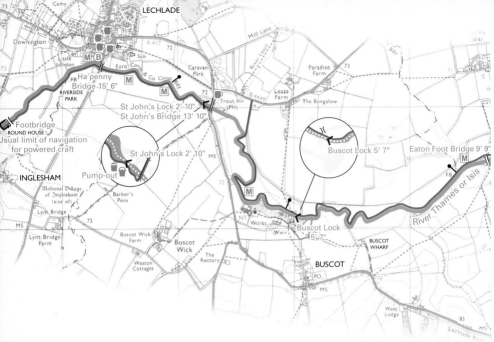

Lechlade

The navigable Thames begins at the Round House, at the junction with the unnavigable Thames & Severn Canal near Inglesham – an attractive group of buildings by the river's edge. Moored craft and all the activities of a riverside park are present as the Thames passes Lechlade, flowing under Ha'penny Bridge, so named because a toll was once taken. The church at Lechlade can be seen for miles around – its tall spire always visible as the river meanders to St John's Lock, the highest on the Thames. Note the modern lock house, the quaint miniature buildings in the lock gardens, and the statue of Father Thames, which once marked the river's source at Thames Head, north of Kemble, Gloucestershire. Below the bridge the course of the Thames becomes even more extravagant – at one point even doubling back before passing the church and beautiful rectory at Buscot. Beyond Buscot Lock the river is once again in open country, delightfully rural and lonely. The church at Eaton Hastings is by the river and provides interest before reaching Grafton Lock, a lonely outpost. A very isolated and rural stretch of river then follows, meandering through meadowland and having little contact with civilisation.

NAVIGATIONAL NOTES

The limit of navigation for powered craft is usually at the old junction with the Thames & Severn Canal, marked by the Round House, below Inglesham. Here a full length narrow boat can wind, taking care to avoid the sandbank on the north side. Those not familiar with the river are urged to proceed no further, even though the right of navigation extends to Cricklade, and craft drawing 2ft 6in may be able to proceed as far as 3 miles above Lechlade.

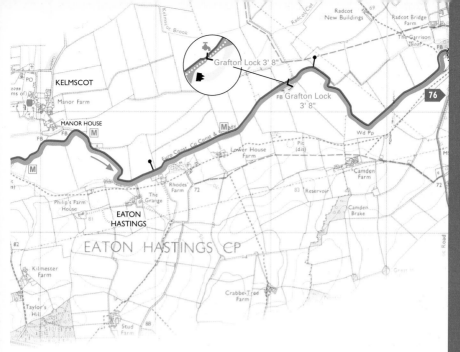

NATURAL HISTORY IN THE THAMES VALLEY

The Thames is a lowland river throughout its length with few of the striking changes in scenery or gradient that one associates with rivers of the north or west of the country. As a result its landscape is gentle and its flood plain contains woodlands, water meadows and grassland with appropriately modest plant and animal inhabitants. However, the scenery is enriched by the Goring Gap, between Goring and Reading, where during the Ice Ages the river cut a new channel through the south western end of the Chilterns, isolating the Berkshire Downs on the south bank. The river here passes through chalk hills with rich grassland and beech woods of spectacular appearance. Through most of its length the water meadows overlie river gravels; in many places these have been excavated to win gravel for roads and buildings, leaving water-filled pits in which the richest animal life of all the Thames valley can be found. As a result of these natural and man-made habitats there is a great deal of fascinating natural history interest in the Thames and its surroundings.

Boatyards

Ⓑ **Riverside Lechlade** Park End Wharf, Lechlade (01367 252229). 🛏 ♨ P D E Gas, narrow boat and cruiser hire, day hire boats, overnight mooring, long-term mooring, winter storage, slipway, dry dock, crane, chandlery, boat and engine sales and repairs, gifts, books and maps, toilets, café. *24 hour* mechanic. Pub *open all day*, serving meals, and with a children's room.

Abingdon (see page 88)

● **Inglesham**

Wilts. A marvellous architectural group around the tiny church. Although of Saxon origin, the present building is largely 13thC with later additions: note the bell tower and the 17thC box pews. William Morris is responsible for the remarkably original state of the building – he loved it and saved it from 19thC restoration. A brass to the right of the entrance commemorates his work. The adjoining farm was once the priory. On the north bank the Inglesham Round House is a notable land-mark. It once belonged to the lock keeper on the now unnavigable Thames & Severn Canal, which joins the river at this point.

● **Lechlade**

Glos. EC Thur. PO, shops. A golden grey market town dominating the river in all directions and best seen from St John's Bridge, with the tall spire of the Perpendicular wool church rising above the surrounding cluster of buildings. Shelley's Walk leads from the river to the church, where his *Stanzas in a Summer Churchyard* is quoted on a plaque in the churchyard wall. Shelley, Peacock, Mary Godwin and Charles Clairmont stayed in Lechlade in 1815 after rowing from Windsor.

Little Faringdon Mill One mile outside Lechlade on the A361 to Burford. A perfect 18thC mill in its original state, with farm and outbuildings. Private.

● **Buscot**

Oxon. A small village off the A417, notable for the very beautiful Queen Anne rectory (private) which stands on the riverside by the church, itself unremarkable apart from its Burne-Jones windows. The National Trust owns a picnic site by the weir pool.

Buscot Old Parsonage Buscot, Faringdon, Oxon. A Cotswold stone building of 1703 on the river bank. *Open by written appointment with the tenant.* NT.

Buscot Park (01367 240786). Built about 1780 in the Adam style, with a park and gardens laid out by Harold Peto. Fine furniture and paintings by Rembrandt and Murillo. Burne-Jones room. *Open 14.00–18.00 Wed to Fri and 2nd and 4th weekends in the month, Apr–Sep.* Groups should ring to book. There is a tearoom on site. Charge. NT.

Buscot Wharf Little trace remains of the wharf from which brandy was shipped to France. The short arm was known as Buscot Pill.

Tourist Information Centre 5 Market Place, Faringdon (01367 242191).

● **Kelmscot**

Oxon. A pristine village of elegant greystone houses, firmly entrenched against development. The quiet 15thC church has a strong medieval atmosphere.

Kelmscot Manor 01367 252486. A beautiful 16thC house behind high walls, which was the home of William Morris from 1871 until his death in 1896. He shared it with Dante

Gabriel Rossetti until 1874. William Morris was buried in the churchyard at Kelmscott after his death in Hammersmith; his tomb is the work of Philip Webb. The Manor is *open 11.00–13.00 and 14.00–17.00 every Wed, and 14.00–17.00 on the 3rd Sat of each month, Apr–Sep.* Charge.

● **Eaton Hastings**

Oxon. Quite inaccessible from the river. The 13thC church is well situated by the water – the rest of the village is a mile away.

The towpath
Practical walking along the Thames begins at Inglesham. The path is in good shape throughout the length of the river to London.

Pubs and Restaurants

The Swan Burford St, Lechlade (01367 253571). A cosy stone-built pub, the oldest in Lechlade, serving Boddingtons, Flowers and guest real ales, and a selection of good wines. Bar meals are available *all day*, with vegetarian menu. Children are welcome and there is a garden. Regular entertainment.

Crown Inn High St, Lechlade (01367 252198). An excellent choice of real ales including Wells, Morland and guests are always available. Good food, such as home-made soups and hamburgers, make this a very popular pub. Meals are served in the bar or dining area *lunchtimes and evenings (every day in summer, less in winter)*, and there are always vegetarian options. Children are welcome and there is a garden. Regular quiz nights.

New Inn Hotel Market Square, Lechlade (01367 252296). An attractive pub by the church, where Morland, Bass, Arkell's and guest real ales are served. Bar and restaurant meals from traditional dishes to the exotic, are available *lunchtimes and evenings*, with vegetarian choices available. Children are welcome and there is a large garden with a play area. There are shower facilities here.

Red Lion Lechlade (01367 252373). A fine old coaching inn with open fires. Arkell's real ales are served and bar and restaurant meals are available *lunchtimes and evenings*, with a vegetarian menu. Children are welcome and there is outside seating in the patio area.

British Raj Burford Street, Lechlade (01367 252956). A wide choice of Indian food. *Open 12.00–14.30 & 18.00–23.30.*

Connect Coffee Shop Burford Street, Lechlade (01367 253464). A friendly tearoom and coffee shop, with prints and paintings on the walls. *Open 09.30–17.00 Mon-Sat, 11.30–17.00 Sun.*

Trout Inn St John's Bridge, Lechlade (01367 252313). A justly famous 13thC Cotswold stone pub, with plenty of wood panelling, low beams and stuffed fish. There are tasty home-cooked bar meals served in the bar or in a dining area *lunchtimes and evenings every day*, with a vegetarian menu always available. Courage and John Smith's real ales are served. Live jazz *Tue and Sun evening*. The large riverside garden borders the weir stream and there is a boules pitch, and a marquee available for special events. Also an intriguing old Oxfordshire game called Aunt Sally is played in the garden. Children are welcome, and there are fishing rights on two miles of the Thames. *On either the first or second weekend in June* the pub holds a tractor and steam rally. A National Music weekend (*last weekend June*) is celebrated, and a jazz festival is usually held on the following weekend (*usually the first weekend in July*).

Plough Inn Kelmscot (01367 253543). A fine 16thC pub with flagstone floors, serving Morland and guest real ales. Restaurant, with à la carte menu, and home-made bar meals served *lunchtimes and evenings*, with vegetarian options. Children are welcome, and there is a garden. Entertainment with music on *Sat evenings*.

Tadpole

A very isolated, rural stretch of river, meandering through meadowland and having little contact with civilisation. The river divides at Radcot where two fine bridges, the ever popular Swan Hotel and a large picnic area opposite are always busy with pleasure seekers on summer afternoons. Caravans line the north bank as once more the Thames enters open meadowland around Radcot Lock. The river then meanders on to the splendid Rushey Lock, with its charming house and fine garden, and the handsome 18thC Tadpole Bridge. Then once again the Thames enters lonely country, passing to the south of Chimney. It is about as far away from it all as you can get on the Thames.

NAVIGATIONAL NOTES

Radcot Bridge: the approach needs care – note that the navigation channel is the north-ernmost of the two, through the single arched bridge, and that the approach is blind and the current sometimes difficult.

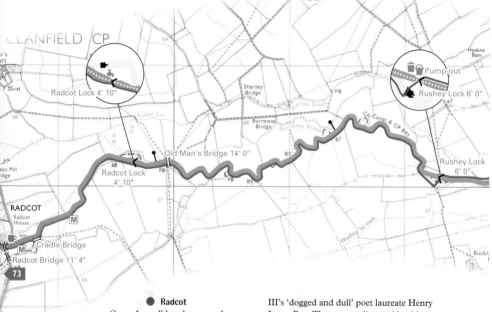

● Radcot

Oxon. A small hamlet centred around the popular Swan Hotel. The triple-arched 13thC bridge is the oldest surviving on the Thames. The single-arched bridge spanning the navigation channel, an artificial cut, was built later, in 1787. The old bridge, made of Taynton stone, was the scene of a Civil War skirmish, when Prince Rupert's Royalist cavalry pounced on Cromwell's men, marching to an attack on Faringdon. Upstream caravans line the north bank – to the south picnics and tents sprawl across the meadow.

Faringdon House *Oxon.* 2¹/₂ miles south of Radcot Bridge. An 18thC house built by George III's 'dogged and dull' poet laureate Henry James Pye. The surrounding parkland is reputedly haunted by a headless Hampden Pye, an earlier member of the family decapitated at sea. His story is recalled in *The Ingoldsby Legends*, 1840. The folly on Faringdon Hill, an octagonal Gothic lantern, was built by the artist and author Lord Berners in 1935.

● Bampton

Oxon. PO, tel, stores. A very attractive greystone town 1¹/₂ miles from the river, easily approached by a variety of footpaths or by road from Tadpole. It has a timeless appearance in that much of the new development is built from the same materials as, and often in a style

Pubs and Restaurants

🍺 **Swan Hotel** Radcot Bridge (01367 810220). A very comfortable and friendly old inn of great character. The interior is decorated with stuffed fish, plenty of brass and features a William Morris oak chair. Morland real ales are served, and bar meals are available *lunchtimes and evenings every day*, with vegetarian choices. There is a pleasant garden. Children are welcome.

🍺 ✕ **Trout Inn** Tadpole Bridge (01367 870382). A fine traditional riverside pub serving Archers, Gibbs Mew and Morland real ale, and meals *lunchtimes and evenings every day*, with vegetarian choices. Children are welcome, and there is a fine riverside garden. Camping and fishing rights.

It is not difficult to find a pub in Bampton – these are two of those available:

🍺 **Morris Clown** High Street, Bampton (01993 850217). A fine 12thC pub with a wonderful sign and superb garden full of mangles (which is visited regularly by school parties). Courage, Wadworth and guest real ales are served. Children are welcome.

🍺 ✕ **Romany Inn** Bridge Street, Bampton (01993 850237). There are Saxon arches in the cellar of this fine old pub, which offers a fine choice of real ales, including Hook Norton, Archers, Wadworth, Donnington and guests. Meals are served *lunchtimes and evenings every day*, with vegetarian options. Children are welcome and there is a garden and children's play area.

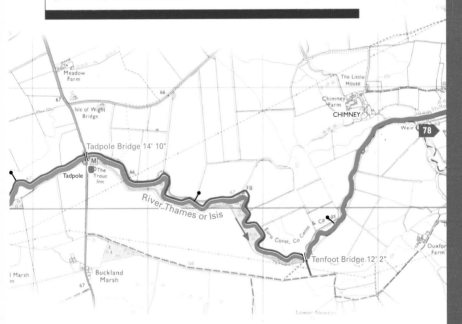

similar to, the old. The result is both unusual and pleasing without being consciously archaic. The church, largely 13thC and 14thC, is dominated by a slightly uneasy octagonal spire. Inside, the 14thC reredos is cut from a single piece of stone, while the Horde Chapel contains excellent Baroque monuments. Beside the church is the old grammar school, founded in 1653. At one time the town was called Bampton in the Bush – this dates from before the 18thC when no roads served the community. Morris dancing is reputed to have originated here.

● **Buckland**
Oxon. PO, tel, stores. About a mile south of Tadpole Bridge. A village intimately connected with Buckland House, and best approached from the river, as there is a fine view over the Thames Valley. The church has an unusually wide 12thC nave. The south transept is splendidly decorated in rich late-Victorian mosaic, dating from about 1890.
Buckland House Built in 1757 by Wood of Bath, it is one of the most imposing 18thC homes in Oxfordshire. The wings were added in 1910, but are nonetheless quite convincing. There is a Gothic stable in the park (private).

Newbridge

The navigation channel passes through a tree-lined cut to Shifford Lock, the last lock to be built on the Thames, in 1898. Again the countryside is flat farmland, glimpsed here and there over the steep river banks, in places heavily overgrown. Electricity pylons do little to improve the scene. Welcome relief appears at Newbridge, with a fine pub on each side of the handsome old bridge. The nearest village is Standlake, a mile to the north. As the hills close in from the east the countryside gradually loses much of the bleakness of the upper reaches and the villages comes a little closer. There are attractive woods below Northmoor Lock, and Bablock Hythe is soon reached. To the north, the grassy banks of the vast Farmoor Reservoir, much loved by anglers, come down to the river's edge.

● **Shifford**
Oxon. A church and a few houses surrounded by lush pastureland are all that remain of a once important town. Alfred held a meeting of the English Parliament here in AD890. The church is situated in the middle of a field less than 1/4 mile from the river.

● **Hinton Waldrist and Longworth**
Oxon. Two pleasant straggling villages up on a ridge overlooking the valley. Longworth church contains a good example of Arts and Crafts stained glass by Heywood Sumner, 1906. The Old Rectory, Longworth, was the birthplace of Dr John Fell, 1625–86, who participated in the early development of the Oxford University Press, especially with regard to printing types; and also Richard Doddridge Blackmore, 1825–1900, author of *Lorna Doone* (1869), who spent only the first four months of his life here – sadly his mother died shortly after his birth.
Harrowdown Hill A very dominant dome-shaped hill, approached by footpath from the river.

● **Newbridge**
Oxon. A fine 13thC stone bridge with pointed arches, one of the oldest on the river and the site of a Civil War battle when the Parliamentarians tried, and failed, to approach Faringdon. The River Windrush joins the Thames here.

● **Northmoor**
Oxon. The 13thC cruciform church contains a restored bell loft, dated 1701 – note the dedication poem. Behind the church is a Tudor rectory.

● **Appleton**
Oxon. PO, store. A meandering thatch and stone village, with new development to the west. Appleton Manor, situated beside a splendid weather-boarded barn and gateway, was built at the end of the 12thC. An astonishing amount remains: note especially the doorway.

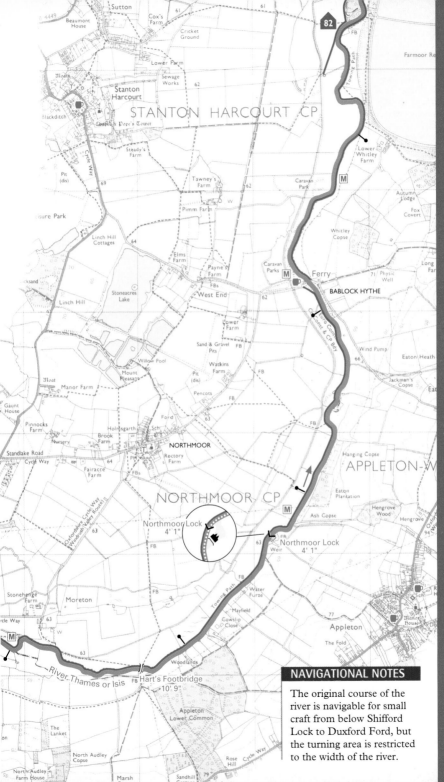

NAVIGATIONAL NOTES

The original course of the river is navigable for small craft from below Shifford Lock to Duxford Ford, but the turning area is restricted to the width of the river.

● **Bablock Hythe**

Oxon. Mentioned by Matthew Arnold in *The Scholar Gypsy*, 1853, who was seen: 'In hat of antique shape, and cloak of grey, crossing the stripling Thames at Bab-lock-hithe'. A Roman stone altar, now in the Ashmolean, was dredged from the river here. There has been a ferry here since AD904, and although it has been a little erratic in recent years, it is, at the time of writing, operating again. The area is surrounded by an estate of temporary homes.

● **Stanton Harcourt**

Oxon. PO, stores. A superb greystone village between the Thames and the Windrush, the waters reflecting the quiet glory of the buildings. The grand cruciform church, still predominantly Early English and Perpendicular, has fine monuments in the Harcourt Chapel.

Stanton Harcourt Manor (01865 881928). The Harcourts built this 15thC manor, but only Pope's Tower, the scene of his translation of the *Iliad*, and the unique Great Kitchen, survive. *Open 14.00–18.00 Thur, Sun & B Hol Mons fortnightly Apr–Sept.* Charge. Well worth the walk from the river.

Pubs and Restaurants

🍺 **Blue Boar** Tuck's Lane, Longworth (01865 820494). Morrells real ale and snacks in a busy 16thC country pub. Home-cooked bar meals *lunchtimes and evenings*, with vegetarian options. Children are welcome, and there is a garden.

🍺 **Maybush Inn** Newbridge (01865 300624). A fine riverside pub serving Morland real ale, with bar meals available *lunchtimes and evenings*. Vegetarian menu. There is a terrace overlooking the river and an attractive grassy garden. The single bar area means that children are allowed in the *garden only*. Entertainment in the summer with music on *Sun evenings*.

🍺 ✗ **Rose Revived Inn** Newbridge (01865 300221). A superb old Cotswold stone inn with a beam and inglenook interior. Excellent bar meals and snacks served *all day noon until 22.00*, with a vegetarian menu. Morland real ales available. Live jazz is played *Sun evenings*. Children are welcome and there is a tidy garden, with a bouncy castle for children *in the summer*, and regular barbecues.

🍺 **Thatched Tavern** Appleton (01865 864814). An attractive tiled pub, where the sign displays its earlier thatched roof, serving Brakspear and Theakston's real ales. Bar meals are available *lunchtimes and evenings*, with a vegetarian menu. Children are welcome and there is some occasional entertainment.

🍺 **Red Lion** Northmoor (01865 300301). A good village pub by the church, serving Morland real ales. A wide range of meals are available in the bar or dining area *lunchtimes and evenings*, with vegetarian choices. Children are welcome *in the dining area*. Garden. Live music *once a month*.

🍺 ✗ **The Ferry Inn** Bablock Hythe (01865 880028). A famous and welcoming pub, serving Greene King real ale. Meals are available *lunchtimes and evenings every day*, with vegetarian choices. Children are welcome, and there is a riverside garden. In *Sept* they stage a Steamboat Rally, when as many as 33 steam launches can be seen. They also organise a raft race, and the Mikron Theatre visits in *June*.

🍺 ✗ **Harcourt Arms** Stanton Harcourt (01865 881931). A handsome 16thC inn serving John Smith's, Ruddles, Theakston's and a guest real ale. Good, interesting food served *lunchtimes and evenings every day*, with vegetarian choices. Children are welcome, and there is a garden.

🍺 **The Fox** Stanton Harcourt (01865 881551). Morrells real ale is served in this small, friendly pub. Bar meals are available *lunchtimes and evenings*, with a vegetarian and children's menu. There is a garden and a 3½ acre field where the owners are developing a pets corner: it presently boasts Vietnamese pot-bellied pigs. Occasional entertainment.

🍺 **Vine** Abingdon Road, Cumnor (01865 862567). A pretty pub with the aforementioned vine growing along the front wall. Tetley real ale is served, and bar meals are available *lunchtimes and evenings*, with vegetarian choices. Children are welcome and there is a very large garden with a play area. There are regular quiz nights and entertainment of a more active sort: on *B. Hols in summer* bungee jumping, for example.

🍺 ✗ **Bear & Ragged Staff** Appleton Road, Cumnor (01865 862329). A large 16thC building close to the village pond, where Morrells and Bass real ale is served. Good restaurant meals from a varied and imaginative menu, and bar meals available *lunchtimes and evenings every day*, with vegetarian choices. Children are welcome and there is a garden with a play area. There is occasional entertainment with jazz music. *In the summer* there are regular barbecues with, for example, shellfish on the menu.

🍺 **Eight Bells** Eaton (01865 862983). About a mile south east of Bablock Hythe. A welcoming pub serving Morland and guest real ales. Bar meals can be selected from a large menu, including vegetarian and vegan, and are available *lunchtimes and evenings (not all day Mon, or Sun evening)*. Older children are welcome inside the pub *if dining*, and in warmer weather children are welcome *in the large garden*. Regular live folk music.

Godstow

The Thames meanders extravagantly past Farmoor Reservoir and the very pretty Pinkhill Lock, with its picnic site, towards Swinford. Below Eynsham Lock the entrance to the Wharf Stream can be seen on the east side, followed by the Cassington Cut, which bypassed the lower reaches of the Evenlode, when that river was navigable. Opposite are the dense woodlands of Wytham Great Wood, falling steeply down Wytham Hill to the river's edge. The Seacourt Stream leaves the Thames at Hagley Pool, and a short distance below is King's Lock. Access to the Oxford Canal can be gained via a backwater and the Duke's Cut, which join the weir stream. Pixey Mead lies to the west, its peace shattered by the incessant traffic of the Oxford bypass, which crosses the river above Godstow. On the weir stream is the old Trout Inn: overlooking the lock cut are the ruins of Godstow Abbey. By Port Meadow the river is now significantly wider, flowing between sandy banks to Binsey, where a small jetty indicates the presence of the village and its handsome thatched pub. The navigation channel below Binsey becomes comparatively narrow and tree-lined after Medley Footbridge. Soon a water crossroads is reached, with the unnavigable Bulstake Stream running off to the west, while to the east a short, narrow cut to the Oxford Canal branches off under a very low railway bridge. A smart terrace of railway houses stands beside the river, all with doors onto the towpath. The journey through Oxford proper begins at the notoriously low (7ft 6in) Osney Bridge, an obstacle which makes it impossible for the larger Thames cruisers to penetrate upstream.

Swinford Toll Bridge A fine stone balustraded bridge and toll house where a small toll is collected. It was built in 1777.

● **Eynsham**
Oxon. EC Wed. PO, tel, stores, laundrette. ³/4 mile north west of Swinford Bridge. Once a town of considerable importance, boasting a Benedictine Abbey, founded in the 11thC, today Eynsham has a good selection of shops around the old Town Hall, in the Market Square.

Wytham Great Wood A marvellous wood of over 600 acres, owned by Oxford University, whose field station is a good example of English vernacular architecture. A haven for birds; the hobby has nested here, nightingales and warblers sing, and teal visit in winter. There is a heronry at Wytham. (Private, permit required).

● **Godstow**
Oxon. A cluster of buildings around the few remains of Godstow Nunnery, built in 1138 and destroyed by Fairfax, commander of Cromwell's New Model Army, in 1646. The bridge and the Trout Inn make a charming setting.

● **Wytham**
Oxon. A very pretty small village set into the side of Wytham Hill, at its best when approached from the river. Wytham Abbey, originally 16thC, has many later additions: the whole is pleasingly irregular.

NAVIGATIONAL NOTES

1 Access to the Oxford Canal can be gained via the weir stream above King's Lock and through Duke's Cut. Maximum dimensions on this charming rural canal are: length 70ft 0in, beam 7ft 0in, headroom 7ft 0in. The canal is described in detail in Book 1.

2 Take great care at Godstow Bridge, where the arches are narrow and low.

3 Proceeding downstream below Binsey, note that the navigation channel is under the iron footbridge on the west side, by the boatyard. Access to the Oxford Canal can be made along the channel above Osney Bridge.

4 The headroom at Osney Bridge is 7ft 6in at normal levels, less when the river is in spate. Those proceeding upstream who are in any doubt regarding the headroom should consult the lock keeper. And remember, the water levels can change very quickly, so you could get stuck *upstream*.

Pubs and Restaurants

🍺 **Talbot** Oxford Road, Eynsham (01865 881348). North west of Swinford Bridge. A busy and attractive pub on the now unnavigable Wharf Stream, serving a selection of real ales, including Theakston's, Boddingtons, Fuller's and Tetley's. Meals are served *lunchtimes and evenings every day*, with vegetarian options. Children are welcome, and there is a garden.

🍺 **Chequers** Cassington (01865 881390). Morrells real ale is served in this village local, and bar meals are available *lunchtimes and evenings every day*, with vegetarian options. Children are welcome, and there is a garden.

🍺 ✗ **Trout Inn** Godstow Road, Wolvercote, Oxford (01865 554485). A lovely ivy-covered stone building, with a riverside terrace, built in 1138 as a hospice for Godstow Nunnery. Peacocks roam the large gardens, and the weir stream – not fished for the last 20 years – is full of shoals of large fish, swimming tamely near the surface among the ducks. Fork & Pitcher Inn serving Bass, Hancock's and Fuller's real ale at the bar, and hot and cold bar meals *lunchtimes and evenings every day*. There are always vegetarian options. Children are welcome.

🍺 **White Hart** Wytham (01865 244372). An old village pub with flagstone floors, a 16thC dovecote and walled garden. Tetley's, Burton, Ind Coope (ABC) and guest real ales are served.

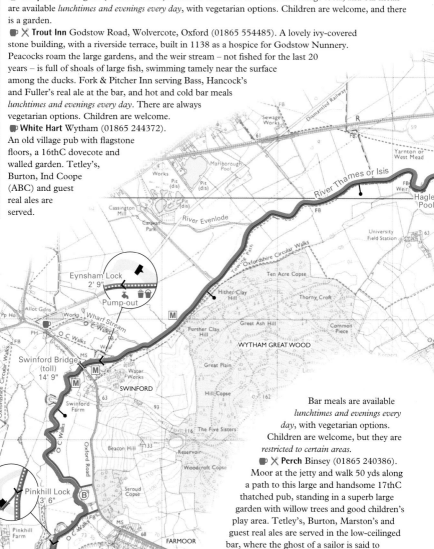

Bar meals are available *lunchtimes and evenings every day*, with vegetarian options. Children are welcome, but they are *restricted to certain areas.*

🍺 ✗ **Perch** Binsey (01865 240386). Moor at the jetty and walk 50 yds along a path to this large and handsome 17thC thatched pub, standing in a superb large garden with willow trees and good children's play area. Tetley's, Burton, Marston's and guest real ales are served in the low-ceilinged bar, where the ghost of a sailor is said to appear. Bar meals from ploughmans to exotic fish dishes (fish is the speciality) are available *lunchtimes and evenings every day (not Sun eve in winter)*, with vegetarian options. *In the summer* there is a barbecue on *Sun and other fine evenings*. Occasional entertainment.

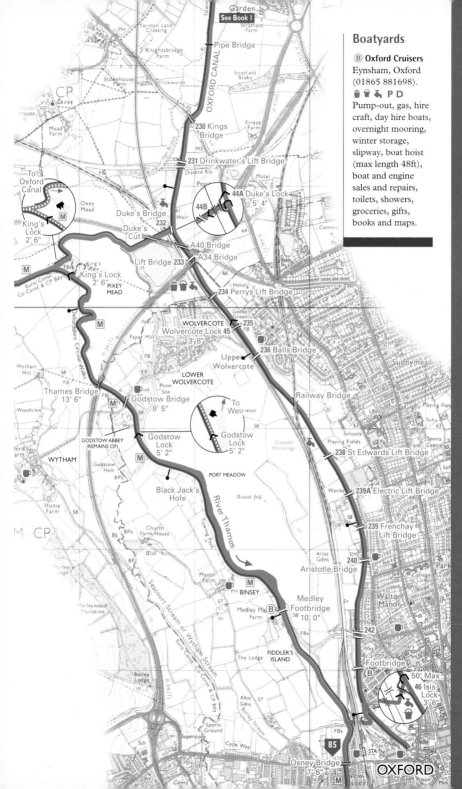

Boatyards

Ⓑ **Oxford Cruisers**
Eynsham, Oxford
(01865 881698).
🚽 🛢 🧹 P D
Pump-out, gas, hire
craft, day hire boats,
overnight mooring,
winter storage,
slipway, boat hoist
(max length 48ft),
boat and engine
sales and repairs,
toilets, showers,
groceries, gifts,
books and maps.

Garden
See Book I
Stratfield
Farm
Pipe Bridge
OXFORD CANAL
230 Kings
Bridge
231 Drinkwater's Lift Bridge
44A Duke's Lock
5' 4"
44B
Duke's Bridge
232
Duke's
Cut
A40 Bridge
A34 Bridge
Lift Bridge 233
King's
Lock
2' 6"
PIXEY
MEAD
234 Perrys Lift Bridge
235
WOLVERCOTE
Wolvercote Lock 45
3' 8"
236 Balls Bridge
Upper
Wolvercote
LOWER
WOLVERCOTE
Railway Bridge
Thames Bridge
13' 6"
Godstow Bridge
8' 5"
To
Weir
Godstow
Lock
5' 2"
GODSTOW ABBEY
(REMAINS OF)
Godstow
Lock
5' 2"
WYTHAM
PORT MEADOW
Black Jack's
Hole
River Thames
238 St Edwards Lift Bridge
239A Electric Lift Bridge
239 Frenchay
Lift Bridge
240
Aristotle Bridge
BINSEY
Medley
Footbridge
10' 0"
Medley
Farm
FIDDLER'S
ISLAND
242
Footbridge
50' Max
46 Isis
Lock
3' 6"
Osney Bridge
7' 6"
85
STA
OXFORD
To
Oxford
Canal
King's
Lock
2' 6"

Oxford

This section, while not particularly picturesque, provides plenty of interest, in stark contrast to the miles of water meadows above the town. Below Osney Bridge is a lovely stretch of urban waterway, with terraced houses facing the river, a handsome pub and a lock – an environment much appreciated by the local work people who spend their lunchbreaks here in the summer. There are many access points to the towpath, which is well used by cyclists, joggers and walkers. Just above Osney Railway Bridge stands a touching memorial to Edgar Wilson who, on 15 June 1889, saved the lives of two boys here, at the cost of his own. Folly Bridge is always a hive of activity during the summer; Salter's Boatyard is here, along with a large riverside pub. Punts are available for hire and small motor and rowing boats proceed up and down. Christ Church Meadow lies to the east, and is thronged with tourists and sunbathers during the summer. Below is a long row of boathouses, facing the mock Tudor of the University Rowing Club building. Downstream of Donnington Road Bridge, suburbia keeps its distance and the river proceeds along a green passage to Iffley Lock, with its pretty balustraded footbridges and fine lock house, all surrounded by trees, with a white-painted pub nearby. There is an area of parkland to the west, on an isthmus created by the Weirs Mill Stream, followed by the functional steel of Kennington Railway Bridge. As the river doglegs past Rose Isle pylons run parallel, but still the houses and factories, for the most part, keep away. Gradually the Oxford conurbation is left behind as the river passes through a mixture of woodland, suburbia and light industry, then curves through a maze of backwaters, used as boat club moorings, to Sandford Lock, the deepest on the river above Teddington and distinguished by the presence of large mill buildings. Below here the Thames passes through open country crisscrossed by electricity pylons. A fascinating stretch of river.

● **City of Oxford**
Oxon. All shops and services. The town was founded in the 10thC and has been a university city since the 13thC. Today it is a lively cosmopolitan centre of learning, tourism and industry.
Oxford Tourist Information Centre The Old School, Gloucester Green (01865 726871). Here you will find a good selection of city guides and maps, and helpful and informative staff.
Colleges
It is, of course, the 39 colleges which give Oxford its unique character – they can all be visited, but opening times vary, so consult with the Tourist Information Centre. Those noted here have been selected as being particularly representative of their periods.
Merton College
One of the earliest collegiate foundations, dating from 1264, the buildings are especially typical of the Perpendicular and Decorative periods. The chapel was begun in 1294 and Mob Quad was the first of the Oxford quadrangles. The library, mainly 14thC, has a famous collection of rare books and manuscripts. During the Victorian era, the college was enlarged, and the Grove Buildings are by William Butterfield, with alterations in 1929 by T. Harold Hughes.
New College
The college was founded by William of

Wykeham, Bishop of Winchester, in 1379. The chapel, a noble example of early Perpendicular, was greatly restored by Sir George Scott in the 19thC. The great west window, after a cartoon by Reynolds, and Epstein's *Lazarus* are noteworthy. The 14thC cloister and the workmanship of the wrought-iron screen, 1684, between the Garden Quad and the Garden, are outstanding memorials of their times.
Keble College
Built by William Butterfield in 1870, Keble is the only Oxford college entirely in the Victorian Gothic style. The frontage of red and grey patterned brickwork and the tracery windows have a god-like self-confidence. The chapel, with its glass and mosaics, bricks, tiles and brass, contains Holman Hunt's *The Light of the World.*
St Catherine's College
An important and interesting example of the new university by the Danish architect, Arne Jacobsen, 1964. The entrance to the college is reached through an unprepossessing car park area, but in the main quadrangle the effect is one of stark impact. The mass of glass windows with their bands of ribbed concrete stretch like concertinas on either side of the quadrangle. All is bleak but full of atmosphere. The furniture and college plate were also designed by Jacobsen.

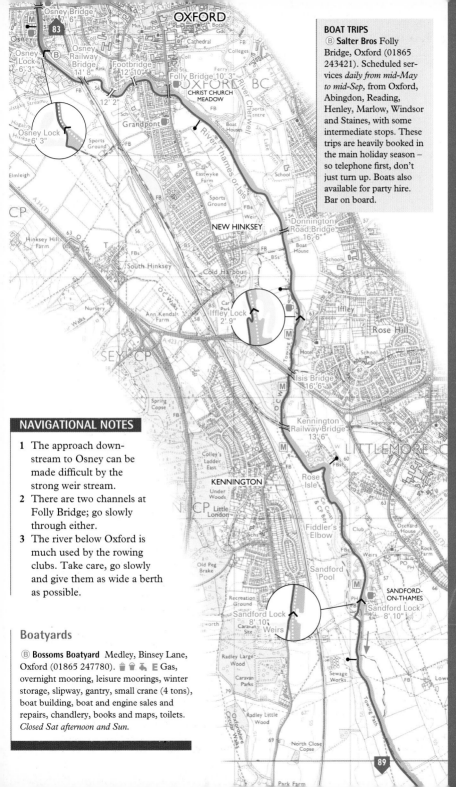

BOAT TRIPS

ⓑ **Salter Bros** Folly Bridge, Oxford (01865 243421). Scheduled services *daily from mid-May to mid-Sep*, from Oxford, Abingdon, Reading, Henley, Marlow, Windsor and Staines, with some intermediate stops. These trips are heavily booked in the main holiday season – so telephone first, don't just turn up. Boats also available for party hire. Bar on board.

NAVIGATIONAL NOTES

1 The approach downstream to Osney can be made difficult by the strong weir stream.
2 There are two channels at Folly Bridge; go slowly through either.
3 The river below Oxford is much used by the rowing clubs. Take care, go slowly and give them as wide a berth as possible.

Boatyards

ⓑ **Bossoms Boatyard** Medley, Binsey Lane, Oxford (01865 247780). 🚽 🚿 🛒 ⒺGas, overnight mooring, leisure moorings, winter storage, slipway, gantry, small crane (4 tons), boat building, boat and engine sales and repairs, chandlery, books and maps, toilets. *Closed Sat afternoon and Sun.*

St Anne's College

This college reflects some of the most exciting modern building in Oxford. The Wolfson block in the main quadrangle was designed by Howell, Killick and Partridge, 1964. With its two curving wings and square jutting windows, all of pre-cast concrete, this building is impressive and original. Facing the block is the Dining Hall by Gerald Banks, 1964, and to one side is Hartland House, mainly 1930s but with 1951 additions by Sir Giles Gilbert Scott.

Other interesting buildings include:

Radcliffe Camera

Radcliffe Square. Dr Radcliffe left £40,000 for the building of this library by James Gibbs, 1739, to house his Physic library. It is a vast domed Italianate rotunda, now a Bodleian reading room, and not open to the public. The staircase and skylight can be admired through the doorway.

Sheldonian Theatre

Broad Street (01865 277299). Built by Christopher Wren in 1669 under the auspices of Gilbert Sheldon, Archbishop of Canterbury, the theatre was designed to be used for university ceremonies and degrees, which are still awarded here. For many years it also housed the work-shops of the University Press. The interior with its ceiling by Robert Streeter is delightful. *Open 10.00–12.30 and 14.00–16.30 (15.30 in winter) Mon–Sat. Closed in the afternoons on concert days, and from mid Nov–mid Feb.* Charge.

The Old Bodleian

Schools Quadrangle (01865 277165). Named after Thomas Bodley, who died in 1613 leaving a fine collection of rare manuscripts, the old Bodleian buildings, mainly 16thC and early 17thC, also incorporate Duke Humphrey's library, dating from the 15thC. Bodley extended Duke Humphrey's library and also financed the entire rebuilding of the Schools Quadrangle. Under the Copyright Act the Bodleian is entitled to claim a copy of every book published in the British Isles. It currently holds some 5½ million volumes and 136,000 manuscripts. *Open for guided tours Nov–mid March every weekday afternoon and Saturday morning, and mid March–Oct tours on weekday mornings also.* The tour lasts 45 mins and tickets are sold in the Divinity School. Charge. Please note that children under 14 years of age *are not permitted on the tours.* The Divinity School and exhibition room are *open 09.00–17.00 Mon–Fri and Saturday morning.* Free.

Christ Church Cathedral

Christ Church. The cathedral, with its inconspic-uous entrance in Tom Quad, was originally part of the Priory of St Frideswide. It is mainly 12thC with later additions and is typically Romanesque. The most splendid feature is the 16thC stone-vaulted fan roof of the choir. There is medieval glass and also 19thC glass by Burne-Jones. The Chapter House is a 13thC masterpiece.

St Mary the Virgin

High Street. The fine 14thC spire is a landmark. The church is typical of the Perpendicular style, apart from the magnificent Baroque porch with its twisted columns by Nicholas Stone, 1637.

Ashmolean Museum

Beaumont Street (01865 278000). The oldest public museum in Britain (opened in 1683) and one of the most rewarding museums outside London. It has an outstanding collection of Near Eastern and European archaeology, as well as the Farrer collection of 17th and 18thC silver. The Herberden Coin Room has a vast display of early coins, while in the Department of Fine Art, the Michelangelo and Raphael drawings are to be admired. The museum also has the bulk of the archaeological material from the Upper Thames. *Open 10.00–16.00 Tue–Sat, 14.00–16.00 Sun, 14.00–17.00 B. Hols.* Free. Café on site *open until 17.00.*

Christ Church Picture Gallery

Christ Church (01865 276172). Built by Powell and Moya, 1968, the gallery displays Christ Church's private collection. Exceptional Renaissance drawings by Michelangelo, Leonardo da Vinci and Rubens, as well as 14th–18thC paintings, mainly Italian. *Open 10.30–13.00 and 14.00–16.30 Mon–Sat, 14.00–16.30 Sun (Easter–end Sept open until 17.30).* Charge. Shop.

Museum of Modern Art

Pembroke Street (01865 728608). Five galleries displaying various art forms from all over the world. No permanent exhibition as displays tend to change every three months. Café and book-shop on site. *Open 10.00–18.00 Tue–Sat, 14.00–18.00 Sun, with late night on Thur until 21.00.* Charge.

The Oxford Story

Broad Street (01865 728822). Automated cars take you on a journey through eight centuries of Oxford University's history. The exhibition also includes a recreation of a 1950s street scene, and an audio visual show of Unviersity life today. *Open 09.30–17.00 Apr–Oct (09.00–18.30 Jul & Aug), 10.00–16.30 Nov–Mar.* Charge.

University Museum

Parks Road (01865 272950). The building by Deane and Woodward, 1855–60, in high Victorian Gothic was much admired by Ruskin. Built to house a collection of the Natural Sciences, the interior is a forest of columns and skeletons covered by a glass roof. One great rarity is the head and claw of a dodo. *Open 12.00–17.00 Mon–Sat.* Free.

Christ Church Meadows

The meadows lie behind Christ Church and Merton and have fine views and a path leading down to the river. The path is lined with college barges, not many remaining, and boathouses. In the afternoons one can watch the rowing Eights. Enter the Meadows from St Aldates.

University Botanic Garden
Rose Lane, by Magdalen Bridge (01865
276920). The oldest botanic garden in Britain
founded by Henry Lord Danvers. In the 17thC
the garden was intended for the culture of
medical plants, but today it fosters an
extensive collection of rare plants for research
and teaching. The gateway is by Inigo Jones.
Open 09.00–17.00 daily. Free (but a charge is
made from mid June to end Aug).

Pubs and Restaurants

There are many fine pubs and restaurants in
Oxford. Those listed here are on or near the
river, with one notable exception.

Old Gatehouse Botley Road (01865 242823).
Situated between Osney Bridge and Oxford
Station, this pub was once a toll house. Bar
meals and snacks are served *lunchtimes and
evenings (not Sun evening)*, with vegetarian
options. Children are welcome, and there is a
large garden.

Watermans Arms South Street, Osney
(01865 248832). A very fine riverside local near
Osney Lock, once used by the bargees. Morland
real ale is served along with bar meals *lunchtimes
and evenings (not Sun evening)*, with vegetarian
options. Children are welcome and there is
outside seating on a patio area. There is also
some grass to sit on by the river, in summer.

Head of the River Folly Bridge (01865
721600). A three-storey pub and dining complex built in a converted grain warehouse, with
an upstairs bar opening onto a balcony, and
which contains the winning 1908 Olympic
twin scull. Fuller's real ale and bar meals are
available *lunchtimes and evenings*, with vegetarian
choices. A sandwich bar in a separate building is
open all day during the summer. Large terrace
with outside seating at the front of the pub.
Punts for hire close by, *Apr–Oct.* Occasional
entertainment.

Folly Bridge Inn Abingdon Road (01865
790106). South of Folly Bridge. A pleasant pub
with garden, serving Wadworth real ale and bar
meals *lunchtimes and evenings*, with vegetarian
options. Children are welcome. Regular
entertainment.

Chequers High Street (01865 726904).
A 15thC inn, with the original panelling and
fireplace in the Monks bar at the front. Serving
Tetley's, Burton and Wadworth real ales and
meals in a dining area or in the bar at *lunchtime
every day.* There is a vegetarian menu. Children
are welcome *if dining.* Garden with seating.
A disco is held on *Fri* and a disco and karaoke
on *Wed.*

Mitre High Street (01865 244563). Parts
of this building date from the 13thC, but the
main part of this well-known hotel is 17thC.
Past patrons include Peel, Gladstone and
Elizabeth Taylor. Boddingtons and a couple of
guest real ales are served. There is a Beefeater
Restaurant *open all day*, with a vegetarian menu,
and bar snacks are available. Afternoon teas are
served *during the summer.* Children are welcome
and there is a garden to the rear. Regular quiz
nights.

Turf Tavern Bath Place, off Holywell Street
(01865 243235). Surprisingly secluded from
the bustle of the city this pub is one of the most
distinctive in Oxford. Made famous through
Hardy's *Jude the Obscure*, the 13thC tavern has
become popular with both students and tourists
and is consequently expensive. There is a large
choice of real ales. Bar meals and snacks
available *all day.* Outside seating. Children
welcome *in the back bar only.*

Restaurant Elizabeth St Aldates (01865
242230). A restaurant in a very old building of
great character, specialising in French traditional
cuisine. Some excellent dishes, including
vegetarian. Delicious sweets and a good wine
list. Just a short walk up from Folly Bridge.
L & D, closed Mon.

Munchy Munchy Park End Street (01865
245710). East of Osney Bridge. Exciting
Indonesian cooking. *L & D, closed Sun & Mon.*
Can cater for vegetarians.

Heroes Ship Street (01865 723459). Home-
made soup, filling sandwiches and breakfasts.
*Open 08.00–19.00 Mon–Fri, 08.30–18.00 Sat,
and 10.00–17.00 Sun.*

Isis Iffley Lock (01865 247006). A large,
white, isolated pub, once a farmhouse, in a
pleasant garden with mature trees and a
children's play area. With no direct road access,
the beer was once delivered from the river. The
bars contain memorabilia of university boat
races. Morrells real ale and meals *lunchtimes
and evenings every day (not Sun evening)*, with
vegetarian choices.

King's Arms Church Road, Sandford
Lock, Sandford-on-Thames (01865 777095).
A fine lockside pub, with ceiling beams of old
barge timbers, serving Courage and
Theakston's real ales. Bar meals and a family-
style restaurant serving food *lunchtimes and
evenings every day*, with vegetarian choices.
Extensive indoor and outdoor facilities for
children, with a garden that has a bouncy castle
in good weather.

Abingdon

Hills close in from the east as Radley College Boathouse is passed and the landscaped grounds of Nuneham House come into view, followed by the steeply wooded slope of Lock Wood. After Nuneham Railway Bridge the river passes the entrance to the Swift Ditch – once the main navigation channel – where one of the earliest pound locks on the Thames was built in about 1620. Its remains were incorporated into an overspill weir in 1967. Above Abingdon Lock the handsome river frontage faces the open fields and sports grounds of Andersey Island, in an area noted for mute swans. The River Ock enters the Thames under a bridge (dated 1824) by the Old Anchor Inn, a mellow and welcoming building. Now the river heads for open country and enters Culham Reach, passing the wooden bridge across the Swift Ditch, standing beside the old road bridge and its more modern replacement. A sharp turn east marks the entrance to Culham Cut, overlooked by the 17thC greystone manor. There is a footpath to the pub and village from the footbridge, but, of course,

ABINGDON

ABBEY (REMS OF)

Abingdon Lock 6' 2"

Abingdon Bridge 13' 11"

ANDERSEY ISLAND

Swift Ditch

The Warren

Barton Lane

Dismantled Railway

Thrupp House

Nuneham Railway Bridge 15' 9"

Weir

Warren Farm

Abingdon Lock 6' 2"

Pump-out

Culham Hill
Culham Bridge

The Knoll

The Toot

Sloven Copse

Thame Lane

Culham Lock 7' 11"

Schola Europaea

Pol Ho

CULHAM CP

Culham House

The Green

CULHAM

Footbridge

Manor House 12' 5"

Culham Cut

Culham Lock 7' 11"

Sutton Bridge 14' 9"

Sutton Pools

Station

Zouch Farm

River Thames or Isis

Cycle Way

Works

Appleford Railway Bridge 13' 0"

THE ABBEY

Cross Tree Farm

SUTTON COURTENAY

APPLEFORD

NAVIGATIONAL NOTES

1 Go slowly at west entrance to Culham Cut – blind corner.
2 Go slowly through Culham Lock Bridge – narrow.

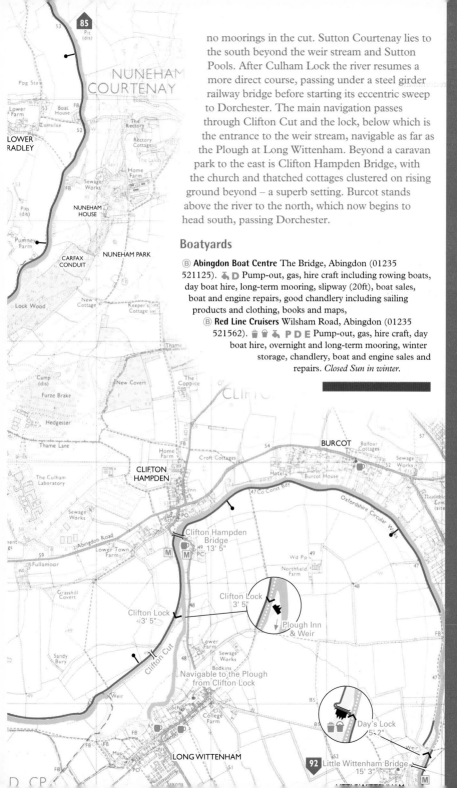

no moorings in the cut. Sutton Courtenay lies to the south beyond the weir stream and Sutton Pools. After Culham Lock the river resumes a more direct course, passing under a steel girder railway bridge before starting its eccentric sweep to Dorchester. The main navigation passes through Clifton Cut and the lock, below which is the entrance to the weir stream, navigable as far as the Plough at Long Wittenham. Beyond a caravan park to the east is Clifton Hampden Bridge, with the church and thatched cottages clustered on rising ground beyond – a superb setting. Burcot stands above the river to the north, which now begins to head south, passing Dorchester.

Boatyards

Ⓑ **Abingdon Boat Centre** The Bridge, Abingdon (01235 521125). ⚓ D Pump-out, gas, hire craft including rowing boats, day boat hire, long-term mooring, slipway (20ft), boat sales, boat and engine repairs, good chandlery including sailing products and clothing, books and maps,

Ⓑ **Red Line Cruisers** Wilsham Road, Abingdon (01235 521562). 🛏 🏠 ⚓ P D E Pump-out, gas, hire craft, day boat hire, overnight and long-term mooring, winter storage, chandlery, boat and engine sales and repairs. *Closed Sun in winter.*

● **Radley**

Oxon. PO, shop. A straggling commuter suburb on the main London-Oxford railway, with much indiscriminate new development. The church is predominantly Perpendicular, with unusual wooded pillars in the aisle. Note the 15thC pulpit canopy, reputedly from the House of Commons, and the 17thC choir stalls.

Radley College Founded in 1847. The college is based on Radley Hall, 1721–7, with many later additions. It is famed as a rowing school.

Nuneham Park Nuneham Courtenay, Oxon. An 18thC Palladian mansion by Leadbetter, splendidly situated in landscaped grounds (see Nuneham Courtenay, below) by Mason and Brown. Rousseau stayed here in 1767, and planted foreign wild flowers in the gardens. The Temple is by Athenian Stuart. Particularly noticeable from the river, standing on a wooded slope, is the Carfax Conduit, an ornamental fountain built in 1615 and once part of Oxford's water supply system. Originally situated in Carfax, it was moved here in 1786. In times of celebration wine and beer were run through it. The house and grounds are owned by the University of Oxford and are *opened for a few days in Aug & Sep.*

● **Nuneham Courtenay**

Oxon. PO. An 18thC model village of startling regularity along the main road, the result of a mass upheaval around 1760 when the 1st Earl of Harcourt required the original village site as part of his landscaped garden. Oliver Goldsmith (1730–74) wrote bitterly of this practice in *The Deserted Village* (1770):
'The man of wealth and pride
Takes up a space that many poor supplied'.
However, whether the early villagers, moving from ancient clay-built cottages into far more modern houses would have seen it that way is open to question. The site of the original village is by the estate road.

● **Abingdon**

Oxon. EC Thur. All shops and services, and an extensive shopping precinct with laundrette. A busy and attractive 18thC market town which grew up around the abbey, founded in AD675. Little of the original building now remains, except the Gateway, Long Gallery and Checker, which has a 13thC chimney, and is used as an Elizabethan-style theatre. What appear to be remains, in the park, is a folly, built about 100 years ago. Abbey Meadow, by the river, is a public park with a swimming pool, toilets, café and putting green. The best views of the town are from the river or the bridge, which is of medieval origin but was rebuilt in 1927. The river is dominated by the gaol, an impressive stone bastille built 1805–11 (now a leisure and sports centre) and St Helen's Church. Set among almshouses, the church has five aisles, making it broader than it is long. Perpendicular in style with a 17thC painted roof, it has a notable pulpit (1636), and the reredos is by Bodley (1897). Long Alley Almshouses, beside the Old Anchor Inn, were built 1446–7 by the Fraternity of the Holy Cross. John Mason of Abingdon created Christ's Hospital, which has been administered them since. The porches and lantern were added in 1605 & 1618. Each year in Abingdon, *on the Saturday closest to 19 June,* the people of Ock Street elect a Mayor for the day. Morris dancers perform outside each inn along the street, a custom of uncertain origin.

Abingdon Museum (01235 523703). What is recognised as one of the finest town halls in England stands in the Market Place. Built 1678–82 by Christopher Kempster, one of Wren's city masons, it is high and monumental with an open ground floor, once used as a market. The upper floor, which was a court room, now houses a local museum. *Open 11.00–17.00 Tue–Sun (16.00 in winter).* Free.

St Michael's Church Park Road. A quiet and dignified design by Gilbert Scott 1864–7.

Tourist Information Centre Bridge Street, Abingdon (01235 522711). Very helpful and friendly service.

● **Culham**

Oxon. A pretty village with a fine green and replica stocks.

● **Sutton Courtenay**

Oxon. A large village, both wealthy and reward-ing, built around a green. The well-kept church has late Norman works, a fine Jacobean pulpit and pleasantly naive 17thC inscriptions. Eric Blair (George Orwell) and Henry Asquith (Prime Minister of the Liberal government, 1908–16) are buried in the churchyard. Overlooking the weir stream is Norman Hall, a remarkably original late 12thC manor house. The 14thC abbey was never used as such, but as a grange. There are excellent walks across the weirs by Sutton Pools.

● **Long Wittenham**

Oxon. PO. Access by boat along the weir stream from Clifton Lock. A fine straggling village along the original course of the river. The 13thC church contains choir stalls from Exeter College, Oxford, and a late Norman font.

Pendon Museum At the far end of Long Wittenham village (01865 407365). A museum of miniature landscapes and transport. The main display is an ambitious recreation of the Vale of White Horse area in the 1930s, and there are also miniature recreations of a Great Western Railway branch on Dartmoor, and John Ahern's famous Madder Valley layout. The models have been under construction for 40 years, and build-ing continues. *Open weekends 14.00–17.00 & B. Hols 11.00–17.00 including Good Fri to Easter Mon, May and Aug B. Hols.* Charge.

● **Clifton Hampden**

Oxon. EC Tue. PO, store. A cluster of thatched cottages away from the brick bridge (a Norman folly built in 1864). The small church on a mound was delicately re-made by Gilbert Scott. Very picturesque.

Pubs and Restaurants

There are many pubs and eating places to be found in Abingdon.

🍺 **The Mill House** Abingdon (01235 536645). Well situated on the bridge, this friendly pub serves Bass, Worthington and Abingdon real ale, along with food *lunchtimes and evenings every day*. There are always vegetarian choices, and children are welcome. Barbecues are held in the gardens *in summer*, and fortnightly theme nights include Mexican and Chinese evenings.

🍺 ✕ **Crown & Thistle** Bridge Street, Abingdon (01235 522556). A hotel, pub and Country Grill restaurant in an old 19thC coaching inn, with an attractive cobbled courtyard. Courage and Theakston's real ales are served. Bar meals are available *lunchtimes* and restaurant meals *L & D*, both with vegetarian and children's menus. There is outside seating in the courtyard.

🍺 **Broad Face** Bridge Street, Abingdon (01235 524516). A friendly corner pub with a lovely sign, serving Morland real ales. Bar meals are available *lunchtimes and evenings Mon–Sat, with a Sun lunchtime roast*. There is a vegetarian menu. Children are welcome *if dining*. Patio.

🍺 ✕ **Old Anchor** St Helens Wharf, Abingdon (01235 521726). A very handsome pub by the confluence of the Rivers Ock and Thames, but alas, no mooring outside. Morland and guest real ales are served, and bar and restaurant meals are available *lunchtimes and evenings*, with vegetarian choices. Children are welcome and there is outside seating. Live entertainment on *Sun*, jazz on *Wed* and regular quiz nights.

✕ 🍷 **Upper Reaches** Thames Street, Abingdon (01235 522311). A smart restaurant/hotel in a converted mill on the Abbey Stream, serving John Smith's real ale. The restaurant has a vegetarian and children's menu and serves *L & D*. There is also a garden.

🍺 ✕ **George & Dragon** High Street, Sutton Courtenay. A cosy black and white pub serving Morland real ale. Bar meals are available *lunchtimes Mon–Fri*, and restaurant meals are served *L & D (not Sun D)*, with vegetarian options. Children are welcome (but *not in the bar*), and there is a large garden.

🍺 **Swan** The Green, Sutton Courtenay (01235 847446). A red brick local with a large garden, which has a play area featuring a bouncy castle *in the summer*. Morrells real ale is served here, and bar meals are available *lunchtimes and evenings Mon–Fri and all day Sat and Sun*, with a vegetarian menu. Occasional entertainment with music and quiz nights.

🍺 **Fish Inn** Appleford Road, Sutton Courtenay (01235 848242). A large pub serving Morland real ale. Excellent freshly cooked food with an à la carte and vegetarian menu available *lunchtimes and evenings (not Sun evening)*. Fish dishes are a

speciality here. A short walk across the field takes boaters to the huge garden and then the aptly named garden room (where muddy boots are to be removed!). Children are welcome *in the garden room*.

🍺 **Carpenters Arms** Appleford (01235 848328). Morland real ale and bar meals are available *lunchtimes and evenings*, with vegetarian choices. Children are welcome, and there is a garden.

🍺 **Lion** Culham (01235 520327). A village pub just a short walk from Culham Cut serving Morrells real ale. Home-cooked bar meals are available *lunchtimes and evenings*, with vegetarian choices. Garden with a children's play area.

🍺 **Waggon & Horses** Culham (01235 525012). On the main road. Morrells and Felinfoel real ales are served, and meals are available in the bar or in a separate eating area *lunchtimes and evenings*, with vegetarian choices. Children are welcome, and there is a garden with a play area. Regular entertainment with a karaoke and disco, *mainly at weekends*.

🍺 ✕ **Plough Inn** High Street, Long Wittenham (01867 207738). The weir stream is navigable from Clifton Lock to this attractive pub. Websters and Ushers are amongst the real ales offered, and meals are served *lunchtimes and evenings every day*, with vegetarian choices. It is a family pub, so children are welcome – they will enjoy the massive garden. The folk club meets here every *Wed*, and it is handy for the Pendon Museum.

🍺 **The Vine** Long Wittenham (01865 407832). A cosy pub, bedecked with flowers in the summer. Morland real ale, and bar meals served *lunchtimes and evenings every day*, with vegetarian choices. Children are welcome. Garden.

🍺 ✕ **Barley Mow** East of Clifton Hampden Bridge (01865 407847). A deservedly famous and superbly old-fashioned thatched pub built in 1350. It was described by Jerome K. Jerome as having 'quite a story book appearance'. Webster's, Theakston's and Ushers real ales are served, and bar and restaurant meals are available *lunchtimes and evenings every day*, with vegetarian choices. Children are welcome in the family room, and there is a pleasant garden.

🍺 **Chequers** Burcot (01865 407771). Well worth the walk from Clifton Hampden or Dorchester to visit this handsome and totally civilised thatched pub. A large log fire is surrounded by settees, bookcases, and settles, spaciously arranged. The grand piano is occasionally played live. Excellent food with fresh bread baked on the premises, served *lunchtimes and evenings every day (but not Sun evening)*, with vegetarian choices. Brakspears, Ushers and Ruddles real ale can be enjoyed, children are welcome, and there is a garden.

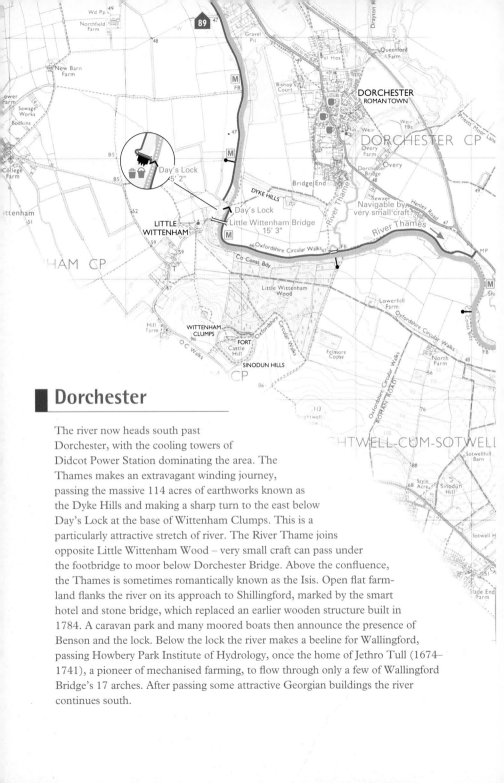

Dorchester

The river now heads south past
Dorchester, with the cooling towers of
Didcot Power Station dominating the area. The
Thames makes an extravagant winding journey,
passing the massive 114 acres of earthworks known as
the Dyke Hills and making a sharp turn to the east below
Day's Lock at the base of Wittenham Clumps. This is a
particularly attractive stretch of river. The River Thame joins
opposite Little Wittenham Wood – very small craft can pass under
the footbridge to moor below Dorchester Bridge. Above the confluence,
the Thames is sometimes romantically known as the Isis. Open flat farmland flanks the river on its approach to Shillingford, marked by the smart
hotel and stone bridge, which replaced an earlier wooden structure built in
1784. A caravan park and many moored boats then announce the presence of
Benson and the lock. Below the lock the river makes a beeline for Wallingford,
passing Howbery Park Institute of Hydrology, once the home of Jethro Tull (1674–
1741), a pioneer of mechanised farming, to flow through only a few of Wallingford
Bridge's 17 arches. After passing some attractive Georgian buildings the river
continues south.

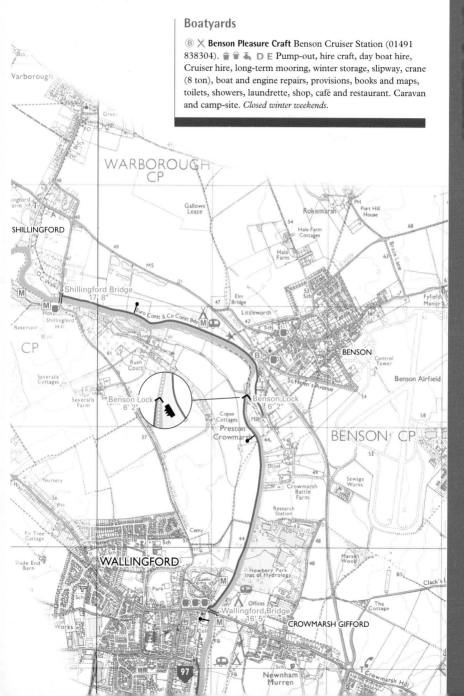

NAVIGATIONAL NOTES

1 Take care at the blind corner below Little Wittenham Bridge.

2 Wallingford Bridge – use the central arch.

Boatyards

Ⓑ ✕ **Benson Pleasure Craft** Benson Cruiser Station (01491 838304). 🛏 🎁 ⚓ D E Pump-out, hire craft, day boat hire, Cruiser hire, long-term mooring, winter storage, slipway, crane (8 ton), boat and engine repairs, provisions, books and maps, toilets, showers, laundrette, shop, café and restaurant. Caravan and camp-site. *Closed winter weekends.*

● **Little Wittenham**
Oxon. The church is well situated among woods, and there are good walks through Little Wittenham Woods to the summit of Castle Hill, topped with an Iron Age hill fort.

● **Dorchester**
Oxon. PO, stores. This large village of antique shops and hotels was once a small Roman town sited on the River Thames. It is accessible from the Thames by footpath over Dyke Hills from Day's Lock. Today only the abbey Church of SS Peter and Paul, founded in the 7thC, shows that it was once the cathedral city of Wessex, then Mercia. Approached through a Butterfield lych gate, the mostly decorated abbey gives little clue to the splendid size and proportion of its interior. The most important feature is the Jesse window, with stonework imitating trees. The figures seem to grow organically from the body of Jesse. Note also the tomb of Sir John Holcombe: the realism and fluidity of the effigy has inspired many modern sculptors. The Old Monastery Guest House, built circa 1400 and used in the 17thC as a grammar school, now houses the:
Dorchester Abbey Museum (*open daily Tue–Sat, Sun afternoons and B Hols May–Sept only, plus Easter weekend*), although most Roman finds are in the Ashmolean, Oxford. Small craft may navigate up the River Thame to Dorchester Bridge. The town is quite quiet, now the by-pass has opened.

● **Shillingford**
Oxon. Tel. The extremely handsome triple-arched bridge and the hotel stand away from the village, a discreet residential area to the north.

● **Benson**
Oxon. EC Wed. PO, shops. A friendly town with a pleasant river frontage, although it is hard to believe this was once a seat of the Kings of Mercia. The 13thC church has Saxon foundations.

● **Wallingford**
Oxon. EC Wed. All services. One of the oldest Royal Boroughs, the town received its charter in 1155. Well-preserved banks and ditches of Saxon defences still remain. From the river the town is dominated by the unusual openwork spire of St Peter's Church, built by Sir Robert Taylor in 1777. At the rear of the George Hotel is the entrance to the splendid Castle Gardens, where footpaths lead to the remains of the Norman castle built on a mound by Robert D'Oilly in 1071, held for the Empress Matilda during her fight with King Stephen for the English crown, and finally destroyed by Fairfax in 1646. The Town Hall, built in 1670, has a typical open ground floor. The 17-arched bridge is of medieval origins (possibly as early as 1141), and was rebuilt in 1809 when the balustrade was added. It still has a Bridge Chamberlain, appointed each year by the town council. There is a music festival held at St Peter's Church *May–Sept*, and an illuminated river pageant in *Sept*.
Wallingford Museum (01491 835065). Housed in Flint House, in the traffic-choked High Street. *Open 14.00–17.00 Tue–Fri Mar–Nov, 10.30–17.00 Sat Jun–Aug. Also open 14.00–17.00 Sun and B. Hols.* For large groups advance notice is required and a special rate may be given: information on (01491) 651127.
The Corn Exchange Wallingford (01491 825000). Theatre and cinema.
The Cholsey and Wallingford Railway St Pauls Halt, 15 minutes walk west of Wallingford (01491 835067 for information). This line opened in 1866 to link the Great Western Railways' main line with the Wycombe Extension Railway. The last British Rail service ran on 31 May 1981. Now 2 1/2 miles of track have been purchased, and steam and diesel trains are run.
Wallingford Tourist Information Centre Town Hall, Market Place (01491 825844). *Open 10.00–16.00 Mon–Fri.*

AND BABY MAKES THREE . . .

Babies who are not yet walking can be coped with fairly easily on a boating holiday. Children between the ages of one and five are probably the most difficult to deal with, and the following points may be helpful:

1 Mum, Dad and two toddlers on a heavily locked length of canal will have problems. If you cannot gather a larger crew to help, a river such as the Thames, where the locks are operated by keepers, is ideal.
2 Ensure buoyancy aids are worn by children when they are up on deck.
3 Avoid traditional style narrow boats with a small unprotected rear deck. Thames cruisers, with an enclosed cockpit, are ideal.
4 Airing cupboards are useful for drying all the washing produced by small children.
5 Pack the favourite toys and games.
6 Allow time for plenty of stops, where children can run off their excess energy.

From the age of six, children, properly supervised, can become useful crew members.

Pubs and Restaurants

George Hotel High Street, Dorchester (01865 340404). Built in 1495 as the brewhouse of the nearby abbey, this comfortable galleried inn was once a coaching stop. Brakspear real ale is served, along with bar meals, and a restaurant serving English à la carte *lunchtimes and evenings*, with vegetarian options. The hotel is set in pleasant grounds.

Fleur de Lys High Street, Dorchester (01865 340502). A pub dating from 1520, opposite the abbey.

White Hart Hotel High Street, Dorchester (01865 340074). A 17thC coaching inn serving Morland real ale. Bar meals are available, and there is a restaurant serving traditional English fare *lunchtimes and evenings,* with vegetarian choices. Children are welcome. There is live music *on Fri.*

Dorchester Abbey Tea Room High Street, Dorchester. Next to the abbey. Delicious biscuits, cakes and scones, all home baked. *Open from 15.00 'until the food runs out' Wed, Thur, Sat & Sun during the summer (May–Sept).*

Chesters Queen Street, Dorchester. A charming coffee shop, serving fine cakes.

Shillingford Bridge Hotel and Restaurant (01865 858567). A very smart riverside hotel with excellent moorings (modest fee). Patrons may use the squash courts, and the outdoor heated swimming and paddling pools, which are *closed after 19.00.* Ansell's, Brakspear and Whitbread real ales are served, and bar and restaurant meals, with vegetarian choices, are available *lunchtimes and evenings every day.* Children are welcome, and there is a pleasant riverside garden. *Every Sat* there is a dinner and dance, but you will need to wear evening dress!

Crown Benson (01491 838331). A large, comfortable inn serving Morland and occasionally a guest real ale. Bar meals are available *lunchtimes and evenings (not Mon),* with vegetarian choices. Children are welcome and there is outside seating on a patio area. Pub games, regular quiz nights and live music and karaoke nights make up the entertainment.

Three Horseshoes Benson (01491 838242). A small traditional pub serving Brakspear and three guest real ales. The restaurant is open *L & D every day,* with vegetarian choices. Children are welcome and there is a garden.

Sun Watlington Road, Benson (01491 835087). Courage real ale is served and bar meals are available *lunchtimes and evenings every day,* with vegetarian options. Children are welcome and there is a garden. Regular entertainment with quiz and live music nights.

The Boathouse By Wallingford Bridge (01491 833188). A lively riverside pub, with a terrace and a conservatory.

Town Arms by Wallingford Bridge (01491 835411). A friendly 200 year old pub serving pub snacks and Ushers real ales. Outside seating.

Stoneys High Street, Wallingford (01491 836249). Family run restaurant serving French and English cuisine, specialising in seafood, with a vegetarian menu. Children are welcome. *Open Tue–Sun L and Mon–Sat D.*

George Hotel High Street, Wallingford (01491 836665). A smart Tudor hotel with restaurant. The Teardrop Room recalls a Civil War story of the landlord's daughter's grief at the loss of her love, a Royalist sergeant. There are two bars serving guest real ales, and bar meals are available *lunchtimes (not Sun),* with restaurant meals *D, including Sun D.* Both serve vegetarian options. Children are welcome and there is outside seating in a courtyard area.

Prince of India High Street, Wallingford (01492 835394). A traditional Indian restaurant *open L & D.* Vegetarian options.

Bell Crowmarsh (01491 835324). Morland and guest real ales (including the 1996 addition of Bill's Spring Brew, which was specially brewed to acknowledge the 50 year commitment of one of the brewery workers). Bar and restaurant meals available *lunchtimes and evenings every day,* with vegetarian choices. Large garden with children's play area*, although children are only permitted inside the pub if visiting the restaurant.* Regular entertainment with quiz nights and live music on *Sat evenings.*

Queen's Head Crowmarsh (01491 825082). Low beams and open fires feature in this pub, which serves Bass, Tetley's, Wadworth and guest real ales. Bar and restaurant meals are available *lunchtimes and evenings (not Sat lunchtime or Sun evening),* with vegetarian choices. Garden with children's play area. There is a quiz on *Tue night* and in summer regular barbecues are held.

Moulsford

A broad stretch of river, pleasant but unremarkable. The buildings of Carmel College stand in wooded grounds in Mongewell Park, which fronts the Thames for a mile. North Stoke lies back from the river to the east, while the Fair Mile Hospital for the Disabled is passed to the west. The islands above Brunel's lovely skewed brick arched railway bridge are supposedly haunted. Gradually the hills close in as the valley narrows towards Goring. The Beetle & Wedge Hotel marks the site of the old ferry which once linked Moulsford and South Stoke, facing each other across the river, but now totally separate.

● **North Stoke**
Oxon. An attractive red brick village among trees. The church is pleasingly original and unrestored, with notable wall paintings and a canopied pulpit.

● **Cholsey**
Oxon. PO. Store. An undistinguished village, except for the pub and shop.

● **Moulsford**
Oxon. A roadside village with large houses by the river. The small, secluded church was rebuilt by Gilbert Scott in 1846: his fee was reputedly £64.

● **South Stoke**
Oxon. A pretty residential village among trees. St Andrew's Church is 13thC. Access can be gained from the river opposite the Beetle & Wedge Hotel.

ROW, ROW, ROW YOUR BOAT . . .

In the early part of the 20thC it was not uncommon for those who were lucky enough to live by the river to own a camping boat. The Thames Gig was typical of such craft, and could have been 25ft long with a 4ft beam, constructed perhaps by Hammertons of Thames Ditton. Clinker built in mahogany and propelled by two pairs of sculls, it would have two rowing thwarts, passenger seats in the stern and bows, a camping cover and, for comfort, a carpet! A crew of two could propel such a craft at 6mph over still water for considerable distances, with the added options of a small sail on a mast stepped at the bow if the wind was favourable, or a tow line to haul from the bank when the current was adverse.

Pubs and Restaurants

🍴 ✕ **Morning Star** Papist Way, Cholsey (01491 651413). Morland real ale is served in this unspoilt village pub. Bar and restaurant meals are available *lunchtimes and evenings every day,* with vegetarian options. Children are welcome and there is a garden. Occasional entertainment.

🍴 ✕ **Beetle & Wedge Hotel** Ferry Lane, Moulsford (01491 651381). A *beetle* is a mallet used to hit the *wedge* which split trees into planks for floating down river to London; a practice last recorded in 1777 but recalled in the name of this justly famous pub, where H.G. Wells stayed while writing *Mr Polly* – it features in the book as the Potwell Inn. The building is a former manor house, standing in a superb riverside situation, with a lovely garden and a jetty. A choice of two (three in summer) smart restaurants offering excellent cuisine and vegetarian menus. The Boat House has a large open fire on which many of the items on the à la carte menu are cooked,

and a there is a choice of Wadworth, Adnams and Hall & Woodhouse (Tanglefoot) real ales. The Dining Room is more formal, and has a set price menu, although you still have plenty of choice, and is situated in the main hotel building. *Open L & D (not Sun D or Mon all day except on B. Hols).* Also, in the summer, The Water Garden is open *weather permitting* serving an à la carte menu. Booking is advisable for all three restaurants. Children are welcome and the large garden is a plus. Moorings.

🍴 **Perch & Pike Inn** South Stoke (01491 872415). Brakspear and two other real ales in a cosy 17thC red brick and flint pub, with low beams and open log fires. Extensive home-cooked menu served in the bar *lunchtimes and evenings every day (not Sun evening)*, with vegetarian choices. Children are welcome in one area of the pub, and there is a pleasant garden.

Boatyards

Ⓑ Sheridan UK Marine
Moulsford (01491
652085). ⚓ **D E** Calor
gas, rowing boat hire,
long-term mooring,
winter storage, slipway,
boat lift (30ft), boat
and engine sales and
repairs, chandlery,
some groceries, gifts,
books and maps.
*Closed Fri in summer
and weekends in
winter.*

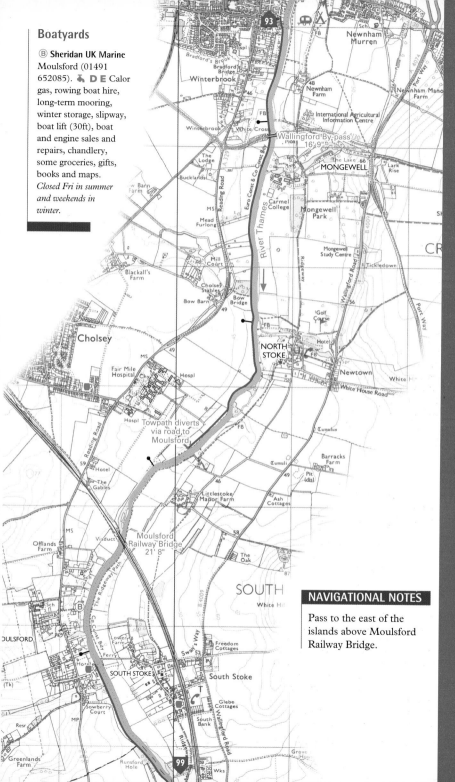

NAVIGATIONAL NOTES

Pass to the east of the
islands above Moulsford
Railway Bridge.

Goring

Approaching Cleeve Lock the valley narrows, with Lardon Chase rising steeply to the west behind Streatley. Little of Goring can be seen from the river – boathouses, the mill and a glimpse of the church as the river enters one of its most attractive parts. In the meadows to the east of Basildon there is a picturesque group of buildings around a church, while on the east bank beech woods rise steeply from the river's edge. The brick Gatehampton Railway Bridge was built by Brunel – beyond this Basildon House stands in wooded grounds, to the west of Beale Park.

Pubs and Restaurants

✕♀ **Leatherne Bottle Restaurant** Bridle Way (01491 872667). Riverside, above Cleeve Lock. There was a well here in Roman times which produced medicinal water. Now it is a smart riverside restaurant with a bar. Food is served *L & D*, with vegetarian options. Garden.

◗ ✕ **Swan Diplomat Hotel** Streatley-on-Thames (01491 873737). A beautifully situated and very smart hotel/restaurant serving brasserie light lunches *L & D (not Sat)* and *Sun brunches* and meals *every evening*, with vegetarian options. Plush interiors and fine riverside gardens. Children are welcome.

◗ ✕ **Bull** Reading Road, Streatley (01491 872507). A 16thC restaurant/pub at a busy crossroads, serving John Smith's, Eldridge Pope, Flowers and guest real ales. Bar meals are available *lunchtimes and evenings Mon–Fri*. The restaurant serves food *Mon to Sat D and Sun L*. There are always vegetarian options. Both children and dogs are welcome, and there is a large garden. Occasional live bands.

◗ ✕ **Miller of Mansfield** High Street, Goring (01491 872829). Up the road from the bridge, this is a very comfortable brick and flint pub,

where parts of the building are 13thC. Courage, Ruddles and Wadworth real ales are served. Separate restaurant and excellent bar meals *lunchtimes and evenings, and breakfast in winter*, with vegetarian choices. Children are welcome, and there is occasional entertainment in winter.

◗ ✕ **John Barleycorn** Manor Road, Goring (01491 872509). Brakspear real ale is dispensed, and bar and restaurant meals are available *lunchtimes and evenings every day*, with vegetarian choices. Children are welcome *in the dining area and restaurant only*. Garden.

◗ **Catherine Wheel** Station Road, Goring (01491 872379). Brakspear real ale is served in this attractive 15thC pub, which has foreign food evenings about *once a month*. Excellent meals are available *lunchtimes and evenings every day (but not Sun evening)*, with lots of vegetarian choices. Children are welcome, and there is a garden.

● **Goring**
Oxon. EC Wed. Shops and supermarket in High Street, laundrette. One of the most important prehistoric fords across the river, linking the Icknield Way and the Ridgeway. The village is set in a splendid deep wooded valley by one of the most spectacular reaches on the river. A holiday paradise of indeterminate age, it retains many pretty brick and flint cottages. The church, of handsome proportions, is well situated by the river. Its bell, dating from 1290, is one of the oldest in England. Goring Mill stands below the bridge, an approximate replica (built 1923) of the earlier timber structure. Between Goring and Henley, the

Thames passes through the Chilterns Area of Outstanding Natural Beauty, covering 309 square miles.

● **Streatley**
Berks. Shops. A continuation of Goring on the west bank, its 18thC charm is diminished by the traffic roaring through. Of note are the old malt houses converted into a village hall by W. Ravenscroft in 1898. Lardon Chase (NT) rises to the north.

● **Lower Basildon**
Berks. An attractive group of buildings surround the church in a superb riverside situation. The 13thC church is over restored, but note the

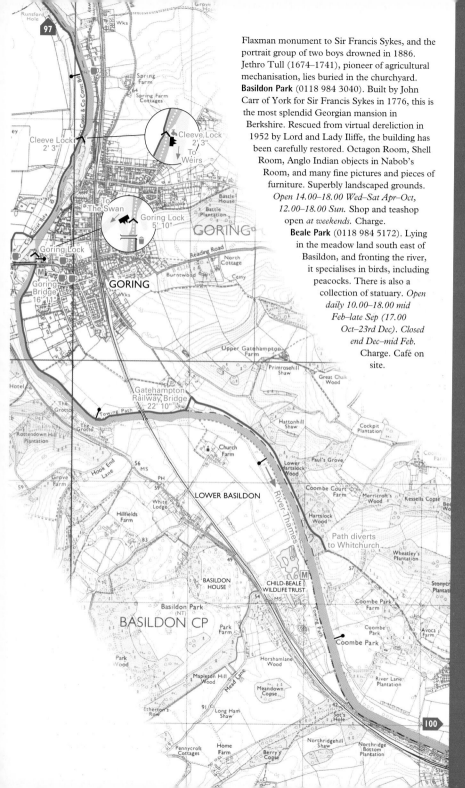

Flaxman monument to Sir Francis Sykes, and the portrait group of two boys drowned in 1886. Jethro Tull (1674–1741), pioneer of agricultural mechanisation, lies buried in the churchyard. **Basildon Park** (0118 984 3040). Built by John Carr of York for Sir Francis Sykes in 1776, this is the most splendid Georgian mansion in Berkshire. Rescued from virtual dereliction in 1952 by Lord and Lady Iliffe, the building has been carefully restored. Octagon Room, Shell Room, Anglo Indian objects in Nabob's Room, and many fine pictures and pieces of furniture. Superbly landscaped grounds. *Open 14.00–18.00 Wed–Sat Apr–Oct, 12.00–18.00 Sun.* Shop and teashop open *at weekends.* Charge.

Beale Park (0118 984 5172). Lying in the meadow land south east of Basildon, and fronting the river, it specialises in birds, including peacocks. There is also a collection of statuary. *Open daily 10.00–18.00 mid Feb–late Sep (17.00 Oct–23rd Dec). Closed end Dec–mid Feb.* Charge. Café on site.

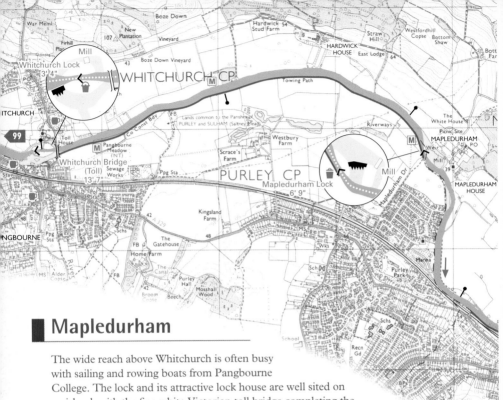

Mapledurham

The wide reach above Whitchurch is often busy with sailing and rowing boats from Pangbourne College. The lock and its attractive lock house are well sited on an island, with the fine white Victorian toll bridge completing the scene. Open farmland flanks the river below here. Hardwick House can be glimpsed through trees on the north bank while to the south, the vineyards of Westbury Farm can be seen as Mapledurham is approached. The weir probably dates from the 13thC and the pound lock from 1777 – it was the first lock on the Thames to be mechanised, in 1956. The mill, church and house are in a superbly romantic setting. Now the residential outskirts of Reading begin, and the main railway line joins the river on an embankment – the trains rush by, a vivid contrast with the pace of the river. The entrance into Reading from the west is, however, not unpleasant. The railway parts company below Appletree Eyot, while the river curves round to Norcot Scours and on past St Mary's Island, becoming quite wide and often busy with rowing and sculling boats. Well-kept chalets and tidy gardens line the north bank, followed by landscaped public gardens above Caversham Bridge.

● **Pangbourne**
Berks. EC Thur. All services. A large, well-equipped commuter town, still preserving traces of Edwardian elegance, built at the confluence of the Thames and the Pang, a famous trout stream. The Nautical College, an imposing William and Mary style mansion, is by Sir John Belcher, built 1897–8. Pangbourne Meadow is now a National Trust property of 7 acres. The Scottish author of *The Wind in the Willows*, Kenneth Grahame (1859–1932), who was also Secretary to the Bank of England, lived in Church Cottage, Pangbourne, and told this story to his four-year-old son Alastair in 1904.

● **Whitchurch**
Oxon. EC Sat. PO, store. Quiet and attractive with a good group of mill buildings, overlooked by the mainly Victorian church. A small toll for cars is collected at the Victorian iron bridge.
Hardwick House *Oxon.* The gardens almost reach down to the river, with the house nestling among trees. Mainly Tudor, it was restored after the Civil War, and has two real tennis courts. Queen Elizabeth I slept in one of the bedrooms. Private.

● **Mapledurham**
Oxon. A cluster of period houses and cottages stand in the water meadows close to the restored and working water mill, one of the oldest corn and

grist mills on the Thames. The scene is typical of an early 19thC landscape painting and should be visited (but see below).

Mapledurham House (0118 972 3350). Still occupied by descendants of the Blount family, who purchased the original manor in 1390 and built the present Elizabethan manor house, with grounds sweeping down to the Thames. The estate is private and there are no rights of way from the river to the village, nor any footpaths alongside the river on the north bank. Mapledurham has interesting literary connections with Alexander Pope, Galsworthy's *Forsyte Saga* and Grahame's *The Wind in the Willows*. More recently it has been the setting for the film *The Eagle has Landed*, and has appeared in various television series including *Inspector Morse*. *The Country Park is open 12.30–17.00, The Water Mill is open 13.00–17.00, and the House is open 14.30–17.00 between Easter and the end of Sep on weekends and B. Hol afternoons only.* Charge. On these days a boat can be taken from Caversham Pier (0118 948 1088) to the landing stage on the Mill island. All passengers alighting do have to purchase an entrance ticket, as do any passengers from private boats, who are allowed to moor only for this purpose, and *only on open days*.

● **Purley**

Berks. EC Thur & Sat. Stores. A straggling village approached from Mapledurham Lock, marking the western extremity of the Reading conurbation.

Pubs and Restaurants

🍺 ✕ **Swan** Above Pangbourne Weir (0118 984 4494). A well-known, rambling, and beautifully situated riverside pub and restaurant serving food *all week 12.00–22.00*, with vegetarian choices. Children are welcome, and have their own menu. Morland real ales are served. It was here that Jerome K. Jerome, his two colleagues and a 'shamed looking dog' abandoned their *Three Men in a Boat* journey (on the way back), and took the train to London.

🍺 ✕ **Copper Inn Hotel** Church Road, Pangbourne (0118 984 2244). A good choice of real ales in an old coaching inn with a restaurant. Bar meals and à la carte available *lunchtimes and evenings every day*, with vegetarian choices.

🍺 ✕ **George Hotel** The Square, Pangbourne

(0118 984 2237). South of the bridge and under the railway. Courage real ale, and restaurant meals with a set menu and *lunchtime* carvery *L & D (not Sat L)*, with vegetarian choices. Children are welcome.

🍺 **Greyhound** North of Whitchurch Bridge (0118 984 2160). A friendly pub with a collection of brasses, serving a selection of real ales. Good selection of bar food available *lunchtimes and evenings every day (not Sun evening)*, with vegetarian options. Garden.

🍺 ✕ **Ferryboat** North of Whitchurch Bridge (0118 984 2161). Morland and John Smith's real ale in a country pub.

Reading

Caversham Bridge was built in 1926. The original bridge on this site was erected in the 13thC, and at one time had a chapel on it. Fry's Island is situated between the bridges; on it are two boatyards. Reading lies to the south, a busy modern town which does little to welcome visitors from the river. Just below Reading Bridge is Caversham Lock, on the edge of King's Meadow. A little further down, to the east and under the railway bridge, is the entrance to the Kennet & Avon Canal (see page 27). Beyond this junction the scenery is initially uninspiring but this all changes when Sonning Lock and Mill appear among the willows. The 18thC bridge and the large white hotel beside it mark the western extremity of Sonning village, which lies back from the river. About a mile below Sonning, St Patrick's Stream (unnavigable, with the River Loddon flowing in), makes its detour around Borough Marsh. The main course of the river passes numerous islands and skirts Warren Hill, a chalk ridge, before reaching Shiplake Lock. It then passes Shiplake and weaves through a group of islands to the west of Wargrave Marsh, a low-lying area enclosed by the Hennerton Backwater (navigable only by small boats).

BOAT TRIPS
Thames River Cruises Mapledurham House, Mapledurham (0118 948 1088). *Caversham Lady* available for private charter. Also regular *summer* trips to Mapledurham, when the house is open.
Salter Bros Caversham Bridge Road, Reading (0118 957 2388). Scheduled *summer* service up and down river, with various stops. *The Waterman* is available for private charter for up to 100 people. Food and a bar can be provided, with a disco if required. Telephone (0118) 9402161 for details.

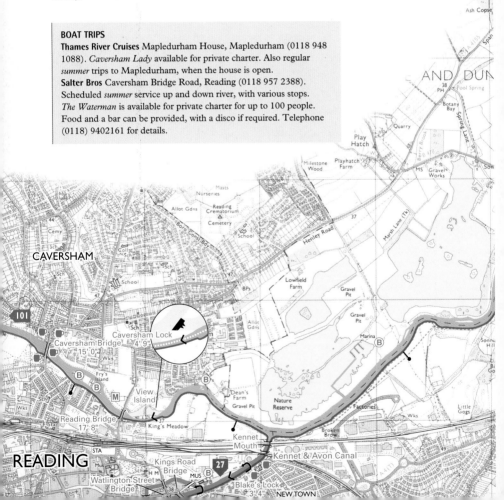

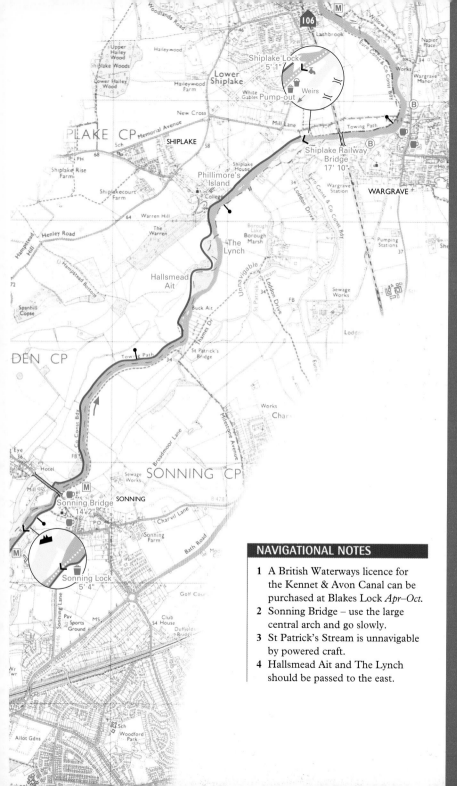

NAVIGATIONAL NOTES

1 A British Waterways licence for the Kennet & Avon Canal can be purchased at Blakes Lock *Apr–Oct.*
2 Sonning Bridge – use the large central arch and go slowly.
3 St Patrick's Stream is unnavigable by powered craft.
4 Hallsmead Ait and The Lynch should be passed to the east.

Boatyards

Ⓑ **Bridge Boats** Fry's Island, Reading (0118 959 0346). 🛢 E Pump-out, Super gas, hire craft, overnight and long-term mooring, winter storage, slipway, boat building, boat and engine repairs, boat sales, books and maps. *Closed winter weekends.*

Ⓑ **Caversham Boat Services** Fry's Island, Reading (0118 957 4323). 🛢 🛢 D E Pump-out, Calor gas, hire craft, day hire boats, overnight and long-term mooring, books and maps, boat and engine repairs (breakdown service), toilets.

Ⓑ **Better Boating** Mill Green, Caversham, Reading (0118 947 9536). 🛢 🛢 🛢 D Pump-out, Shell and Calor gas, long-term mooring, winter storage, boat sales and repairs, outboard sales and repairs, crane, chandlery, toilets, books and maps, gifts.

Ⓑ **Thames & Kennet Marina** Caversham Lakes, Henley Road, Reading (0118 948 2911). 🛢 🛢 🛢 D E Pump-out, Calor gas, long-term mooring, winter storage, crane (30 ton), chandlery, boat sales, boat and engine repairs, some groceries, gifts, books and maps, toilets, showers.

Ⓑ **Swancraft** George and Dragon Boathouse, Hurley Road, Wargrave (0118 940 2577). 🛢 D E Pump-out, hire craft, day boat hire, cruiser hire, long-term mooring, winter storage, electric boat sales, boat repairs, books and maps. *Closed weekends in winter.*

● **Reading**
Berks. All services. A very busy town lacking a cohesive centre – it is an amalgam of university and industry – but historically and architecturally it has interest. The university buildings are disappointing, but there are numerous Victorian buildings and the museum houses one of the most fascinating archaeological collections in the country.
Abbey Ruins Fragmentary remains of the 12thC abbey, built by Henry I, lie on the edge of Forbury Park. The Abbey was one of the largest in England and at one time comparable with Bury St Edmunds. The 13thC gatehouse still stands. It was once the Abbey School where Jane Austen studied in 1785–7, although the structure was greatly altered by Gilbert Scott in 1869. The Church of St Lawrence near the Market Place was originally attached to the outer gate.
Gaol Forbury Road. Designed by Scott & Moffat, 1842–4 in Scottish Baronial style. Oscar Wilde (1854–1900) wrote *De Profundis* in 1897 while imprisoned here for homosexual practices (the *Ballad of Reading Gaol* was actually written in Paris in 1898).
The Museum of Reading The Town Hall, Blagrave Street (0118 939 9800). Features *The Story of Reading*, tracing the town's development from a Saxon settlement on the River Kennet to the present day. Special features include a reconstructed section of the abbey and the Oracle gates entrance to the 17thC work-house. In the upper gallery is a full 70 metre sweep of Britain's Bayeux Tapestry, Reading's faithful replica of the 11thC original. *Open 10.00–17.00 Tue–Sat, 14.00–17.00 Sun. Closed Mon but open most B. Hols – ring for details.* Free.
Museum of English Rural Life Royal History Centre, Whiteknights, University of Reading (0118 931 8660). All aspects of rural life in England as it was lived about 150 to 175 years ago, before the invention of the tractor. *Open 10.00–13.00 and 14.00–16.30 Tue–Sat. Closed Sun, Mon & B. Hols.* Small charge.
Reading Tourist Information Centre Town Hall, Blagrave Street (0118 956 6226).

● **Caversham**
Berks. EC Wed. PO, stores, laundrette, fish & chips. A residential continuation of Reading, at its best by the river, where parks and gardens stretch alongside. The library in Church Street is worth a look – it is an amusing Edwardian building, built in 1907, with a central green copper clock supported by an angel.

● **Sonning**
Berks. EC Tue. PO, stores and café. A very pretty and meticulously preserved village. The largely 19thC church by Woodyer and Bodley has remarkable monuments, and some 15thC brasses. The most interesting house in the town is Lutyens' Deanery Gardens, built for Edward Hudson in 1901. To the west of Sonning is Holme Park – the Reading Blue Coat School – its wooded grounds drop steeply to the river. The railway passes in a spectacular cutting to the south, built by Brunel.
Thames Valley Vineyards Stanlake Park, Twyford (0118 934 0176). These vineyards may be visited by groups of a *minimum of 25 people*. Book in advance for a tour and wine tasting. The shop is *open 09.00–17.00 Mon–Fri, 11.00–17.00 Sat, 12.00–17.00 Sun.* Charge for the tours.

● **Wargrave**
Berks. EC Wed. PO, stores. A well-situated town on rising ground among trees, overlooking the Thames. The church was burnt down in 1914 by the Suffragettes – some say it was because the vicar refused to take the word obey out of the

marriage service. Rebuilt, the church has a pleasing architectural unity – note particularly the woodwork. In the churchyard the Hannen Mausoleum was designed by Lutyens. The striking Woodclyffe Hall, in the High Street, was built in 1901. Henry Kingsley (1830–76), the novelist, often stayed here. East of the town is Wargrave Manor, an early 19thC building. The River Loddon joins St Patrick's Stream to the south west – here, in black swampy soil, the Loddon Lily (*Leucojum aestivum*), or summer snowflake, is native. Loddon Pondweed (*Potamogeton nodosus*), its leaves beautifully veined, may also be found.

Pubs and Restaurants

If you do not mind dodging the traffic, there are plenty of pubs in Reading – those on the river may wish to travel a couple of miles up – or downstream, where the surroundings are a little more congenial.

✕ �️ **Three Men in a Boat** By Caversham Bridge. A modern restaurant in a fine situation. Real ale is served. *Open L daily & D Sun–Thur.*

♙ **Pipers Island Bar** (0118 948 4573). A pub in a lovely situation – right in the middle of the river. Real ales available are Brakspear's, Fuller's and Flowers, and food is served *lunchtimes and evenings every day,* with vegetarian choices. Children are welcome, and there is a riverside patio. Plenty of entertainment, including karaoke *on Tue,* live bands *on Thur,* and discos *on Fri or Sat during the winter.*

♙ ✕ **Griffin** Church Road, Caversham (0118 947 5018). North of Caversham Bridge. Courage, John Smith's and Theakston's real ale are served, along with bar meals *lunchtimes and evenings every day,* with vegetarian options. Children are welcome and there is a conservatory to the rear of the pub. Folk club on *Sun evenings.*

♙ ✕ **Holiday Inn Hotel** Richfield Avenue, Reading (0118 925 9988). A smart riverside hotel with a real ale pub, Three Men in a Boat, down below. Bar meals, with vegetarian options, are served *lunchtimes every day, and evenings Sun–Thur.* There is a riverside terrace.

♙ ✕ **Great House Hotel** Thames Street, Sonning Bridge (0118 969 2277). A beautifully situated riverside hotel and restaurant/wine bar of great character, with fine gardens and lawns, and a terrace lined with lime trees. One dining room is 700 years old; the main bar is a beamed room with a stone fireplace. The Ferryman's Bar has a choice of six real ales. Hideaway 96 is an informal wine bar. Meals are served *lunchtimes and evenings every day,*with vegetarian choices. Children are welcome. (Mooring free to residents, £5 for non-residents for 24 hrs, redeemable if you have a meal or drink in the bar).

♙ **Bull Inn** By Sonning church (0118 969 3901). A lovely old half-timbered pub, used by locals and visitors alike. Comfy cushioned settles, massive beams and inglenook fireplaces inside, with wooden tables in a flower-decorated courtyard facing the church outside. A good selection of real ale available, and hot and cold bar meals are served *lunchtimes and evenings every day,* with vegetarian choices. Children are welcome and there is a garden. Traditional pub games, and a quiz night on *Sun in winter.*

♙ ✕ **St George & Dragon** Henley Road, Wargrave (0118 940 3852). A Harvester restaurant and pub, once visited by Jerome K. Jerome. Bass real ale is served. There are views over the Thames from the restaurant, which has the old hotel sign displayed inside. Restaurant meals available *L & D and all day Sat and Sun,* with vegetarian options. Children are welcome and there is a garden and terrace. Quiz on *Tue night in winter.*

♙ ✕ **Bull** High Street, Wargrave (0118 940 3120). A 15thC inn serving Brakspear's real ale and excellent bar and restaurant meals *lunchtimes and evenings every day,* with vegetarian choices. Children are welcome *in the restaurant only,* and there is outside seating on a patio and in the garden.

♙ ✕ **White Hart** High Street, Wargrave (0118 940 2590). A fine old inn serving Brakspear, Flowers and Fuller's real ale, and bar and restaurant meals *lunchtimes and evenings (not Sun evening),* with vegetarian options. Children are welcome.

♙ **Greyhound** High Street, Wargrave (0118 940 2556). A half-timbered corner pub serving Courage and a guest real ale. *Lunchtime* snacks and meals, with vegetarian choices. Children are welcome, and there is a family room, garden and outside seating on a patio area. Regular quiz nights and pub games. There is an old forge at the back of the pub.

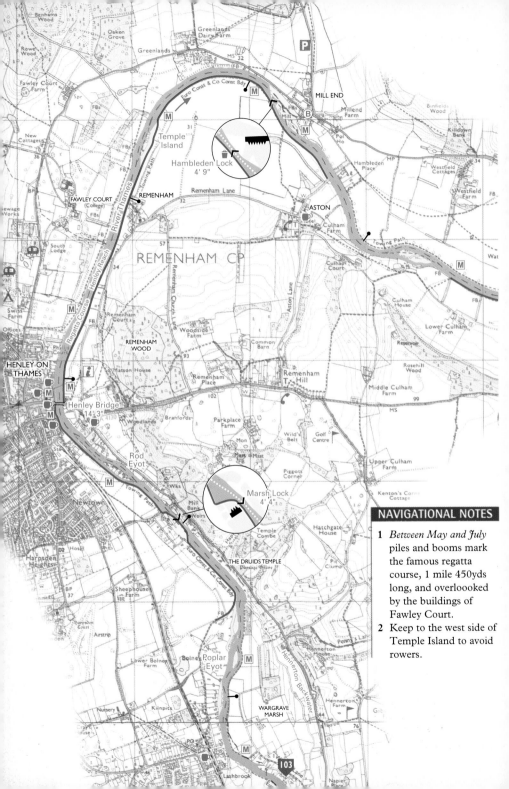

NAVIGATIONAL NOTES

1 *Between May and July* piles and booms mark the famous regatta course, 1 mile 450yds long, and overloooked by the buildings of Fawley Court.

2 Keep to the west side of Temple Island to avoid rowers.

Henley on Thames

The river continues north towards Temple Combe Woods, rising steeply to the east. This part of the river is noted for Brent

Geese and some handsome wooden boathouses. To the north east of Marsh Lock is Park Place; in the grounds is part of Wren's original spire for St Bride's Church, Fleet Street. The house was once occupied by General Conway, whose daughter, Mrs Damer, sculpted the masks of Thames and Isis on Henley Bridge. Henley lies to the west of the river, with an attractive waterfront, many moored boats and resident swans, facing the rise of Remenham Wood to the east. Below Temple Island the river passes the immaculate grounds of the Administrative Staff College (Greenlands) before reaching Hambleden Lock, beautifully situated with an extensive weir (footpath over) and a fine weatherboarded mill, now converted into flats. The tiny village of Aston can be seen on a hillside to the south below the lock; the Thames then divides around thickly wooded islands and meanders past Medmenham and St Mary's Abbey. Beyond the next group of islands a large caravan site heralds the approach of Hurley, where the weir streams rush among more islands by the lock. To the north, on top of the chalk cliffs, is a Ministry of Defence police training base, behind Danesfield, a home built at the turn of the century by a Manchester millionaire.

Boatyards

Ⓑ **Hobbs & Sons** Station Road, Henley (01491 572035). 🛥 P D Rowing boat hire, motor boat hire, long-term mooring, winter storage, slipway, boat and engine sales and repairs, chandlery, gifts, books and maps, toilets. *Closed Sat afternoon and Sun in winter.*
Alf Parrott Thameside, Henley (01491 572380). Useful shop with long-term mooring, fishing tackle and bait. *Closed Wed.*

Ⓑ **Hambleden Mill Marina** Mill End, Henley (01491 571316). Private marina. Craning.
Ⓑ **Peter Freebody's Boatyard** Mill Lane, Hurley (01628 824382). 🛥 E Calor gas, long-term mooring, winter storage, slipway, boat and engine sales and repairs, chandlery. Primarily a boat builder, this is a very famous yard, building many boats, including steam launches for the Henley regatta.

Shiplake

Oxon. Stores. A village of desirable commuter houses climbing up into the hills that border the river. The splendidly situated Church of SS Peter and Paul contains some medieval Belgian glass of great beauty. Tennyson married Emily Sellwood here in 1850. In the village note the White House, built by George Walton in 1908. Further north, near the station, George Orwell lived as a boy at Roselawn, Station Road.

Henley on Thames

Oxon. All shops and services, laundrette, swimming baths, theatre. A fine market town and one of the most popular resorts on the river, described by Dickens as 'the Mecca of the rowing man'. The main street, running down to the Thames from the Victorian Town Hall, has a feeling of timelessness and Edwardian elegance almost out of place today. From the river the most obvious features are the 18thC stone bridge (note the masks of Thames and Isis) and the Decorated and Perpendicular church, a large and gloomy building. The Red Lion Hotel, near the church, has received some notable visitors, including King Charles I (1632 and 1642), the Duke of Marlborough (early 18thC), the poet William Shenstone (1750) and Johnson and Boswell (1776). The Kenton Theatre in New Street is the fourth oldest in the country, being built in 1805. The first Oxford and Cambridge boat race was rowed between Hambleden and Henley on 10 June 1829 – it is now rowed between Putney and Mortlake. The first Henley Regatta was held in 1839, becoming Royal in 1851, with Prince Albert as patron. This is now held *annually in the first week of July;* the town becomes very busy indeed, and everyone seems to be on a picnic. The epitome of an English summer (when the sun shines).

Henley on Thames Tourist Information Centre Town Hall, Market Place (01491 578034).

Fawley Court *Bucks.* (01491 574917). A fine riverside situation. The court was designed by Wren and built in 1684, later to be decorated by Grinling Gibbons and classicised by James Wyatt. The grounds were laid out by Capability Brown in 1770. It now houses the Divine Mercy College and a museum consisting of a library, various documents of the Polish monarchy and Polish militaria, and paintings and sculpture illustrating ancient history and the Middle Ages.

Open 14.00–17.00 Wed, Thur & Sun afternoons Mar–Oct, but closed Whitsun & Easter weekends, and other times – it is wise to telephone and check in advance. Charge. Teashop and gift shop. Very limited moorings in the old canal, and nearby.

Temple Island The temple was built by James Wyatt in 1771 as a vista for Fawley Court, and has a set of hand-painted wall decorations by him. It is thought to be the earliest example in England of the Etruscan style. Owned by the Mackenzie family for over 130 years, the island was sold in 1988. Visited by King Edward VII and Queen Alexandra, it is a pretty ornament, with views down the river to Henley.

Greenlands A sumptuous 19thC Italianate mansion in impeccable grounds, once owned by the first Viscount Hambleden, better known as W.H. Smith. Now an Administrative Staff College.

Hambleden

Bucks. PO, store. Set back from the river and surrounded by heavily wooded hills, this is one of the most attractive villages in Buckinghamshire, and worth the walk up from the river. All mellow flint and brick with a marvellous original unity. The 14thC church and the houses round the green make it a perfect village setting with the 17thC Manor House in the background. The church tower was built in 1721.

Hambleden Mill The white weatherboarded mill, converted into flats, and mill house form a fine group by the lock and weir.

Medmenham

Bucks. A village straggling up from the now defunct ferry into the woods behind.

Medmenham Abbey (St Mary's Abbey) is a charming agglomeration of building styles: 1595, 18thC Gothic and mostly 1898. It was the house of the orgiastic Hell Fire Club, under the auspices of Sir Francis Dashwood. It was decorated in a suitably pornographic and sacrilegious style, but understandably none of this survived the 19thC.

Hurley

Berks. PO, stores. In the old part of the village the long, dark and narrow nave of the church is all that remains of Hurley Priory (St Mary's), founded before 1087 for the Benedictine Order. Opposite the church are a 14thC tithe barn (now a dwelling) and a dovecote.

Harleyford Manor On the north bank opposite Hurley. The manor was built in 1755 by Sir Robert Taylor for Sir William Clayton.

BOAT TRIPS
Hobbs & Sons They have three boats available for trips for private hire , including the largest passenger vessel on the Upper Thames, with a capacity for up to 175 people. They also run regular public trips lasting *1 hour and leaving at 15.00 Apr, May & Sep, and 14.30 & 15.45 July and Aug. During the peak season additional trips are made according to demand.*

Pubs and Restaurants

Baskerville Arms Station Road, Shiplake (0118 940 3332). Brakspear and guest real ales are served, and there is a restaurant with wide-ranging menu *L & D*, with vegetarian choices. Children are welcome and there is a garden. Quiz on *Wed evenings*.

Henley has a fine selection of pubs, the majority serving real ale brewed by Brakspear in their 18thC brewhouse in New Street, by the river. In warm, calm weather the aroma of malt and hops wafts over the water tempting all devotees of good beer to search hastily for a mooring. None of the pubs in Henley is far from the river – those below are simply the closest, and the rest are easily found.

Anchor Friday Street (01491 574753). Brakspear real ales and bar meals available (with barbecues *in summer*) *lunchtimes and evenings every day*, with vegetarian options. Children are welcome and there is a garden and patio. Regular entertainment. No dogs.

Red Lion Hotel By the bridge (01491 572161). A very auspicious and much-visited (see Henley, above) red brick hotel with a brasserie serving meals *lunchtimes and evenings every day*, with a separate vegetarian menu. Children are welcome.

Angel on the Bridge Henley Bridge (01491 574977). A beautiful and historic 14thC inn adjoining the bridge. Bistro restaurant serving fresh fish from Billingsgate and fresh meat from Smithfield. Bar and restaurant meals available *lunchtimes and evenings (not Sun evening in winter)*, with vegetarian choices. Brakspear's real ale is served, and children are welcome. There is a riverside garden.

Little White Hart Hotel Riverside (01491 574145). Half-timbered riverside inn with jetty moorings across the street, serving Brakspear's real ale.

Rose & Crown New Street (01491 578376). Close to the Brakspear brewery and the Kenton Theatre, serving Brakspear's real ale. Bar meals *lunchtimes and evenings (not Sun evening)*, with vegetarian options. Garden.

Little Angel East of Henley Bridge (01491 574165). A 300 year old pub serving Brakspear real ale in the bar, and with a wide-ranging brasserie menu served in the bar or separate dining area *lunchtimes and evenings every day*, with vegetarian choices. Children are welcome and there is outside seating on the patio.

Flowerpot Aston (01491 574721). An attractive, old-fashioned pub serving Brakspear real ales. Bar meals are available *lunchtimes and evenings every day*, with vegetarian choices. Children are welcome and there is a garden.

Stag & Huntsman Hambleden (01491 571227). Brakspear, Wadworth and guest real ales in a fine Victorian pub. A good menu served in both the bar and restaurant *lunchtimes and evenings every day*, with vegetarian options. Children are welcome and there is a large garden. Occasional entertainment with quiz and pub games nights.

Dog & Badger Henley Road, Medmenham (01491 571362). This fine old pub dates from 1390 and has historical associations with the Hell Fire Club (see Medmenham on page 108). Real ales include Brakspear and Flowers. Bar meals are available *lunchtimes and evenings every day*, and the restaurant with an à la carte menu is open *D Tue-Sat*, with vegetarian choices. Children are welcome *in the front bar and restaurant*. Outside seating on the terrace.

Black Boy Hurley (01628 824212). South of Frogmill Farm. An old country pub. Brakspear real ale and extensive bar meals with a range from traditional English to Italian are available *lunchtimes and evenings*, with vegetarian choices (they will happily cater for vegans if prior notice is given). Large garden.

Rising Sun Hurley (01628 824274). A dark and cosy village pub with a log fire, serving Brakspear, Flowers and guest real ales. Bar and restaurant meals *lunchtimes and evenings (not Sun evening, and at Mon lunchtime only snacks are available)*, with vegetarian choices. Children are welcome and there is a garden. Regular theme nights, quiz *on Tue* and music *on Sun.*

East Arms Henley Road, Hurley (01628 823227). Part of the Millers Kitchen group, this pub serves food *all day from 12.00–21.30 and on Fri and Sat until 22.00*, with vegetarian options. Boddingtons, Greenalls and guest real ales are available. Indoor and outdoor children's play areas and a garden. Regular entertainment.

Old Bell Hotel Hurley (01628 825885). Built in 1135 as the guest house for the monastery, it still retains a connecting underground passage, and a fine Norman porch. Fairly expensive French and English food in the restaurant *L & D* with vegetarian menu, and bar snacks. Children are welcome. Garden, with croquet and badminton in the *summer* and specials for the regatta.

Marlow

On the reach below Temple Lock you may well see canoeists and dinghy sailors from the National Sports Centre at Bisham Abbey, so take care. At the end of this long wide stretch is the elegant white Marlow suspension bridge, with the lock just beyond. The Marlow-Bisham bypass crosses below here, followed by the Scouts Boating Centre, so once again the river is often full of small craft.

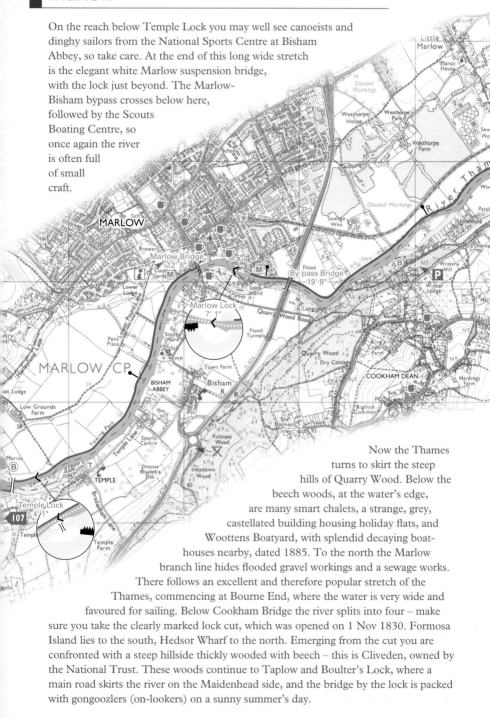

Now the Thames turns to skirt the steep hills of Quarry Wood. Below the beech woods, at the water's edge, are many smart chalets, a strange, grey, castellated building housing holiday flats, and Woottens Boatyard, with splendid decaying boathouses nearby, dated 1885. To the north the Marlow branch line hides flooded gravel workings and a sewage works. There follows an excellent and therefore popular stretch of the Thames, commencing at Bourne End, where the water is very wide and favoured for sailing. Below Cookham Bridge the river splits into four – make sure you take the clearly marked lock cut, which was opened on 1 Nov 1830. Formosa Island lies to the south, Hedsor Wharf to the north. Emerging from the cut you are confronted with a steep hillside thickly wooded with beech – this is Cliveden, owned by the National Trust. These woods continue to Taplow and Boulter's Lock, where a main road skirts the river on the Maidenhead side, and the bridge by the lock is packed with gongoozlers (on-lookers) on a sunny summer's day.

Boatyards

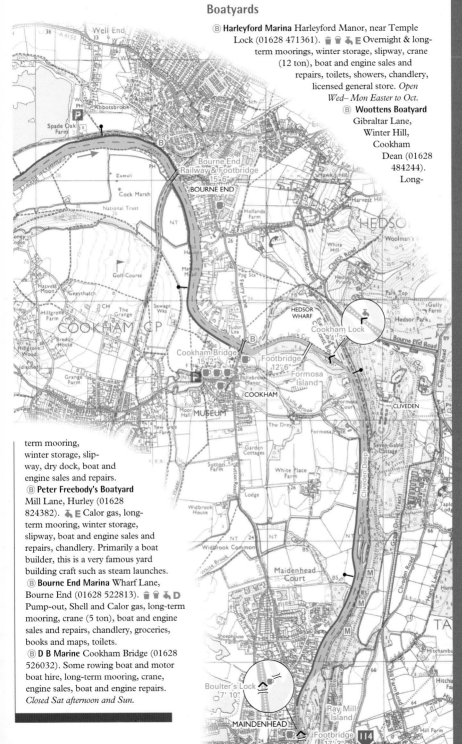

Ⓑ **Harleyford Marina** Harleyford Manor, near Temple Lock (01628 471361). 🚿 🚽 ⚓ E Overnight & long-term moorings, winter storage, slipway, crane (12 ton), boat and engine sales and repairs, toilets, showers, chandlery, licensed general store. *Open Wed– Mon Easter to Oct.*

Ⓑ **Woottens Boatyard** Gibraltar Lane, Winter Hill, Cookham Dean (01628 484244). Long-term mooring, winter storage, slipway, dry dock, boat and engine sales and repairs.

Ⓑ **Peter Freebody's Boatyard** Mill Lane, Hurley (01628 824382). ⚓ E Calor gas, long-term mooring, winter storage, slipway, boat and engine sales and repairs, chandlery. Primarily a boat builder, this is a very famous yard building craft such as steam launches.

Ⓑ **Bourne End Marina** Wharf Lane, Bourne End (01628 522813). 🚿 🚽 ⚓ D Pump-out, Shell and Calor gas, long-term mooring, crane (5 ton), boat and engine sales and repairs, chandlery, groceries, books and maps, toilets.

Ⓑ **D B Marine** Cookham Bridge (01628 526032). Some rowing boat and motor boat hire, long-term mooring, crane, engine sales, boat and engine repairs. *Closed Sat afternoon and Sun.*

Pubs and Restaurants

✕☐ **Compleat Angler Hotel** By Marlow Bridge, Marlow (01628 484444). A restaurant and hotel with a riverside terrace, by the famous suspension bridge. It used to be The Anglers Rest; now the name commemorates Izaak Walton's famous book, published in 1653. The Valaisan Restaurant serves an à la carte menu, with vegetarian options, in a romantic atmosphere. *L & D.* Booking is preferred. Conservatory where *lunch and afternoon tea* can be served. Children are welcome.

🍺✕ **George & Dragon** The Causeway, Marlow (01628 483887). A Beefeater restaurant and pub serving Flowers, Brakspear, Castle Eden and Marston's real ales. Bar and restaurant meals are available *lunchtimes and evenings every day*, with vegetarian options. Children are welcome.

🍺✕ **Chequers Inn** High Street, Marlow (01628 482053). Brakspear and Theakston's real ale in a 17thC inn facing the old Wethered brewery, now sadly closed down. Restaurant and bar meals, with vegetarian choices, are available *lunchtimes and evenings every day.* Children are welcome *in the restaurant only.* Outside seating.

🍺 **The Crown** At the top of the High Street, Marlow (01628 483010). John Smith's real ale is served in what was once the market, with the Town Hall above. Bar meals *lunchtimes (not Sat)*, with vegetarian options. Children are welcome.

🍺 **Prince of Wales** Mill Road, Marlow (01628 482970). Four guest real ales in a locals pub, serving meals in the bar or dining area *lunchtimes and evenings*. They can cater for vegetarians. Children are welcome *in the dining area only.* Outside seating. Quiz *on Sun evenings*. Opposite is the excellent Jolly Frier fish and chip shop.

🍺 **Marlow Donkey** Station Road, Marlow (01628 482022). Flowers, Fuller's and Boddingtons real ale in a Victorian pub near the station. The Donkey was a famous local train, as the sign indicates. Bar meals from a full menu are available *lunchtimes and evenings (not Sun evening)* with vegetarian options. Garden with children's play area.

✕☐ **Pizza Piazza** West Street, Marlow (01628 482544). Pizza and pasta in a restaurant with wooden beams, tiled floors and open fires. Vegetarian selection, and children's menu. *Open 11.00–23.30 Sun–Thur (Fri & Sat closing at midnight).*

🍺✕ **Jolly Farmer** Church Road, Cookham Dean (01628 482905). Opposite the local church, this pub and restaurant offers a range of real ale, including Courage and four changing guests. Bar and restaurant meals served *lunchtimes and evenings (except Sun evening)* with a vegetarian menu. Large garden with children's play area. Barbecues are held in good weather *in the summer.* This pub was bought by the village, for the village, in 1987.

🍺 **Chequers Brasserie** Dean Lane, Cookham Dean (01628 481232). Good selection of wines and real

ale including Fuller's and Marston's. Meals from a daily changing menu *lunchtimes and evenings*, and there is a vegetarian option (the chef will take suggestions for other vegetarian dishes). Children are welcome. Seats outside.

🍺✕ **Hare & Hounds** Cookham Dean Common (01628 483343). The locally brewed Rebellion Smugglers real ale is served here along with Wadworth and Brakspear. Bar and restaurant meals *lunchtimes and evenings* with vegetarian menu. Children are welcome and there is a small garden. Quiz night *every other Wed.*

🍺 **The Walnut Tree** Hedsor Road, Bourne End (01628 520797). A cottagey pub with a garden, serving Morland real ale. Bar meals *lunchtimes*, with vegetarian choices. Children are welcome.

🍺✕ **Firefly** Station Approach (01628 521197). A wide range of real ale including Fuller's, Wadworth, Burton and guests is available. Bar and restaurant meals are served *lunchtimes (not Sun)*, with vegetarian choices. Children are welcome and there is a large garden.

🍺✕ **Ferry Harvester** By the bridge, Cookham (01628 525123). Harvester restaurant with separate low-ceilinged pub. The restaurant has a terrace, river views and children are welcome. Worthington and Bass real ale is served , and bar meals and restaurant meals are available from separate menus *all day every day in summer and in winter Mon–Fri lunchtimes, and all day Sat & Sun.* There is a vegetarian options.

🍺✕ **Bel & the Dragon** High Street, Cookham (01628 521263). An attractive pub dating from 1417, serving Brakspear's real ale. Restaurant *L & D (closed Sun D & Mon)*, with vegetarian options. Children are welcome, and there is a garden.

🍺✕ **King's Arms** High Street, Cookham (01628 530667). Very smart red plush old coaching inn with a Beefeater Steak House, serving a wide range of real ale, including Flowers, Boddingtons and guests. Bar meals are available *12.00–22.30* and the restaurant is open *L & D* – both have vegetarian selections. Children are welcome and there is a superb garden with a play area.

🍺 **Royal Exchange** High Street, Cookham (01628 520085). Tetley, Benskins, Tasco (the house ale) and guest real ales are served, and bar meals are available *lunchtimes and evenings*, with vegetarian options. Children are welcome *if dining*, and there is a garden.

✕☐ **Boulters Lock Hotel** Boulters Island, Maidenhead (01628 21291). Right by the lock in the Old Ray Flour Mill, built 1726 and converted in 1950. The Terrace Bar upstairs serves light meals, and the restaurant serves English and French cuisine *L & D (closed Sun D)*, with vegetarian choices. Children are welcome.

Bisham

Berks. A largely Georgian village set back from the river, behind the abbey. The church is set apart from both, being superbly sited almost at the river's edge. Although rebuilt, it still has a Norman tower. Inside are the fine 17thC Hoby monuments, especially that to Margaret, one of the most unusual of the period.

Bisham Abbey The abbey, built mainly in the 14th and 16thC, was a private house from 1540. It is now a sports centre of the Central Council of Physical Recreation, a hive of activity where young players and coaches come together under the aegis of their respective governing bodies of sport. They train in the sport of their choice, ranging from archery to weight lifting. River activities feature strongly in the training programme. The centre is not open to casual visitors.

Marlow

Bucks. EC Wed. All shops and services, laundrette. A very handsome and lively Georgian town, with a wide tree-lined High Street connecting the bridge with the Market Place. A marvellous view of the weir can be had from the white suspension bridge, built by Tierny Clarke in 1831–6 and reconstructed, retaining its original width, in 1966. Holy Trinity Church is by Gilbert Scott, 1852, and the Roman Catholic church is a surprisingly uninspired design by Pugin. The town's most ancient building is the Old Parsonage, once part of a great 14thC house and containing panelled rooms and beautifully decorated windows. West Street, at the top of the High Street, has great literary associations – Thomas Love Peacock wrote *Nightmare Abbey* at no. 47, Shelley wrote *Revolt to Islam* in Albion House, while his wife Mary Godwin created *Frankenstein* there. T. S. Eliot also lived in West Street for a while after World War I.

Cookham Dean

Berks. PO, stores. Large parts of Cookham Dean are owned by the National Trust. The village stands above steep beech woods by the river. Winter Hill has one of the best views over the Thames Valley, and is well worth the steep walk. Kenneth Grahame, who wrote *The Wind in the Willows*, published 1908, lived at Mayfield between 1906–10. It is thought that Quarry Wood may have been the wild wood mentioned in the story.

Bourne End

Bucks. EC Wed. PO, shops. A riverside commuter village, famous for Bourne End Sailing Week. Cock Marsh opposite, 132 acres, is owned by the National Trust.

Cookham

Berks. EC Wed. PO, no grocery shops. A pretty village of pubs, antique shops, restaurants and boutiques, with bijou cottages filling the gaps in between. Cookham is famous as the home of the artist Stanley Spencer – the quite amazing variety of his work is splendidly exhibited in the old Wesleyan Chapel, open *daily Easter–Oct 10.30–17.30 and Sat, Sun & B. Hols in winter 11.00–17.00.* Modest admission charge. His *Last Supper,* painted in 1920, hangs in the splendid square-towered Holy Trinity Church, built by the Normans in 1140 on the site of a Saxon building. There are fine 16thC monuments, and the church is floodlit after dark. The bridge, an iron structure, was built in 1867. David Barber is Her Majesty's Swan Keeper – a unique appointment. In the *third week of July* he takes to his boat with a supply of 'tea' (an intoxicating mixture of dark rum and milk) to mark the swans, together with representatives of the Vintners' and Dyers' Companies, in their double sculling skiffs. This colourful event is known as Swan Upping.

Hedsor

Bucks. A priory and an over-restored church on the hill. It is worth the walk up for the splendid views over the beech woods. Hedsor House was rebuilt in 1862 in an Italianate style. Lord Boston's Folly, an 18thC structure, faces the church from the opposite hill.

Hedsor Wharf An important shipping point for timber, paper and coal for over 500 years until the lock cut bypassed it in 1830. At the lower end of Hedsor Water there was once a lock – the original cottage still stands, a single room cut from the chalk and fronted with brick. Hedsor Water is private.

Cliveden Taplow (01628 668561). A most marvellous stretch of beech woods from Hedsor to Taplow surrounds the house. Built in 1862 for the Astor family, it was the background to many 20thC political intrigues and scandals, ending with the Profumo affair in 1963. Fine tapestries and furniture, and a theatre which heard the first performance of *Rule Britannia.* It is now a stately home (hotel), leased from the National Trust. B & B prices start at £245 per night.

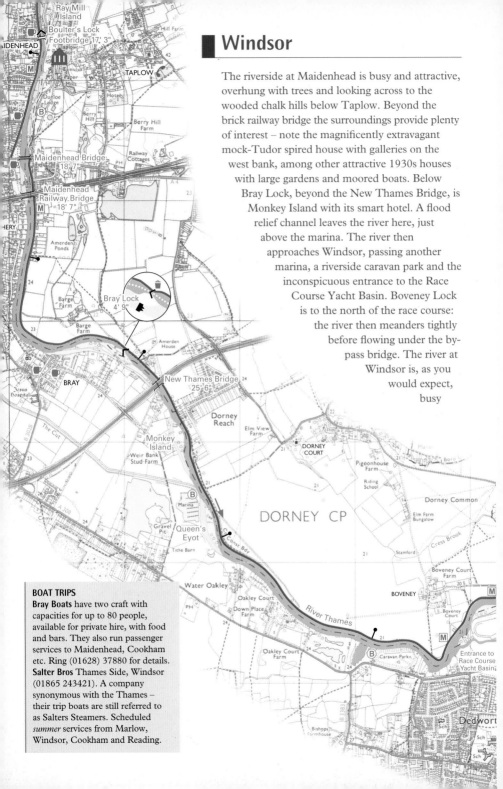

Windsor

The riverside at Maidenhead is busy and attractive, overhung with trees and looking across to the wooded chalk hills below Taplow. Beyond the brick railway bridge the surroundings provide plenty of interest – note the magnificently extravagant mock-Tudor spired house with galleries on the west bank, among other attractive 1930s houses with large gardens and moored boats. Below Bray Lock, beyond the New Thames Bridge, is Monkey Island with its smart hotel. A flood relief channel leaves the river here, just above the marina. The river then approaches Windsor, passing another marina, a riverside caravan park and the inconspicuous entrance to the Race Course Yacht Basin. Boveney Lock is to the north of the race course: the river then meanders tightly before flowing under the by-pass bridge. The river at Windsor is, as you would expect, busy

BOAT TRIPS

Bray Boats have two craft with capacities for up to 80 people, available for private hire, with food and bars. They also run passenger services to Maidenhead, Cookham etc. Ring (01628) 37880 for details. **Salter Bros** Thames Side, Windsor (01865 243421). A company synonymous with the Thames – their trip boats are still referred to as Salters Steamers. Scheduled *summer* services from Marlow, Windsor, Cookham and Reading.

with trip boats, rowing and motor boats, walkers and children feeding the ducks. On the north bank is the smart Eton College Boat House, while the magnificent Windsor Castle dominates the river for miles around. Leaving Windsor, the Thames winds around the Home Park, passing the playing fields at Eton, and the famous college, on the north bank.

Boatyards

Ⓑ **Bray Boats** Lockbridge Boathouse, Ray Mead Road, Maidenhead (01628 37880). 🚽 🚻 ♿ Pump-out, day boat hire, long-term mooring, outboard repairs, toilets. Tug hire. *Closed Sun in winter.*

Ⓑ **Peter Freebody** Boulters Island, Maidenhead (01628 824382). Boat building and repairs. This is the Maidenhead yard of the very famous boatbuilders, who construct steam launches for the Henley regatta, amongst others.

Ⓑ **Bray Marina** Monkey Lane, Bray (01628 23654). 🚽 🚻 ♿ P D E Calor gas, long-term mooring, winter storage, crane (10 ton), boat sales, boat and engine repairs, chandlery, groceries, gifts, books and maps, toilets, showers. Café open *10.00–16.00 weekends and 10.00–15.30 weekdays.*

Ⓑ **Windsor Marina** Maidenhead Road, Oakley Green, Windsor (01753 853911). 🚽 🚻 ♿ P D Pump-out, Calor gas, long-term mooring, winter storage, slipway, dry dock, crane (10 ton), boat and engine sales and repairs, chandlery, gifts, books and maps, toilets, showers.

Ⓑ **Race Course Yacht Basin** Maidenhead Road, Windsor (01753 851501). 🚽 🚻 ♿ P D E Gas, overnight & long-term mooring, winter storage, slipway, dry dock, crane, boat and engine sales and repairs, toilets, showers, large chandlery, books and maps, gifts.

Ⓑ **Tom Jones (Boat Builders)** Romney Lock Boat House, Windsor (01753 860699/mobile 0831 862729). Long-term mooring, winter storage, crane, boat building, boat and engine sales and repairs.

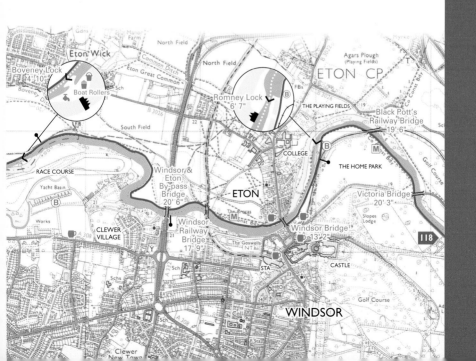

Pubs and Restaurants

Taplow House Hotel Berry Hill, Taplow (01628 70056). A Georgian mansion standing in 6 acres of grounds and housing a residential hotel, an excellent restaurant and two bars. The restaurant serves meals *L & D (closed Sun)* with a vegetarian menu. Children are welcome.

Thames Hotel Ray Mead Road, Maidenhead (01628 28721). A modernised riverside hotel and restaurant with an à la carte menu, served *lunchtimes and evenings every day*, with a vegetarian menu. Bar meals are served overlooking the river. Children are welcome and there is a terrace with outside seating.

Franco's Ray Mead Road, Maidenhead. (01628 33522). By the bridge. Intimate Italian restaurant with some vegetarian dishes *L & D (booking advisable). Closed Sat L & Sun.*

Thames Riviera Hotel (River Bar) Bridge Road, Maidenhead (01628 74057). A residential hotel overlooking the Thames below Maidenhead Bridge. Bar meals are served *lunchtimes and evenings every day*, with vegetarian options. There is also a coffee shop open *09.00–17.00*. Children are welcome and there is a garden.
Maidenhead town centre, where you will find more pubs and eating places, lies about 3/4 mile south west of the bridge.

Old Station Inn Bath Road, Taplow (01628 22922). Known locally as the Tin Shack, this friendly pub serves Flowers and also, *in summer*, a guest real ale. Bar meals are available *lunchtimes and evenings (not Sun evening)*, with vegetarian dishes available. There is a garden with a children's play area. On *Sun evening* the Buskers play acoustic guitar, and the pub has a sing-along.

Waterside Inn Ferry Road, Bray (01628 20691). A very smart riverside restaurant in a beautiful setting, run by Michel Roux – considered by some to be the best restaurant in the country. Exciting menu, attentive waiters, expensive wine. *Closed Mon, Tue L & Sun D in winter. Booking essential.*

Crown High Street, Bray (01628 21936). A beamy old pub serving Courage and Wadworth real ales. There is good bar food and a separate restaurant serving meals *lunchtimes and evenings (not Sun or Mon evenings)*. Children are welcome and there is a sheltered courtyard with vines.

Sir Christopher Wren's House Hotel Thames Street, Windsor (01753 861354). Thames-side residential hotel with cocktail bar and restaurant overlooking the river. The *Orangery* restaurant serves *L & D* and *afternoon teas* with vegetarian menu. Children are welcome. Outside seating.
Windsor has many fine pubs, the following are those nearest the river:

Royal Oak Datchet Road (01753 865179). Wide range of real ale including Courage, John Smith's, Ruddles, Marston's and guests. Meals are served in the bar and a separate restaurant *lunchtimes and evenings every day* with vegetarian choices. Children are welcome. Garden.

Adam & Eve Thames Street (01753 864359). Bass real ale is served in this pub, which has close associations with the Theatre Royal. Bar meals are available at *lunchtimes*, with vegetarian options. Children are welcome and there is a garden and outside seating in a courtyard.

William IV Thames Street (01753 851004). Courage, Wadworth and Morland real ale in a beamy pub. Also *lunchtime* bar meals, with vegetarian menu. Children welcome *at lunchtime if dining*. Morris dancers *Sundays in summer*.

La Taverna River Street (01753 863020). Excellent Italian food and wine *L (Mon–Fri) & D (Mon–Sat). Prefer booking.*
The following five pubs are easily found in Eton High Street, straight up from the bridge:

Crown & Cushion Eton (01753 861531). Wide selection of real ale including Courage, John Smith's, Fuller's and Morland. Bar meals are available *lunchtimes and early evenings every day*, with vegetarian options. Children are welcome *in the back bar*, and there is a garden.

Christopher Hotel Eton (01753 852359). A selection of real ale is served, and bar restaurant meals are available *lunchtimes and evenings every day*. Vegetarian options are on the menu, but if advance notice is given other dishes can be prepared. Children are welcome.

College Arms Eton (01753 865516). A friendly pub serving Boddingtons and Marston's real ale, with bar meal available *lunchtimes and evenings every day*, with vegetarian options. Children are welcome and there is outside seating.

Hog's Head Ale House Eton (01753 861797). A wide choice of 12 regularly changing real ales including Flowers, Boddingtons, Brakspear, Wadworth and Castle Eden. A traditional breakfast is served from *10.00–12.00*, with *lunchtime* bar meals, *early evening* snacks and *18.00–21.30* bar meals. Vegetarian options are served. Children are welcome *if dining*, and there is a large garden. Live jazz on *Thur evenings*.

House on the Bridge By Windsor Bridge, Eton (01753 860914). International restaurant with its own moorings. *L & D*, with vegetarian choices. Children are welcome and there is outside seating on a riverside terrace.

Watermans Arms Brocas Street (01753 861001). Near the Eton College Boat House. The restaurant serves traditional English cuisine *L & D (not Sun D)*. Bar meals are also available *lunchtimes and evenings (not Sun evening)*. Both the bar and restaurant offer vegetarian and vegan options. A selection of seven real ales, including Brakspear, Courage, Wadworth, Morland and Ruddles. Children are welcome, and there is a conservatory seating area.

● **Maidenhead**
Berks. MD Fri, Sat. All services. A dormitory suburb of London, close to the M4 motorway, and with much new development.
Maidenhead Tourist Information Centre The Library, St Ives Road (01628 781110).
Maidenhead Railway Bridge The two beautiful arches, each 123ft long, are reputedly the largest brickwork spans in the world. They were built in 1839 by Brunel.

● **Bray**
Berks. EC Wed. PO, stores. Although there is much commuter development, Bray still retains its village centre. The well-preserved largely 13thC church is approached via a fine brick gatehouse of 1450. Simon Alwyn, the 16thC vicar of Bray, who changed his creed three times to hold the living under Henry VIII, Edward VI, Mary and Elizabeth I, was immortalised in song, and now lies buried in the churchyard. Just outside the village is the Jesus Hospital, founded in 1627.
Monkey Island *Berks.* On the island are the fishing lodge and pavilion of the 3rd Duke of Marlborough, built in 1744, and now a hotel. In one of the restaurant rooms there are monkey paintings on the ceiling, by Clermont. The name of the island, however, is a derivation of Monk's Eyot.
Down Place A pretty 18thC riverside mansion, once the meeting place of the Kit Kat Club. Steele, Addison, Walpole and Congreve were members. It now houses Bray Studios. Nearby is Oakley Court, a magnificent Victorian Gothic castle of 1859. All the elements of romantic medievalism are present. Now a hotel.
Dorney Court and Church (01628 604638). A gabled and timbered house built with soft pink Tudor brick around 1500. It has been occupied by the present family for 400 years. Many restorations have not altered the original feeling of the house which contains fine furniture and paintings. The church forms a perfect unit with the court, and contains a Norman font, 17thC woodwork and a Garrard monument. Cream teas and shop. *Open 13.00–16.30, Sun & B Hols in May, Mon–Thur July & Aug.* Charge.

● **Boveney**
Bucks. A village scattered around a green. There are some over-restored Tudor buildings, which still remain attractive. The pretty flint and clapboard church nestles in trees by the river.

● **Windsor**
Berks. All shops and services. A clean and tidy town. The castle is a splendid fairy-tale edifice, and the changing of the guard ceremony in the morning is conducted with a uniquely British mixture of military authority and showman-ship. The main street curves around the castle, and is full of pubs, restaurants and souvenir shops. There are many fine buildings in the town, most of them 19thC. The Church of St John the Baptist in the High Street, built 1820–2, has three galleries supported by delicate cast iron piers. The town hall, built by Wren in 1689–90 after a design by Sir Thomas Fitch, has the usual open ground floor. The ceiling is supported by four Tuscan columns which stop two inches short: a private joke of the architect's at the expense of a doubting mayor. To the west of the town there is a fine riverside park. Theatre at the Theatre Royal (01753 853886).
Windsor Tourist Information Centre High Street (01753 852010).

● **Windsor Castle**
The largest inhabited castle in the world, first built by Henry II, 1165–79. Most succeeding monarchs have left their mark, notably Charles II, and Queen Victoria who spent over £1 million on modernisation. The building falls into three sections:
Lower Ward St George's Chapel, the finest example of Perpendicular architecture in the country, rebuilt after a disastrous fire in 1993. The Albert Memorial Chapel, originally built by Henry VII and turned into a Victorian shrine.
Middle Ward The Round Tower, with a panoramic view over 12 counties.
Upper Ward The Private Apartments and the State Apartments, containing a collection of paintings. The castle is surrounded by parks; Home Park borders on the river and contains Frogmore House, built by Wyatt in 1792 out of an earlier house, and the Royal Mausoleum. *The castle precincts are open daily – other parts of the castle are open to the public but times vary: telephone for a recorded message on (01753) 831118.* Charge.
Windsor Leisure Pool Stovell Road. Right beside the river (01753 850004). Flumes, a wave machine, fitness suite, sauna and steam rooms, gymnasium, sunbeds, massage, aromatherapy, café, bar. *Open daily – times vary.*

● **Windsor Great Park**
A total area of 4800 acres between the Thames and Virginia Water. There has been a starling roost in the park for over 100 years, and a heronry at Fort Belvedere.

● **Eton**
Berks. PO, shops. Windsor Bridge is now used by pedestrians only, and the lack of through traffic has made the long and rambling High Street a very pleasant place to walk. The famous college is very much the heart and soul of Eton. It was founded by Henry VI in 1440 and the buildings date from 1441 to the present day. The magnificent 15thC Eton College, chapel and cloisters are *open to the public 14.00–16.00 daily Apr–Oct during term-time, 10.30–16.00 during school holidays.* Charge.

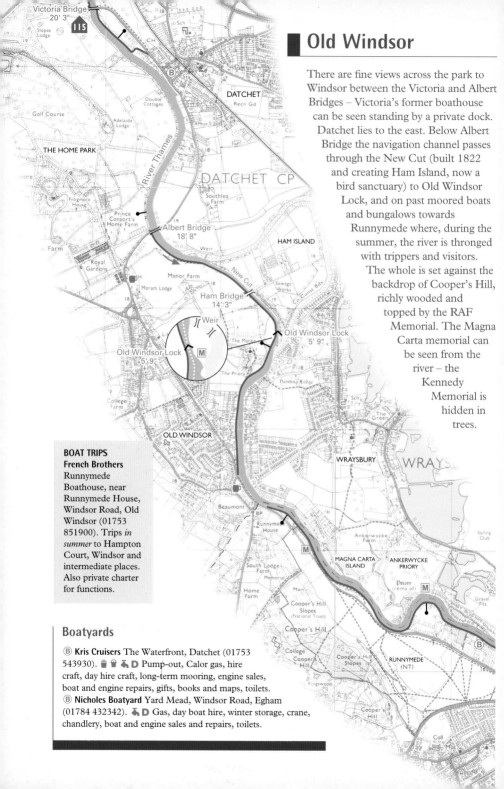

Old Windsor

There are fine views across the park to Windsor between the Victoria and Albert Bridges – Victoria's former boathouse can be seen standing by a private dock. Datchet lies to the east. Below Albert Bridge the navigation channel passes through the New Cut (built 1822 and creating Ham Island, now a bird sanctuary) to Old Windsor Lock, and on past moored boats and bungalows towards Runnymede where, during the summer, the river is thronged with trippers and visitors. The whole is set against the backdrop of Cooper's Hill, richly wooded and topped by the RAF Memorial. The Magna Carta memorial can be seen from the river – the Kennedy Memorial is hidden in trees.

BOAT TRIPS
French Brothers
Runnymede Boathouse, near Runnymede House, Windsor Road, Old Windsor (01753 851900). Trips *in summer* to Hampton Court, Windsor and intermediate places. Also private charter for functions.

Boatyards

Ⓑ **Kris Cruisers** The Waterfront, Datchet (01753 543930). 🚽 🚿 ⚓ **D** Pump-out, Calor gas, hire craft, day hire craft, long-term mooring, engine sales, boat and engine repairs, gifts, books and maps, toilets.

Ⓑ **Nicholes Boatyard** Yard Mead, Windsor Road, Egham (01784 432342). ⚓ **D** Gas, day boat hire, winter storage, crane, chandlery, boat and engine sales and repairs, toilets.

To the north are the remains of Ankerwyke Priory. Passing Holm Island, the London Stone stands by the river: this marked the former limit of the jurisdiction of the City of London over the Thames. There is some smart and mellow new housing on the north bank above Staines Bridge, but for the most part the riverside is lined with a wonderful, and sometimes ludicrously eccentric, array of holiday chalets and bungalows, with houseboats and moored craft of indiscriminate vintage.

● **Datchet**
Berks. EC Wed. PO, shops, fish & chips. At its best around the green, where there is still a village feeling.

● **Old Windsor**
Berks. PO, shop. A great expanse of suburban houses with no sign of the 9thC village, built around the site of a Saxon royal palace. The 13thC church, hidden among trees, was restored by Gilbert Scott in 1863.

● **Runnymede**
Surrey. Beside the river on the south bank – a stretch of open parkland backed by the wooded slope of Cooper's Hill. The paired gatehouses, by Lutyens, introduce an area of memorials. The inspiration is the sealing of the Magna Carta in 1215. On top of the hill is the Commonwealth Air Forces Memorial. This quadrangular structure, built by Sir Edward Maufe in 1953, perfectly exploits its situation. Below are the Magna Carta Memorial and the Kennedy Memorial, the latter built on an acre of ground given to the American people. There are many good walks. The area is owned by the National Trust, and is a popular venue in summer.

Ankerwyke Built on the site of a Benedictine nunnery is Ankerwyke Priory, a low, early 19thC mansion surrounded by trees, among which is the Ankerwyke Yew, whose trunk is 33ft in circumference.

● **Staines**
Surrey. EC Thur. All services, laundrette, fish & chips. A commuter town which has expanded hugely over the last 30 years. However, the area around the pleasantly situated church has remained virtually unchanged. Clarence Street, which culminates in Rennie's stone bridge, built 1829–32, still has the feeling of an 18thC market town. To the north are huge reservoirs.

Pubs and Restaurants

🍺 ✕ **Bells of Ouzeley** Straight Road, Old Windsor (01753 861526). A busy pub near the river, serving Bass real ale. Bar meals are available *lunchtimes and evenings every day*, and a separate restaurant serves *L & D all day Sat & Sun*. Both serve vegetarian dishes. Children are welcome and there is a garden.

🍺 ✕ **Runnymede Hotel** Windsor Road, Egham (01784 436171). A very smart hotel with riverside gardens and conference facilities. English restaurant and the River Room à la carte restaurant serve *L & D*, with vegetarian choices. The bar serves a selection of real ale. Children are welcome.

🍺 ✕ **Thames Lodge Hotel** Thames Street, Staines (01784 464433). Marston's real ale is served here, and bar meals are available *lunchtimes and evenings every day.* English restaurant meals from an à la carte menu are served *every D and Sun L.* With both the bar and restaurant meals there are vegetarian options, but alternatives can also be arranged with the chef on the day (telephone to book any special requirements). Children are welcome *in the conservatory*, and there is also a patio seating area.

🍺 **Bells** Church Street, Staines (01784 454240). Close to the supposedly haunted churchyard, this pub serves Courage, John Smith's and Ruddles real ale. Bar meals are available *12.00–20.00 (not Sun)*, and vegetarian options are always on the menu. Garden.

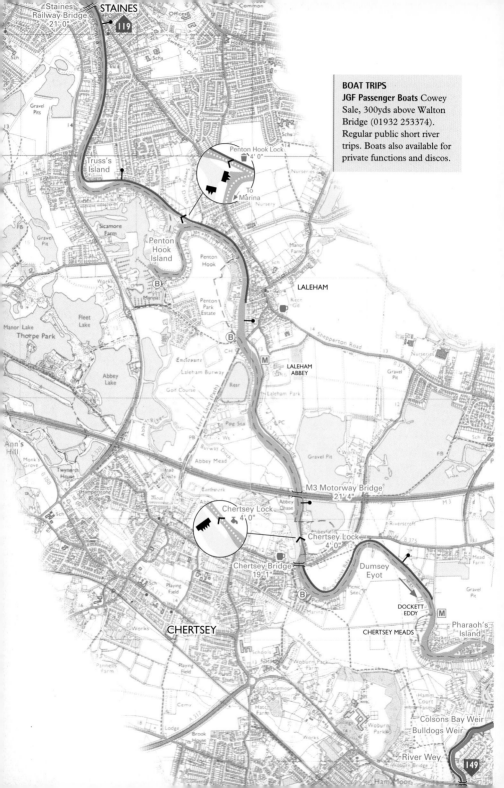

BOAT TRIPS
JGF Passenger Boats Cowey Sale, 300yds above Walton Bridge (01932 253374). Regular public short river trips. Boats also available for private functions and discos.

Weybridge

At Penton Hook a large marina has been established in flooded gravel pits – it is approached from below the lock. Laleham follows, and soon the bungalows disappear and Laleham Abbey and park provide a brief breathing space before Chertsey looms large. The river twists and turns on its way to Weybridge, where the River Wey (see page 149) flows in from the south. Desborough Cut removes two large lops from the navigable course before the rivers makes a direct run for Sunbury, leaving Walton-on-Thames to the east.

NAVIGATIONAL NOTES

1 Note that Penton Hook Marina is approached from *below* the lock.
2 The River Wey joins the Thames *below* Shepperton Lock.
3 The old course of the river north of Desborough Island is navigable, but it may be shallow in places. Nauticalia runs a ferry service below Shepperton Lock for the National Trust, so walkers can enjoy this ancient crossing, noticing that 'droves of sheep will be carried at the fare of one shilling per score (shepherd to clean up afterwards)'.

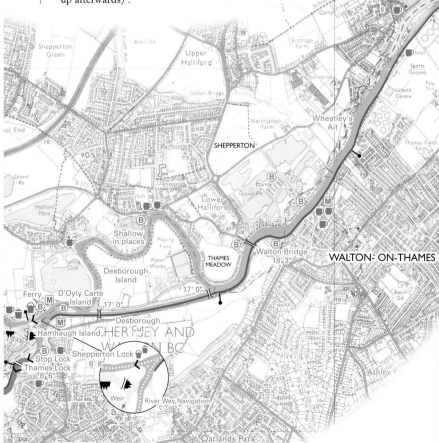

SUNBURY
124

Boatyards

Ⓑ **Penton Hook Marina** Staines Lane, Chertsey (01932 568681). A vast marina in flooded gravel pits.🛏 🛒 🔧 P D E Pump-out, gas, overnight and long-term mooring, winter storage, two mobile cranes, slipway, dry dock, chandlery, books and maps, boat and engine sales and repairs, toilets, showers.

Ⓑ **Harris Boatbuilders** Laleham Road, Chertsey (01932 563111). 🛏 🛒 🔧 D Pump-out, gas, hire craft, day hire craft, long-term mooring, winter storage, slipway, boat building, boat and engine repairs, café, books and maps. *Closed winter weekends.*

Ⓑ **Chertsey Meads Marine** Mead Lane, Chertsey (01932 564699).🔧 D E Gas, hire craft, day hire boats, long-term mooring, crane, winter storage, slipway, boat and engine sales and repairs, boat building, small chandlery, books and maps.

Ⓑ **Nauticalia** Ferry Lane, Shepperton (01932 254844). 🛏 🔧 E Gas, long-term mooring, winter storage, slipway, crane, boat and engine sales and repairs, boat building, chandlery, gifts, books and maps.

Ⓑ **Eyot House** D'Oyly Carte Island, Weybridge (01932 848586).🛏 🛒 🔧 Gas, long-term mooring, winter storage, slipway, boat sales, boat and engine repairs, telephone, toilets.

Ⓑ **Gibbs Marine Sales** Sandhills, Russell Road, Shepperton (01932 220926). 🔧 E Overnight and long-term mooring, winter storage, slipway, crane, boat and engine sales and repairs, electric boat sales, gifts, books and maps, telephone, toilets.

Ⓑ **Walton Marine Sales** Walton Bridge, Walton (01932 226266). 🛒 Gas, overnight and long-term mooring, crane, boat and engine sales and repairs, chandlery, gifts, books and maps, toilets, showers, café.

Ⓑ **Bridge Marine** Thames Meadow, Shepperton (01932 245126). 🔧 Gas, dry mooring, winter storage, slipway, boat hoist, chandlery, boat and engine repairs, gifts, books and maps.

Ⓑ **Shepperton Marina** Felix Lane, Shepperton (01932 243722).🛏 🛒 🔧 P D Pump-out, gas, overnight and long-term mooring, winter storage, crane, chandlery, boat and engine sales and repairs, books and maps, toilets, showers.

Ⓑ **DBH Marine** Angler's Wharf, Manor Road, Walton (01932 228019). Day hire craft, overnight and long-term mooring, boat building, boat and engine sales and repairs, books and maps.

● **Laleham**
Surrey. PO, stores. The first impression of Laleham is one of bungalows and houseboats. The village does not exploit the river at all, and the centre lacks the riverside feeling of some other towns hereabouts. The 18th and 19thC church is well placed in a wooded graveyard, which contains the tomb of Matthew Arnold. In the church, note the Norman arcades on both sides of the nave, and the expressionist window by W. Geddes, 1926. To the south of the town is Laleham Park. Formerly the grounds of Laleham House, built about 1805, it is now a wooded public park reaching down to the river.
Thorpe Park Staines Road, Chertsey (01932 562633). A popular theme park for all ages. Rides and attractions include the highest log flume ride in the UK, Thunder River, Phantom Fantasia, the Canada Creek Railway which takes visitors to Thorpe Farm – a 1930s traditional working farmyard, as well as a Medieval town square and castle. *Open 10.00–16.00 Easter–Oct. Charge.*
● **Chertsey**
Surrey. All shops and services. From the river the first sight of Chertsey is James Paine's stone bridge, built 1780-2. Chertsey just manages to retain a feeling of the 18thC, especially around

Windsor Street, which runs past the site of the abbey. Today nothing remains of what was one of the greatest abbeys in England. Founded in AD666, rebuilt during the 12thC, it was finally destroyed during the Reformation. It is thought likely materials from the abbey were used in the construction of Hampton Court. In the town centre the large and airy church is mostly 19thC. The interior is painted in pleasing Adamesque colours.
● **Weybridge**
Surrey. All shops and services, laundrette. A commuter town in the stockbroker belt, built around the confluence of the rivers Wey and Thames – the junction is marked by a pretty iron bridge of 1865. Weybridge represents the frontier of the suburbia that now spreads almost unbroken to London.
● **Shepperton**
Surrey. All shops and services, laundrette. Recognisable from the river by the lawns of the 19thC Manor House, Shepperton is a surprising example of village survival. The square contains a number of relatively intact 18thC inns. The church, with its fine brick tower, was built in the 17th and 18thC – note the box pews. To the north of the church is the rectory, which has an excellent Queen Anne front of about 1700. The

famous film studios are to the north, near the vast Queen Mary Reservoir.

- **Walton-on-Thames**
Surrey. PO. All shops and services, laundrette, fish & chips and Lees, baker of the year 1996. There is much new development here, including a huge straggling shopping centre, but there is little to see.

- **Sunbury**
Surrey. PO. Shops and laundrette. Sunbury has a pleasant village feeling, but the parish church is a 19thC disaster. Sunbury Court, the grand mansion of the town, was built in 1770, and is now a Salvation Army Youth Centre.

Pubs and Restaurants

Three Horseshoes Shepperton Road, Laleham (01784 452617). An attractive and comfortable pub, once patronised by Sir Arthur Sullivan and Marie Lloyd. Webster's, Ruddles and Fuller's real ale. Excellent home-made snacks and meals *lunchtimes and evenings*. Separate à la carte restaurant *L & D (not Sat L or Sun D)*. Both the bar and restaurant menus have vegetarian options. Children are welcome, and there is a conservatory and a large garden.

The Boat House Bridge Road, Chertsey (01932 565644). A busy wood and tile riverside pub, with a nautical theme.

Thames Court Hotel Shepperton Lock (01932 221957). Oak-panelled and balconied pub serving Hancocks and Bass real ale, with meals *lunchtimes and evenings every day*. There are always vegetarian choices, and children are welcome. Garden.

Anchor Hotel Church Square, Shepperton (01932 221618). A 400 year-old wood-panelled pub serving Morlands real ale, and good food *lunchtimes and evenings every day*, with vegetarian choices. Children are welcome, and there are seats outside.

Lincoln Arms 104 Thames Street, Weybridge (01932 842109). A large, friendly riverside pub with a family room, garden and play area. Mexican-American and traditional English food is served *lunchtimes and evenings every day*, with vegetarian choices, and you can choose Tetley's, Burton or a changing guest real ale to wash it down. Live music for special events, such as halloween and Christmas.

Old Crown 83 Thames Street, Weybridge (01932 842844). A rambling weather-boarded pub by the old course of the River Wey, with charming nautical decor. Courage, Theakston's and Young's real ale are served, along with meals *lunchtimes and evenings every day*. There are always vegetarian choices. Children are welcome, and on fine days you can choose between the riverside garden or patio.

Ship Russell Road, Shepperton (01932 227320). Adnam's, Morlands and Whitbread real ales are served, along with food *lunchtimes and evenings every day*, with vegetarian choices. Children are welcome.

Swan Manor Road, Walton (01932 225964). An imposing and friendly riverside pub, licensed since 1770, and serving Young's real ale. Meals are available *lunchtimes and evenings every day*, with vegetarian choices. Children are welcome, and there is a garden.

Anglers Inn Anglers Wharf, Manor Road, Walton (01932 223996). A fine river-side pub serving Courage, Marston's and Wadworth real ales, and bar meals *lunchtimes and evenings every day*. A separate French restaurant upstairs overlooks the river, and specialises in shellfish. *L & D*. There is a range of vegetarian meals. Children are welcome, and there are riverside seats.

Old Manor Inn Manor Road, Walton (01932 221359). Courage and Marston's real ale in a pub with a fine floral display. Bar meals are served *lunchtimes and evenings Mon–Fri*, with vegetarian options. There is a garden.

Flower Pot Hotel Thames Street, Sunbury (01932 780741). A 14thC pub, offering Bass, Brakspear's, Greene King, Young's and Tetley's real ale. Food is served *lunchtimes and evenings every day*, with vegetarian choices. Children welcome if eating.

Magpie Thames Street, Sunbury (01932 782024). Gibbs Mew real ale in a friendly riverside pub, with mooring. Good food is served *lunchtimes and evenings every day*, with vegetarian choices. Children are welcome, they have their own menu, and free ice cream for sweet! Patio.

Phoenix Thames Street, Sunbury (01932 785358). Courage and Theakston's real ale is served, and meals are available *lunchtimes and evenings every day*, with vegetarian choices. There is a garden.

Hampton Court

Sunbury Court Island is lined with immaculate chalets and bungalows: opposite and to the east is a vast area of reservoirs and waterworks. Below Platt's Eyot is Hampton, where the ferry still survives. Hampton Church stands on the north bank opposite Garrick's Ait. Bushy Park stretches away to the north east of the river. Tagg's Island and Ash Island are lined with smart moored craft and eccentric houseboats – the large Swiss chalet behind Tagg's Island is part of Hucks Boatyard. Below Hampton Bridge is Hampton Court Palace, standing close to the river, and separated from it by an extremely long red brick wall. Further downstream, Thames Ditton Island is absolutely packed with bungalows and chalets. The river then becomes very wide as it curves past the village of Thames Ditton, flanked by the

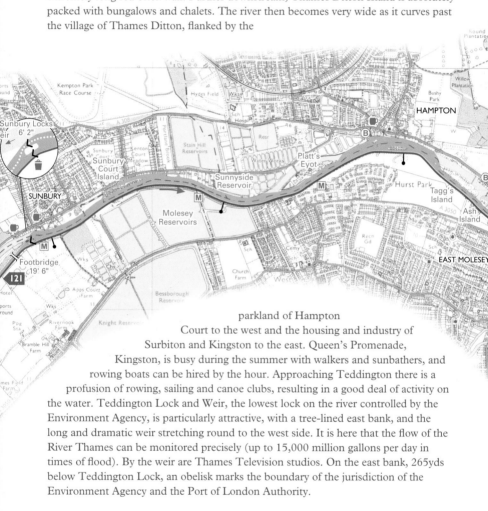

parkland of Hampton Court to the west and the housing and industry of Surbiton and Kingston to the east. Queen's Promenade, Kingston, is busy during the summer with walkers and sunbathers, and rowing boats can be hired by the hour. Approaching Teddington there is a profusion of rowing, sailing and canoe clubs, resulting in a good deal of activity on the water. Teddington Lock and Weir, the lowest lock on the river controlled by the Environment Agency, is particularly attractive, with a tree-lined east bank, and the long and dramatic weir stretching round to the west side. It is here that the flow of the River Thames can be monitored precisely (up to 15,000 million gallons per day in times of flood). By the weir are Thames Television studios. On the east bank, 265yds below Teddington Lock, an obelisk marks the boundary of the jurisdiction of the Environment Agency and the Port of London Authority.

Turk's Launches Run a public service to Hampton Court, Kingston and Richmond in *summer*. Also private charter up to 175 people. Telephone 0181 546 2434 for details.

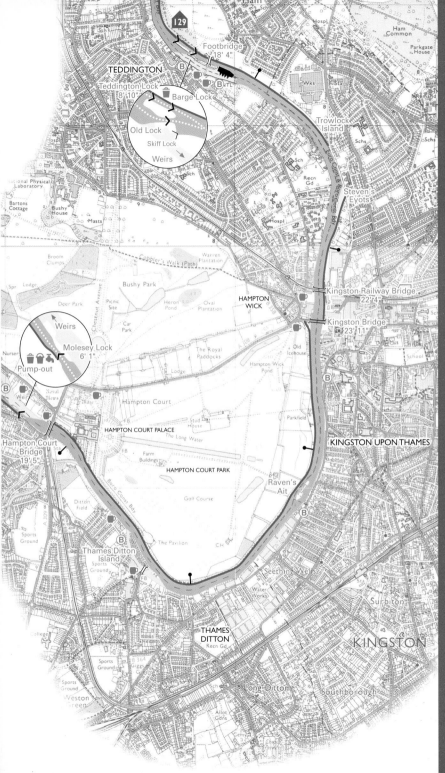

129

Footbridge
18' 4"

TEDDINGTON

Teddington Lock
8' 10"
Barge Lock

Old Lock

Skiff Lock

Weirs

National Physical
Laboratory

Bartons
Cottage

Bushy
House

Masts

Cobbler's Walk (Path)

Broom
Clumps

Warren
Plantation

Spr

Lodge

Deer Park

Bushy Park

Picnic
Site

Chestnut Avenue

Heron
Pond

Oval
Plantation

Car
Park

HAMPTON
WICK

Weirs

Molesey Lock
6' 1"

Pump-out

Nurser

Weir

Royal
Mews

The Royal
Paddocks

Lodge

Hampton Wick
Pond

Old
Icehouse

Hampton Court

HAMPTON COURT PALACE

Stud
House

The Long Water

Parkfield

Hampton Court
Bridge
19' 5"

F.B.

Farm
Buildings

HAMPTON COURT PARK

KINGSTON UPON THAMES

Ditton
Field

Sports
Ground

Golf Course

Raven's
Ait

The Pavilion

Thames Ditton
Island

Sports
Ground

F.B.

THAMES
DITTON

Recn Gd

Seething Wells

Water
Works

Surbiton

College

Sports
Ground

A 309

Boro Const Bdy

A 364

Sports
Ground

Weston
Green

Allot
Gdns

Long Ditton

Southborough

KINGSTON

Steven's
Eyots

Kingston Railway Bridge
22' 4"

Kingston Bridge
23' 11"

Schs

Trowlock
Island

Ham
Common

Parkgate
House

Hospl

Wks

Hospl

1 Teddington Locks (0181 940 8723). Traffic moving upstream *must* observe the light signals at the end of the lock island.
Two red diagonal crosses – both locks *closed*. Do not proceed.
One red diagonal cross – lock *closed*.
White Arrow – *proceed* in direction indicated.

2 Those using the Skiff Lock should follow the lock keeper's instructions.

3 The river below Teddington Lock is tidal for two hours either side of high water.

4 **Teddington to Brentford** – leave Teddington 20 minutes before high water.

5 **Teddington to Limehouse** – leave Teddington 30 minutes before high water.
Note for both 4 & 5 Arrival time must fall within normal working hours. If it will not, the passage **must** be booked *24 hours* in advance with the appropriate lock keeper.
If you fail to do this, you will be left in the tideway. Times are approximate and depend upon the speed of your boat. If in any doubt – *check before you leave.*

Boatyards

Ⓑ **Geo Wilson & Sons** Sunbury (01932 782067). 🚣 Day hire craft, overnight and long-term mooring, winter storage, slipway, traditional boat repairs, engine repairs, toilets. *Closed Tue.*

Ⓑ **Turk's of Sunbury** 10 Thames Street, Sunbury (01932 782028). 🚻 🚣 Pump-out, long-term mooring, slipway, boat and engine repairs. *Closed winter weekends.*

Ⓑ **George Kenton** Hampton Ferry Boatyard, Thames Street, Hampton (0181 9794712). 🚣 Rowing boat hire, long-term mooring. Also operates the Hampton Ferry.

Ⓑ **T.W. Allen & Son (Yachts)** Ash Island, Hampton Court, East Molesey (0181 979 1997). 🚻 🚻 🚣 Pump-out, gas, overnight and long-term mooring, slipway, boat and engine sales and repairs, toilets, showers.

Ⓑ **Ferryline Cruisers** Ferry Yacht Station, Thames Ditton (0181 398 0271). 🚻 🚻 🚣 D Pump-out, hire craft, overnight mooring, slipway, toilets, books and maps.

Ⓑ **Taggs Boatyard** Summer Road, Thames Ditton (0181 398 2119). 🚣 Day hire craft, long-term mooring, winter storage, slipway, boat and engine sales and repairs, toilets.

Ⓑ **Thames Marina** Portsmouth Road, Thames Ditton (0181 398 6159). 🚻 🚻 🚣 D Gas, overnight and long-term mooring, winter storage, slipway, crane, boat building, boat and engine sales and repairs, toilets, chandlery, books and maps, gifts.

Ⓑ ✕ **Hart's Boatyard** Portsmouth Road, Surbiton (0181 399 2113). 🚻 🚣 Overnight and long-term mooring, winter storage, slipway, boat and engine sales and repairs, toilets. Pub upstairs (0181 399 7515). *Summer* ferry to Hampton Court.

Ⓑ **Turks of Kingston** 68 High Street, Kingston (0181 546 2432). Pump-out, day boat hire, overnight and long-term mooring.

Ⓑ **Tough Bros** Ferry Road, Teddington (0181 977 4494). 🚻 🚣 Pump-out, boat sales, boat and engine repairs. Chandlery nearby.

● **Hampton**
Surrey. PO, shops, laundrette. Despite much new development Hampton remains an attractive late 18thC village, still linked by ferry to the south bank. The church, built in 1831 by Lapidge, is prominent on the riverside. Despite the proximity of Hampton Court, the village owes its existence to Hampton House, bought by David Garrick in 1754, and subsequently altered by Adam. By the river is Garrick's Temple, built to house Roubiliac's bust of Shakespeare. Nearby stands the large and incongruous Swiss chalet which was brought over from Switzerland in 1899 and is owned by Hucks Boatyard. The style of building in Hampton ranges from impressive Italianate to plain 20thC brick.

● **Hampton Court Palace**
Surrey. (0181 781 9500). Probably the greatest

secular building in England. Cardinal Wolsey, son of an Ipswich butcher, was graced by ambition and ability to such an extent that at the age of 40 he had an income of £50,000 a year. He was thus able to build the grandest private house in England. Work began in 1514. Henry VIII was offended by the unashamed ostentation of his lieutenant and in 1529, following Wolsey's downfall and his failure to secure the annulment of Henry VIII's first marriage, the king took over the house. Henry spent more on Hampton Court than on any other building, establishing it as a Royal Palace. Subsequently Wren added to it, but little work, other than repairs, has been done since. In the formal gardens (at their best in *mid-May*) are the Great Vine, planted in 1789, and the Maze where Harris, one of Jerome K. Jerome's *Three Men in a Boat*, got hopelessly lost, along with 20 followers and a keeper. *Open 09.30 (10.15 Mon)–17.15 (15.45 winter) daily. Closed Christmas Eve, Christmas Day and Boxing Day.* Charge. Teas in the grounds. Behind the palace is Bushy Park, enclosing 2000 acres. It is a formal design reminiscent of Versailles, and is famous for deer.

● **Hampton Green**
Surrey. A fine collection of 18thC and earlier buildings surround Hampton Green, just to the north of Hampton Court Bridge. The bridge was built by Lutyens in 1933.

● **Thames Ditton**
Surrey. EC Wed. PO, shops, laundrette. The centre of this unspoilt riverside village has managed to avoid the careless development of the surrounding area. The church here has an interesting graveyard and a lovely garden. A collection of several good brasses inside. Pretty whitewashed houses stand close by the suspension bridge which leads to Thames Ditton Island.

● **Kingston-on-Thames**
Surrey. All shops and services. A Royal Borough where seven Saxon kings were crowned. The coronation stone is displayed outside the Guildhall. There is a good river frontage, centred round the stone bridge built 1825–8 by Lapidge. Away from the river the market place is the centre of the town. The Lovekyn Chapel on London Road dates largely from the Tudor period and is surrounded by many interesting 18thC buildings. The Italianate Town Hall, 1838–40, is one of the most striking buildings in the area. Note also the five conduit houses built by Cardinal Wolsey to supply water to Hampton Court.

● **Teddington**
Middx. PO, shops, laundrette. R. D. Blackmore (1825–1900), author of *Lorna Doone,* lived in Teddington from 1860. The site of his home, Gomer House, is at the end of Doone Close, near the station. The tiny parish church of St Mary's, largely 18thC, is dwarfed by the enormity of the unfinished church of St Alban's which stands opposite. The riverside, viewed from the Surrey bank, is one of Teddington's most pleasing aspects. The Thames Television studios stand in Broom Road, near the weir.

Pubs and Restaurants

⬤ **Bell** Thames Street, Hampton (0181 941 5673). Right by the church and overlooking the river, this small, cosy pub serves Tetley's and a guest real ale, and food.

⬤ **Cardinal Wolsey** The Green, Hampton Court (0181 979 1458). Fullers real ale and *lunchtime bar meals every day,* in a pub by the stables. Children are welcome.

⬤ ✕ **King's Arms** Lion Gate, Hampton Court Road (0181 977 1729). A superbly situated pub adjoining the palace wall, offering Badger real ale and excellent food *lunchtimes and evenings every day,* including a carvery *Sun lunchtimes,* with something for vegetarians. Children and dogs are welcome, and there is outside seating.

⬤ **Crown Inn** Summer Road, Thames Ditton (0181 398 2376). Bar meals *lunchtimes and evenings every day,* with vegetarian choices, in a friendly pub just over the river from Hampton Court. Children are welcome, and there is outside seating.

⬤ ✕ **Old Swan Hotel** Summer Road, Thames Ditton (0181 398 1814). A riverside pub, behind Thames Ditton Island, serving Bass, Brakspear's, Greene King and Webster's real ale. Meals are available *lunchtimes and evenings Mon–Fri, and 12.00–16.00 Sat & Sun.* There are always vegetarian options. Children are welcome, and there is outside seating.

⬤ ✕ **King's Head** Hampton Wick (0181 977 2413). Courage, Marston's and Webster's real ales are available, along with bar meals *lunchtimes only every day,* and full meals in the fish restaurant *L & D (not Mon or Tue).* There are vegetarian choices, children are welcome, and there is outside seating.

⬤ **White Hart** 70 High Street, Hampton (0181 979 5352). A good choice of ever-changing real ales, together with food *lunchtimes every day.* There are vegetarian choices. Seating on the patio.

⬤ **The Swan** 22 High Street, Hampton Wick (0181 977 8426). A friendly local pub serving Shepherd Neame draught and bottled real ale, along with light meals *lunchtimes and evenings every day.* Vegetarian options can be arranged. There is outside seating.

⬤ **Anglers** Broom Road, Teddington (0181 977 8426). Right next door to Thames Television Studios, this friendly family pub offers Burton, Tetley's, Youngs and a guest real ale, along with food *lunchtimes and evenings every day (but not Sun evening).* There are vegetarian choices, children are welcome, and there is a large garden with a children's play area. Barbecues *in summer.*

⬤ **Tide End Cottage** 8 Ferry Road, Teddington (0181 977 7762). There is a choice of Courage, Boddingtons, Brakspear's and Bass real ale, along with food *lunchtimes and evenings every day (but not Sun evening).* There are always vegetarian choices, and children are welcome. Pleasant garden, with a grape vine.

Richmond-upon-Thames

As the river passes Eel Pie Island and enters Horse Reach, Richmond Hill can be seen rising gently from the east bank, with the large Star and Garter Home dominating the view. To the west lies Marble Hill Park. The river is the focal point of Richmond – indeed the view of the river from Richmond Hill is dramatic and much painted and photographed. Richmond Bridge is an elegant, slightly humped, 18thC structure – one of the prettiest bridges on the river. Beyond the railway bridge is Richmond half-tide lock, movable weir and footbridge, built in 1894. Its brightly painted arches belie its more serious function of tide control. Curving around Old Deer Park, Isleworth Ait lies to the west, with the old village and church close by the river to the north. Behind wooded banks is Syon Park, and opposite are the Royal Botanic Gardens, Kew. Immediately below the park is the entrance to the Grand Union Canal, a direct link with Birmingham (see Book 1).

Boatyards

Ⓑ **W. Hammerton Ferry Boat House,** Marble Hill Park, Twickenham (0181 892 9620). **E** Day hire craft, overnight mooring, long-term mooring.

Ⓑ **Swan Island Harbour** Strawberry Vale, Twickenham (0181 892 2861). ⚓ (charge) **D** Gas, overnight and long-term mooring, winter storage, slipway, boat sales, boat and engine repairs, boat building, toilets, showers.

Ⓑ **Brentford Marine Services** Ridgeways Wharf, Brentford (0181 568 0287). On the Grand Union Canal, above Thames Lock. ⛽ ⚓ Gas (close-by), boat and engine sales and repairs, boat building, telephone, toilets. Brentford High Street, with all its shops, is nearby.

Pubs and Restaurants

🍺 **Pope's Grotto** Cross Deep, Twickenham (0181 892 3050). Young's real ale in a comfortable modern pub by the river. Extensive menu of bar meals *lunchtimes and evenings every day*, with vegetarian choices, and a rear patio garden for summer barbecues. Children are welcome while eating.

🍺 **White Swan** Riverside, Twickenham (0181 892 2166). A startlingly attractive black and white balconied pub right by the river's edge. A fine choice of real ale, including Courage, Marston's, Theakston's, Wadworth and Webster's, and excellent bar meals *lunchtimes Mon–Sun and evenings Mon–Fri*, always with vegetarian options. Children are welcome, and there is a garden.

🍺 ✕ **The Barmy Arms** Twickenham (0181 892 0863). A pleasant pub serving Courage, John Smith's and Theakston's real ale, and food *lunchtimes and evenings every day*, with vegetarian dishes. Children are welcome, and there is outside seating.

🍺 ✕ **London Apprentice** Church Street, Old Isleworth (0181 5601915). A 15thC riverside pub with Elizabethan and Georgian interiors, decorated with prints of Hogarth's *Apprentices*. The restaurant upstairs, with views across the river to Isleworth Ait, serves *L & D (not Sun D)*, and bar meals are available downstairs in the conservatory

lunchtimes and evenings every day (not Sun evening). Vegetarian choices are always offered, children are welcome, and there is a patio.

🍺 **Rose of York** Petersham Road, Richmond (0181 948 5867). This used to be the Tudor Close. Large, comfortable bar panelled in English oak and decorated with reproductions of paintings by Turner and Reynolds of the famous turn in the river. Good views of the Thames from the terrace and courtyard. Samuel Smith real ale is available, and food is served *lunchtimes and evenings every day*, with vegetarian options. Children are welcome, and there is a garden.

🍺 **Waterman's Arms** Water Lane, Richmond (0181 940 2893). A small cosy and popular pub in a cobbled riverside street, which was once frequented by the watermen who trudged up from the river. Young's real ale is served, and meals are available *lunchtimes and evenings every day*, with vegetarian dishes offered. Children are welcome in the function room, and there is outside seating.

🍺 ✕ **White Cross** Water Lane, Richmond (0181 940 0909). A friendly riverside pub with a garden, serving Young's real ale, plus meals, and including a large buffet *Mon–Sat until about 19.00, and Sun until about 16.00*. There are always special vegetarian dishes. Children are welcome upstairs.

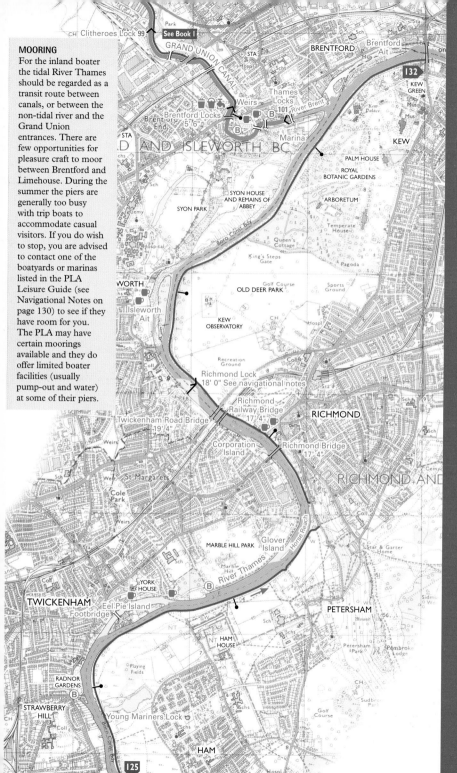

MOORING

For the inland boater the tidal River Thames should be regarded as a transit route between canals, or between the non-tidal river and the Grand Union entrances. There are few opportunities for pleasure craft to moor between Brentford and Limehouse. During the summer the piers are generally too busy with trip boats to accommodate casual visitors. If you do wish to stop, you are advised to contact one of the boatyards or marinas listed in the PLA Leisure Guide (see Navigational Notes on page 130) to see if they have room for you. The PLA may have certain moorings available and they do offer limited boater facilities (usually pump-out and water) at some of their piers.

CH Clitheroes Lock 99

See Book 1

GRAND UNION CANAL

Park

STA

BRENTFORD

Brentford Ait

Hospl

132

KEW GREEN

Thames Locks

Weirs

River Brent

Brentford Locks 5'6"

101

B

River Brent

Brentford End

Marina

KEW

D AND ISLEWORTH BC

B

PALM HOUSE

ROYAL BOTANIC GARDENS

STA

SYON HOUSE AND REMAINS OF ABBEY

ARBORETUM

SYON PARK

Temperate House

Hospital

Queen's Cottage

Pagoda

WORTH

Isleworth Ait

King's Steps Gate

OLD DEER PARK

Golf Course

Sports Ground

KEW OBSERVATORY

CH

Hospl

Recreation Ground

Coll

Richmond Lock 18' 0" See navigational notes

Richmond Railway Bridge 17' 4"

RICHMOND

Twickenham Road Bridge 19' 4"

Weirs

Corporation Island

Richmond Bridge 17' 4"

RICHMOND AND

St Margarets

Cemy

Cole Park

Weirs

Coll

MARBLE HILL PARK

Glover Island

Horse Reach

Star & Garter Home

TWICKENHAM

YORK HOUSE

B

River Thames

PETERSHAM

Eel Pie Island

Footbridge

Marble Hill

HAM HOUSE

NT

Petersham Park

Pembroke Lodge

RADNOR GARDENS

B

Playing Fields

Sudbrook Park

STRAWBERRY HILL

Coll

Young Mariners Lock

Golf Course

CH

Hospl

125

HAM

1 From **Brentford** to **Limehouse** navigation on the Thames is far more complex than on the upper reaches. The river here is a commercial waterway first and foremost, and pleasure craft must take great care. The River Thames below Teddington is controlled by the Port of London Authority (PLA) which produces a useful set of free notes, *The Tidal Thames – A Pleasure Users' Guide*. A separate leaflet (**PLA Leisure Guide**) details facilities available to boaters. For general navigational enquiries about the river contact the Assistant Harbour Master, Devon House, 58–60 St Katharine's Way, London E1 9LB (0171 265 2656). While hire companies do not allow their craft to be taken onto the tideway, owners of pleasure boats may wish to make the passage along the Thames below Teddington Locks and between the canals at Brentford and Limehouse. With proper planning this should present no particular difficulties.

2 **Brentford** to **Limehouse Basin** – leave Brentford ½ hour before high water to gain the benefit of the ebb tide. Limehouse Basin is now fitted with sector gates and is *open Apr–Oct 08.00–18.00 & Nov–Mar 08.00–16.30. (Pre-booked passage within the core hours 05.00–22.00 is available by giving at least 24hrs notice.)* Telephone Limehouse Basin (0171 308 9930) and inform them of your intentions. Limehouse listen and operate on VHF channel 80.

3 **Limehouse Basin** to **Brentford** – pass through the entrance lock at Limehouse 2½ hours before high water, to gain the benefit of the flood tide. Thames Lock, Brentford is manned *for a period before, and following high water (2hrs each side if this falls within normal working hours)* and you should contact the lock keeper to pre-book passage *outside the normal working hours* (which are the same as Limehouse) on 0181 560 1120. The same core hours also apply. Brentford gauging lock is boater operated using a BW sanitary station key. Brentford listen and operate on VHF channel 74.

4 **Brentford** to **Teddington** – pass through Thames Lock, Brentford 2 hours before high water to gain the benefit of the flood tide. Teddington lock keeper can be contacted on 0181 940 8723 and Twickenham lock keeper can be contacted on 0181 940 0634.

5 **VHF Radio** – all vessels of 20 metres or more in length must carry a VHF radio capable of communicating with the harbourmaster at port control – channel 14. An exception is made for narrow boats of between 20 and 25 metres in transit between the Grand Union Canal at Brentford and the non-tidal Thames at Teddington Locks. If no radio is available such vessels must telephone the PLA duty officer (0181 855 0315) immediately before and on completion of transit.

6 **Warning lights** – see PLA publication: *The Tidal Thames – A Pleasure Users' Guide.*

7 **Draught** – The depth at the centre span of Westminster Bridge is approximately 2ft 8in at chart datum (about 4ft 0in at mean low water springs). In practice there is usually a greater depth than this – full details are given in the aforementioned PLA publication. The depth at all the other bridges is greater than Westminster.

8 **Headroom** – on the tidal river the clearance at bridges (see PLA Guide) is given as the maximum at mean high water springs – this is less than the headroom at chart datum (lowest astronomical tide). In practice this means that there will usually be more headroom than that indicated.

9 **Canals** – those who wish to navigate on the adjoining British Waterways canals will require a licence, available from: Craft Licensing Office, Willow Grange, Church Road, Watford WD1 3QA (01923 226422). Full details of the inland waterways encountered at Brentford and Limehouse can be found in Book 1.

● **Ham House** Petersham, Surrey (0181 940 1950). A superb 17thC riverside mansion, the exterior largely by Sir John Vavassour. Lavish Restoration interior with a collection of Stuart furniture. *Open 13.00–17.00 Mon–Wed, 12.00–17.00 Sat & Sun Easter–Oct. Closed Nov–Mar.* Charge. Gardens *open 10.30–dusk daily (except Fri).* Free. Restaurant *open Easter–Oct.*

● **Twickenham**

Middx. All shops and services. Twickenham was one of the most elegant and desirable areas in the 18thC. The church, with its three-storey tower, dates largely from 1714. Alexander Pope has many connections with Twickenham and in the church can be found monuments to him and to his parents. York House, built c1700, and now Municipal Offices, has a rather astonishing collection of statues in its riverside gardens.

Strawberry Hill (0181 240 4114). The surviving glory of Twickenham is Walpole's Gothic fantasy, one of the earliest examples of the 18thC Gothic revival. Designed first by John Chute and Richard Bentley between 1753–63, and later by Thomas Pitt, it expresses Walpole's appreciation of Gothic forms and spirit. Strawberry Hill now houses St Mary's Training College. *Tours 14.00–15.30 Sun Easter–Oct.* Charge.

Marble Hill House Richmond Road (0181 892 5115). A restored Palladian mansion, built in 1720s by George II for his mistress, Henrietta Howard. Fine collection of paintings and furniture dating from the early 18thC. *Open 10.00–13.00, 14.00–18.00 Mon–Sun Mar–Oct; 10.00–13.00, 14.00–16.00 Mon–Sun Nov–Feb.* Charge. Open-air concerts on *Sun evenings in summer.*

Eel Pie Island Twickenham. In Edwardian times the hotel on the island ran tea dances. In the 1960s it housed a noisy night club which featured popular rock groups.

Twickenham Tourist Information Centre 44 York Street (0181 891 1411).

● **Petersham**

Surrey. But for the traffic, this would be one of the most elegant village suburbs near London. It is exceptionally rich in fine houses of the late 17th and 18thC. Captain George Vancouver who sailed with Cook and discovered the island off the coast of Canada which is named after him, lived in River Lane and is now buried in the churchyard here.

● **Richmond-upon-Thames**

Surrey. All shops and services. One of the prettiest riverside towns in the London area. Built up the side of the hill, Richmond has been able to retain its Georgian elegance and still has the feeling of an 18thC resort. Richmond Green is the centre, both aesthetically and socially; it is surrounded by early 18thC houses. Only the brick and terracotta theatre, built in 1899, breaks the pattern; so deliberately that it is almost refreshing. The gateway of Richmond Palace is all that remains of the Royal residence

built by Henry VII, out of the earlier Palace of Shene. Behind the gate, in Old Palace Yard, is the Trumpeter's House. This magnificent building, c1708, was once visited by Metternich and Disraeli. At the top of Richmond Hill stands Wick House, built for Joshua Reynolds in 1772. It is from here that he painted the marvellous views over the Thames.

Richmond Theatre The Green (0181 940 0088). Shows productions from London's West End and touring companies.

Richmond Park The largest of the royal parks, created by Charles I in 1637, it covers 2358 acres. The park remained a favourite hunting ground till the 18thC. Private shooting stopped in 1904 but the hunting lodges can still be seen. White Lodge, built for George II in 1727, now houses the Royal Ballet School. *Open 07.00–dusk.*

Old Deer Park Kew Observatory was built here in 1729, by William Chambers for George III and was used by the Meteorological Office until 1981. The three obelisks nearby were used to measure London's official time.

Richmond Bridge This fine stone bridge with its five arches and parapet is one of the most handsome on the Thames, and was frequently the subject for paintings in the 18th–19thC. Built in the classical style by James Paine, 1777, it replaced the earlier horse ferry, and was a toll bridge until 1859.

Richmond-upon-Thames Tourist Information Centre Old Town Hall, Whittaker Avenue (0181 940 9125).

● **Isleworth**

Middx. PO. The prettiest view of this village is from the stretch of river just before Syon House. The 15thC tower of All Saints' Church, the London Apprentice Inn and a collection of fine Georgian houses all make for a delightful setting. Vincent Van Gogh taught here and used the Thames as the subject for his first attempts at painting.

Syon Park Park Road, Brentford (0181 560 0881). Set in 55 acres of parkland, landscaped by Capability Brown, Syon House is built on the site of a 15thC convent. The present square structure with its corner turrets is largely 16thC, although the interior was remodelled by Robert Adam in 1762. The house itself is mainly of interest on account of the magnificent neo-classical rooms by Adam. Katherine Howard was confined here before her execution in 1542 and Lady Jane Grey stayed here for the nine days preceding her death in 1554. Conservatory (1827) by Charles Fowler. The Butterfly House houses a huge variety of live butterflies and insects from all over the world. There is also an excellent garden centre. House *open 11.00–17.00 Wed–Sun & B. Hol Mon Apr–Sept (Sun only Oct–mid Dec).* Charge. Gardens *open 10.00–18.00 daily Apr–Sept; 10.00–dusk Nov–Mar.* Charge.

West London

Immediately below Brentford Dock Marina is the entrance to the Grand Union Canal, a direct link with Birmingham and places north. On the north bank opposite Kew is Strand-on-the-Green, a cluster of desirable houses and fashionable pubs facing

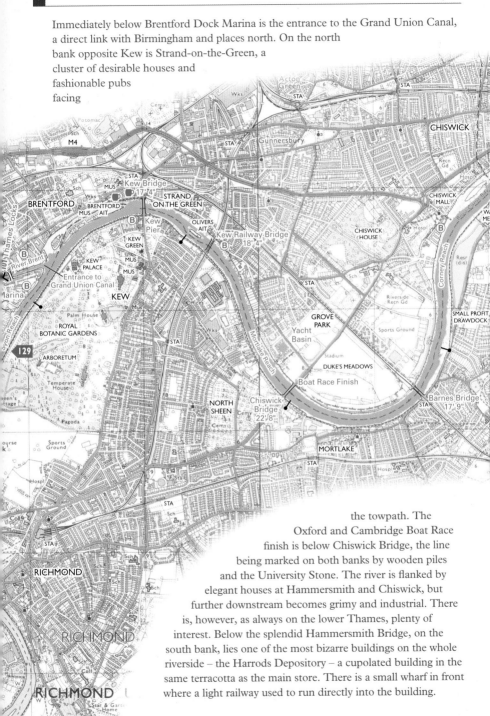

the towpath. The Oxford and Cambridge Boat Race finish is below Chiswick Bridge, the line being marked on both banks by wooden piles and the University Stone. The river is flanked by elegant houses at Hammersmith and Chiswick, but further downstream becomes grimy and industrial. There is, however, as always on the lower Thames, plenty of interest. Below the splendid Hammersmith Bridge, on the south bank, lies one of the most bizarre buildings on the whole riverside – the Harrods Depository – a cupolaed building in the same terracotta as the main store. There is a small wharf in front where a light railway used to run directly into the building.

River Thames West London

NAVIGATIONAL NOTES

Boaters joining the tidal
Thames at Brentford should
read the Navigational Notes
on page 130, and the Mooring
Note on page 129.

HAMMERSMITH

Pier

HAMMERSMITH LB

Hammersmith Bridge
"12' 2"

Cemetery

PLAYING
FIELDS

CASTLENAU

HARROD'S
DEPOSITORY   Wharves

Wharves

BARN ELMS WATER WORKS

Barn Elms
Reach

RESERVOIRS

Wharves

HAMMERSMITH FULHAM BC

FULHAM

Barn Elms
Playing Fields

BARNES   Sports Centre

PARSONS GREEN

FULHAM
PALACE

SOUTH
PARK

BARNES
COMMON

BARNES
STA

Boat Race Start

Putney
Pier

Fulham Railway Bridge
22' 7"

HURLINGHAM
HOUSE

138

Wharves

Putney
Bridge
18' 0"

RIVER THAMES

Wandsworth
Reach

Jetty

New Jetties

WANDSWORTH
PARK

PUTNEY

WANDSWORTH

Barn Elms
Reservoir is now
host to a variety of
watersports and is ideal
for fishing and birdwatching.
On the north bank is
Bishop's Park, home to
Fulham Palace. Putney
Bridge marks the start of
the Oxford and Cambridge
Boat Race and gives way to
a stretch of industry.

Pubs and Restaurants

For Pubs and Restaurants accessible to the boater
entering the canal at either Brentford or
Limehouse see Book 1.

A Thames sailing barge at Greenwich (see page 142)

Notes for walkers

This is an absolutely splendid section for walking. The path keeps to the south side throughout and Kew Gardens and Kew Palace are definitely worth a visit. Across the river is Strand-on-the-Green, with its fine houses and pubs. Barnes Railway Bridge has a foot crossing, and walkers can choose which bank they take to reach Hammersmith – the scenic route is on the south bank, the pubs on the north. After the fascinating walk around Barnes to Putney, the Thames towpath terminates, giving way to road as far as Putney Bridge. The course of the river can best be followed through London by keeping to the north side. *Nicholson's London Streetfinder* or *London Street Atlas* are helpful guides if detours are necessary.

● **Royal Botanic Gardens** Kew Road, Kew, Richmond (0181 940 1171). Superb botanical gardens of 300 acres founded in 1759 by Princess Augusta. Delightful natural gardens and woods bounded by the river on one side, and stocked with thousands of flowers and trees. The lake, aquatic garden and pagoda were designed by Sir William Chambers in 1760 and the magnificent curved glass Palm House and the Temperate House, 1844–8, are by Decimus Burton. Beneath the Palm House is a Marine Display which has examples of flowering marine plants and coral reef. The Princess of Wales Conservatory houses orchids, cacti, and water lilies the size of mattresses. Kew's scientific aspect was developed by its two directors Sir William and Sir Joseph Hooker and the many famous botanists who worked here. Cafeteria and gift shop in the Orangery. *One hour* tours available from the Victoria Gate Visitor Centre. Gardens *open daily 09.30–dusk.* Charge.

Kew Bridge Opened by Edward VII in 1903 and officially called the King Edward VII Bridge. A fine stone structure designed by Sir John Wolfe Barry and Cuthbert Brereton, it replaced the earlier granite bridge of 1789.

Kew Railway Bridge When it was opened in 1869 this five-span lattice girder bridge, designed by W. R. Galbraith, was part of the London and South-Western Railway extension.

● **Kew**

Surrey. Old Kew centres around the Green, the 18thC houses built for members of the Court of George III, and the entrance to the Royal Botanic Gardens. The church of St Anne dates from 1714 but was greatly altered in the 19thC.

Musical Museum St George's Church, 368 High Street, Brentford (0181 560 8108). A fascinating collection of around 200 automatic, old and odd musical instruments. Many of the instruments are played during the *one hour* conducted tour. *Open Jul & Aug 14.00–17.00 Wed–Sat; Sep–Jun 14.00–17.00 Sat & Sun.* Charge. No small children.

Kew Bridge Steam Museum Green Dragon Lane, Brentford (0181 568 4757). Huge Victorian building housing six gigantic beam engines, restored to working order by volunteers. In steam at *weekends.* Also a collection of old traction engines and a working forge. Tearoom *(weekends only). Open 11.00–17.00 Mon–Sun inc B. Hols.* Charge (under 5s free).

● **Chiswick**

W4. Chiswick stretches between Kew Bridge and Hammersmith Terrace and provides some of the most picturesque scenery on the London stretch of the Thames. Georgian houses extend along Strand-on-the-Green and again at Chiswick Mall. Between these points, running down to the riverside, originally stood three 18thC mansions: of the three, only Chiswick House remains. The site of Grove House has been built over, and Duke's Meadows, part of the grounds of Chiswick House, is now a recreation ground. Chiswick Cemetery backs on to St Nicholas Church where Lord Burlington and William Kent are buried.

Chiswick Bridge Built in 1933, designed by Sir Herbert Baker and opened to the public by the Prince of Wales, this bridge has the longest concrete arch of any bridge on the Thames. The centre span measures 150ft.

Chiswick House Burlington Lane W4. 0181 994 3299. Lovely Palladian villa built in the grand manner by 3rd Earl of Burlington 1725–30, modelled on Palladio's Villa Capra at Vicenza.

● **Mortlake**

SW14. In the 17thC Mortlake was famous for its tapestry workshop, established by James I and staffed by Flemish weavers. Some of the Mortlake Tapestries can still be seen in the Victoria & Albert Museum. The riverside here is picturesque along Thames Bank where there is a fine collection of 18thC houses. Mortlake also marks the end of the Oxford and Cambridge Boat Race at Chiswick Bridge (although the first race took place at Henley in 1829).

Barnes Railway Bridge This light and elegant iron bridge by Locke was opened in 1849 to connect with the Richmond line. Similar in design to Richmond Railway Bridge.

Oxford v Cambridge Boat Race On a *Saturday afternoon in March or April* this famous annual event is held over a 4-mile course from Putney to Mortlake. Get to the riverside early for a good view.

● **NORTH BANK**

Hammersmith Terrace *W6*. A terrace of 17 identical houses on the river bank, built c1750. The late Sir Alan Herbert, historian of the Thames, lived in the Terrace.

Upper Mall *W6*. Separated from Lower Mall by Furnivall Gardens, Upper Mall boasts some fine 18thC buildings including the Dove Inn, originally a coffee house. William Morris lived in Kelmscott House between 1878–96.

Lower Mall *W6*. Bustling in the summer months with rowers from the number of boathouses and rowing clubs which have been established here for over a century. Lower Mall is home to the Rutland and Blue Anchor pubs, and a number of pretty 18thC cottages.

Hammersmith Bridge The first suspension bridge in London. The original, built 1824 by William T. Clarke, was replaced in 1883 by the present splendid construction by Sir Joseph Bazalgette.

Fulham In the 18th and 19thC Fulham was the 'great fruit and kitchen garden north of the Thames', a place of market and nursery gardens, attracting the more prosperous Londoners in search of purer air. Today little is left of the fertile village and the area has become quite built-up. Fulham has, however, remained an attractive area, nowadays better known for its abundance of restaurants and bars. Also home to two of London's most famous football clubs, Fulham and Chelsea. Bishop's Park and Hurlingham House can be seen from the river.

Fulham Palace The palace lies behind the long avenues of Bishop's Park, with grounds stretching to the river. The site was first acquired by Bishop Waldhere in 704 and continued as a residence of the Bishops of London until 1973.

A fascinating mixture of architectural styles, from the Tudor courtyard with its mellow red brick to the restrained elegance of the Georgian east front.

Putney Bridge The wooden toll bridge of 1729 was replaced by the present bridge designed by Sir Joseph Bazalgette in 1884. Putney Bridge marks the start of the Oxford and Cambridge Boat Race .

Fulham Railway Bridge This trellis girder iron bridge was part of the Metropolitan extension to the District Railway. Designed by William Jacomb, it was opened in 1889 and connects with a footbridge running parallel to it. Part of the London Transport underground system.

Hurlingham House Ranelagh Gardens *SW6*. This is the only large 18thC residence still surviving in Fulham. The house has a fine river front with Corinthian columns and is now the centre of the Hurlingham Club. Members play tennis, golf and croquet in the grounds.

● **SOUTH BANK**

Barnes Terrace *SW13*. The delightful village of Barnes lies behind the attractive ironwork façade of Barnes Terrace. The terrace was, and still is, a fashionable place to live, with former residents including Sheridan and Gustav Holst.

Castelnau Barnes is rich in Victorian houses and some of the most interesting are to be seen in Castelnau. Remarkably standardised, they are largely semi-detached and typical of early Victorian villa architecture with their arched windows.

Barn Elms Formerly the manor house of Barnes, the estate was later leased to Sir Francis Walsingham, Secretary of State to Elizabeth I. Today, all that remains of the former layout is part of the ornamental pond and the ice house. The Reservoir at Barn Elms now plays host to a variety of watersports, plus fishing and bird-watching.

Putney The Embankment is picturesque. The London Rowing Club and Westminster School have their boathouses here and the eights and sculls can be seen practising most afternoons.

BOAT TRIPS

One of the best ways to understand the layout of a large, water-bound city is to take a boat trip and London is no exception to this rule. There are a large number to choose from, although most originate from Westminster Pier. Broadly speaking the options available encompass a selection of down-river trips as far as the Thames Barrier (and the Visitor Centre) and a range of up-river trips, which can reach as far as Hampton Court. The latter takes a full day. There are also evening dinner and dance cruises. Visit the pier (without your boat) to compare the plethora of options and make a choice.

Central London

The short stretch of intrusive industry, sprawling along the south bank, is soon relieved at Battersea by the splendid St Mary's Church opposite Lots Road Power Station and Chelsea Harbour. Albert Bridge, restored in 1991, is a remarkable sight when illuminated at night by over 4000 bulbs. From here on the River Thames curves through the heart of the capital, and has been London's lifeline for 2000 years. Indeed it was instrumental in the Roman settlement which created London as an international port. Once used as the local bypass, being cheaper and safer than travel by road, it has carried Viking longships, Roman galleys, Elizabethan barges and Victorian steamers. One of the best ways to see London is still from the Thames. The buildings and sights lining its twisting, turning path are as varied as London itself. It is fascinating by day and magical by night.

● NORTH BANK

Wandsworth Bridge In 1938 the 19thC bridge was replaced with the existing structure by E. P. Wheeler, now painted a distinctive bright blue.

Chelsea Harbour A modern development dominated by the Belvedere tower block. The golden ball on its roof slides up and down with the level of the river. The development contains offices, restaurants, a luxury hotel, smart shops, apartments and the marina. Chelsea Wharf, just along the bank, has been transformed from old warehouses into modern business units.

Battersea Railway Bridge The West London Extension Railway, of which this bridge was a part, was opened in 1863 to connect the south of England directly with the north. The line was the only one which did not end at a London terminus and was therefore a target for bombing in the Second World War.

Lots Road Power Station This huge and dominating structure was built in 1904 to provide electricity for the new underground railway.

Battersea Bridge The original Battersea Bridge, 1772, a picturesque wooden structure by Henry Holland, has been portrayed in paintings by Whistler and Turner. The replacement iron structure, opened in 1890, was designed by Sir Joseph Bazalgette.

All Saints Church Chelsea Embankment. Rebuilt in 1964 after severe bomb damage during the war. Contains two 13thC chapels, one restored by Sir Thomas More 1528, a Jacobean altar table and one of the best series of monuments in a London parish church. Henry VIII married Jane Seymour here before their state wedding in 1536.

Cheyne Walk *SW3.* Cheyne Walk, with its houseboats and its row of delightful riverside Queen Anne houses, has been home to Lloyd George, Hilaire Belloc, George Eliot, Isambard Kingdom Brunel, Turner and Whistler.

Carlyle's House 24 Cheyne Row *SW3.* Once the haunt of writers such as Dickens and Tennyson, and the home of Thomas and Jane Carlyle 1834–81.

Albert Bridge A delightful suspension bridge connecting Chelsea and Battersea, built by Ordish 1871–3. The bridge was strengthened in 1973 by a huge solid support under the main span. Illuminated by over 4000 bulbs, the bridge is particularly beautiful at night.

Chelsea Embankment *SW3.* Chelsea Embankment, stretching between Albert Bridge and Chelsea Bridge, was built in 1871. The embankment is bordered on the north bank by the grounds of the Chelsea Royal Hospital where the Chelsea Flower Show is held annually in *May.* Norman Shaw's famous Old Swan House stands at No 17 Chelsea Embankment.

Tate Gallery Millbank *SW1.* Founded in 1897 by Sir Henry Tate, the sugar magnate, and designed by Sidney H. J. Smith. Houses representative collections of British painting from the 16thC to the present day. Fine examples of Blake, Turner, Hogarth, the pre-Raphaelites, Ben Nicolson, Spencer and Francis Bacon; sculpture by Moore and Hepworth. Also a rich collection of foreign paintings and sculpture from 1880 to the present day, including paintings by Picasso, Chagall, Mondrian, Pollock, Lichtenstein, Rothko, Degas, Marini and Giacometti. Policy of annual rotation. The Clore Gallery houses the Turner bequest.

Millbank Tower Millbank *SW1.* The traditional balance of the river bank has been overturned by this 387ft–high office building by Ronald Ward and Partners, 1963.

Victoria Tower Gardens Abingdon Street *SW1.* A sculpture of Rodin's Burghers of Calais, 1895, stands close to the river and near the entrance to the gardens is a monument to Mrs Emmeline Pankhurst and Dame Christabel Pankhurst, champions of the women's suffragette movement in the early 1900s. Emmeline Pankhurst is reputedly the last person to have been incarcerated in the cell at the bottom of Big Ben (1902).

Houses of Parliament Parliament Square *SW1*. Originally the Palace of Westminster, and a principal royal palace until 1512. Became known as parliament or 'place to speak' in 1550. Westminster Hall, one of the few remaining parts of the original royal palace, has an impressive hammerbeam roof. The present Victorian-Gothic building was designed 1847 by Sir Charles Barry and Augustus Pugin specifically to house Parliament and has 1100 rooms, 100 staircases and over 2 miles of passages. The Houses of Parliament and Big Ben – the bell clock housed in the adjoining St Stephen's Tower – make up London's most famous landmark.

Westminster Abbey Broad Sanctuary *SW1*. Original church by Edward the Confessor 1065. Rebuilding commenced in 1245 by Henry III who was largely influenced by the new French cathedrals. Completed by Henry Yevele and others 1376–1506 (towers incomplete and finished by Hawksmoor 1734). Henry VII Chapel added 1503; fine perpendicular with wonderful fan vaulting. The Abbey contains the Coronation Chair, and many tombs and memorials of the Kings and Queens of England. Starting place for the pilgrimage to Canterbury Cathedral. Nave and Cloisters.

Old Scotland Yard Victoria Embankment *SW1*. An asymmetrical building by Norman Shaw,

1888, with fine iron gates by Blomfield. Scotland Yard is now housed in a modern building in Victoria.

Victoria Embankment The Embankment was created by Joseph Bazalgette in 1868, reclaiming 37 acres of mud from the Thames banks, making the river narrower and the water faster flowing, thereby ending the skating era on the once-frozen waters. The building of the embankment provided a wall against flooding, a riverside walk, a new west-east sewerage system and part of the District Line Railway. It was completed in 1870, Bazalgette was knighted, and his bust incorporated into the parapet by Hungerford Bridge.

Cleopatra's Needle Victoria Embankment *SW1*. A 60ft-high ancient Egyptian granite obelisk, presented to Britain by the Viceroy of Egypt, Mohammed Ali, in 1819 and brought to London by sea in 1878. When it was erected various articles were buried beneath it for posterity – the morning's

newspapers, a razor, coins, four Bibles in different languages and photographs of '12 of the best-looking Englishwomen of the day'. The bronze sphinxes were added (facing the wrong way) in 1882.

Savoy Hotel Strand *WC2*. Built on part of the site of the medieval Savoy Palace, the hotel was founded by Richard D'Oyly Carte and built to the designs of T. E. Colcutt. When it opened in 1889 it represented a revolution in comfort and had 70 bathrooms.

Somerset House Strand *WC2*. Built in 1776 by Sir William Chambers on the site of Protector

Somerset's
house, this
magnificent
building with its
arches, terrace,
and river entrances
decorated with lions
and Tuscan columns,
was intended to
compete with the
splendour of Adam's
Adelphi. Once occupied
by the General Register
Office whose records of
birth and death go back to
1836, it now houses offices of
the Inland Revenue and the
Courtauld Institute Galleries. In
the garden stands a bronze statue
of Brunel by Marochetti, 1866.
Brunel was the engineer in charge of
the building of the Great Western
Railway and his ship, the Great Eastern, was
launched on the Thames, at Millwall.

The Temple *EC4*. The name derives from the
Order of Knights Templar who occupied the
site from 1160–1308. In the 17thC the Temple
was leased to the benchers of the Inner and
Middle Temple, two Inns of Court. These inns,
together with Lincoln's Inn and Gray's Inn,
hold the ancient and exclusive privilege of
providing advocates in the courts of England
and Wales. A visit should be made on foot, as
only a few of the Temple Buildings are visible
from the river. On the Embankment, Sir Joseph
Bazalgette's arch and stairs mark the 19thC
access to the Temple from the river.

City of London A thriving and commercial
centre, stretching between Blackfriars Bridge
and London Bridge, which has within its square

mile such famous institutions as the Bank of
England, the Stock Exchange, the Royal
Courts of Justice and the Guildhall.

Mermaid Theatre Puddle Dock *EC4*. The
original theatre, the first in the City since the
16thC, was opened in a converted warehouse
in 1959 following energetic campaigning by
Lord Bernard Miles. It was rebuilt on a new
site and reopened in 1981.

● **Fishmongers' Hall**
King William Street *EC4*. Built in the grand
classical manner in 1831–4 by Henry Roberts
to replace the original hall which was burnt
down in the Great Fire of 1666. The
Fishmongers' Company administers the
annual Doggett's Coat and Badge Race for
Thames Watermen. This race, the oldest
annual contested sporting event and the
longest rowing race in the world (one furlong
short of 5 miles), was introduced in 1715.
Doggett, an Irish comedian and staunch
Hanoverian, who used the services of the
watermen to ferry him to and from the
theatres, decided to mark the anniversary of
the accession of George I to the throne by
instituting an annual race for watermen. The
race is from London Bridge to Cadogan Pier,
Chelsea, and is usually held at the end of *July*.
The victor is presented with a red coat,
breeches and cap, and a silver arm badge
bearing the words 'The Gift of the late
Thomas Doggett'.

Monument *EC4*. A 17thC hollow fluted col-
umn by Wren, built to commemorate the
Great Fire of London. It marked the northern
end of the original London Bridge and stands
at 202ft, a foot in height for every foot in distance from where the fire started in Pudding
Lane. Gives a magnificent view over the city.

Old Billingsgate Market Lower Thames Street
EC3. The yellow-brick Victorian building
with arcaded ground floor was built by
Sir Horace Jones, 1875, although the first
reference to a market at Billingsgate was

made in AD870. A free fish market was established by statute in 1699, but until the 18thC coal, corn and provisions were also sold. The fish porters wore leather hats with flat tops and wide brims, formerly known as bobbing hats. Bobbing was the charge made by the porter to carry fish from the wholesaler to the retailer. These hats enabled the porter to carry about a hundredweight of fish on his head. The market moved down river to new premises on the Isle of Dogs in 1982.

The Custom House Lower Thames Street *EC4*. A custom house has stood beside Billingsgate since AD870. The present building is by Laing, 1813–17, but the river façade was rebuilt by Smirke in 1825. Badly bombed in the war, the building has been restored.

Tower of London Tower Hill *EC3*. Although greatly restored and altered over the centuries, the Tower of London is probably the most important work of military architecture in Britain and has been used as a palace, a fortress and a prison since William the Conqueror built the White Tower in 1078.

Tower Bridge This spectacular bridge was built by Sir John Wolfe Barry in 1894 and the old hydraulic lifting mechanism was originally powered by steam.

● SOUTH BANK

Wandsworth Until the 19thC Wandsworth was a village oasis on the River Wandle – a good fishing river – and was noted for a local silk and hat industry. The course of the Wandle can still be traced near the Church of All Saints. The Surrey Iron Railway, whose wagons were drawn by horses, ran alongside the river. Past residents include Defoe, Thackeray and Voltaire, but today little remains to point to the past. There are a few Georgian houses in Church Row, but the river bank has become a grimy industrial scene.

Battersea Many of the old riverside warehouses are now gone and tall tower blocks dominate.

St Mary's Church Church Road *SW11*. The church is one of the few relics of Battersea's 18thC village. Built in 1775 by Joseph Dixon, it is strangely Dutch in character.

Battersea Park *SW11*. The park was laid out by Sir James Pennethorne as a public garden and opened by Queen Victoria in 1858. Redesigned in the 1950s for the Festival of Britain, there is a boating lake, a deer park, an Alpine showhouse, herb garden and greenhouse, a children's zoo and sculptures by Moore, Hepworth and Epstein. The London Peace Pagoda which stands close to the river was built by monks and nuns of the Japanese Buddhist order Nipponzan Myohoji and was completed in 1985.

Battersea Power Station *SW8*. One of the most potent buildings on the river bank, this vast oblong of brick with its four chimneys was designed by Sir Giles Gilbert Scott, 1932–4, and was one of the finest examples of contemporary industrial architecture. Redundant as a power station, plans for its conversion have faltered, and it now stands as an empty shell.

Albert Embankment *SE1*. Designed as a broad footwalk by Sir Joseph Bazalgette, 1867, the Embankment stretches between Vauxhall and Westminster Bridges. The upper Embankment was once the site of the 18thC Vauxhall Gardens, whose Chinese pavilions and walks were the envy of Europe.

Lambeth Palace Lambeth Palace Road *SE1*. The London residence of the Archbishop of Canterbury since 1197. Remarkable Tudor gate-house, fine medieval crypt. 14thC Hall with a splendid roof and portraits of archbishops on its walls. The Guard Room, which houses the library, was rebuilt in medieval style in 1633.

County Hall Westminster Bridge *SE1*. Designed by Ralph Knott in 1911, this was once the imposing headquarters of the Greater London Council but is now to become a hotel and leisure complex.

Shell Centre *SE1*. Part of the area known as the South Bank, the Shell Centre was designed by Sir Howard Robertson, 1962. Of greyish white concrete with monotonous little square windows, the flat surface is totally unrelieved – it seems more in character to view it as a physical feature rather than as architecture. The central 351ft-high skyscraper rises like a huge grey mountain.

South Bank Arts Centre *SE1*. Royal Festival Hall, the Queen Elizabeth Hall, the Purcell Room, the National Theatre, the National Film Theatre, the Hayward Gallery and the Museum of the Moving Image make up the complex which originated with the Festival of Britain in 1951. The Festival Hall, completed in 1951 and built by Sir Robert Matthew and Sir Leonard Martin, seats 3400. The Queen Elizabeth Hall by Hubert Bennett, 1967, is much smaller and intended for recitals. Bennett also designed the Hayward Gallery which opened in 1968. The Purcell Room is the smallest of the three concert halls; ideal for chamber music and solo concerts. However, the buildings are dreary and the maze of tunnels and winding staircases which lead to the terrace area can be overwhelming, the blind corners in many instances blocking the view and giving a sense of isolation. Nevertheless, the range of cultural activities on offer at the South Bank Centre is diverse and can be enjoyed by everyone.

Upper Ground *SE1*. The decrepit warehouses that used to line the south bank have been demolished, and replaced by the impressive London Weekend Television building and Gabriel's Wharf – South Bank's answer to Covent Garden. To the east of Gabriel's Wharf stands the fine art deco OXO tower, built in 1928 and decorated thus because advertising was forbidden on buildings.

Bankside *SE1*. In the 16thC the Rose Theatre, the Swan and the Globe were all situated around Bankside, and until the 19thC the area was the site of playhouses and amusement gardens. Today the area has been developed and almost all is changing apart from the site of the now disused Bankside Power Station, the few remaining 17thC and 18thC houses and the Anchor pub, an historic tavern with strong smuggling connections. A tudor theatre has been reconstructed near the site of the original Globe Theatre as part of the International Shakespeare Globe Centre, and the Shakespeare Globe Museum illustrates the theatre of the age. From Bankside are fine views of St Paul's Cathedral and the City and it is thought that Wren lived in No 49 Bankside during the construction of St Paul's.

Shakespeare Globe Museum 1 Bear Gardens, Bankside *SE1*. Converted 18thC warehouse on the site of a 16thC bear-baiting ring and the Hope Playhouse.

Bankside Power Station *SE1*. Designed in 1935 by Sir Giles Gilbert Scott, architect of the Battersea Power Station. Like its counterpart, Bankside Power Station now stands redundant, its distinctive single chimney dominating the landscape.

Southwark Cathedral Borough High Street *SE1*. Built by Augustinian Canons but destroyed by fire in 1206 and greatly restored. The tower was built c1520 and the nave, by Blomfield, 1894–7. In the Middle Ages the cathedral was part of the Augustinian Priory of St Mary Overie. Despite its 19thC additions, it is still one of the most impressive Gothic buildings in London. Apart from the wealth of monuments, the model in the retro-choir showing the priory and Winchester Palace in 1540 is of special interest, as is the collection of carved wooden bosses from the 15thC roof.

Kathleen & May St Mary Overy Dock. Last surviving three-masted, topsail, trading schooner and now a floating museum.

● **BRIDGES**

Chelsea Bridge The original bridge designed by Thomas Page, 1858, was rebuilt as a suspension bridge in 1934 by Rendel, Palmer & Tritton.

Victoria Railway Bridge When it was opened in 1859, this was the widest railway bridge in the world – 132ft wide and 900ft long – and it provided 10 separate accesses to Victoria Station. It has now been widened further to meet the demands of modern transport.

Vauxhall Bridge James Walker's Regent's Bridge which opened in 1816 was the first iron bridge to span the Thames in London. The present structure, designed by Sir Alexander Binnie, was opened in 1906. The bronze figures alongside the bridge represent Agriculture, Architecture, Engineering, Learning, the Fine Arts and Astronomy.

Lambeth Bridge Originally the site of a horse ferry, the first bridge was built here in 1861, designed by P. W. Barlow. This was replaced in 1932 by the present steel-arch bridge designed by George Humphreys and Sir Reginald Blomfield.

Westminster Bridge Built in 1750, Westminster Bridge was the second bridge to be built across the Thames in central London. The present bridge, by Thomas Page, replaced the old stone one in 1862.

Charing Cross Railway Bridge Also known as Hungerford Bridge, it has replaced the original suspension bridge which was demolished in 1864. A separate footbridge runs alongside to Waterloo Station with excellent views of the City.

Waterloo Bridge John Rennie's early 19thC bridge, a beautiful design of Greek columns and nine elliptical arches, was replaced in 1945 by Sir Giles Gilbert Scott's concrete bridge, faced with Portland stone.

Southwark Bridge Built in 1814, this was the largest bridge ever built of cast iron. Replaced 1912–21 by the present five-span steel bridge of Mott and Hay, with Sir Ernest George as architect. Southwark Causeway, the steps on the south side, were used by Wren when he travelled across the river to supervise work on St Paul's.

Cannon Street Railway Bridge Built in 1866 as part of the extension of the South-Eastern Railway, the bridge's engineers were J. Hawkshaw and J. W. Barry. A prominent structure on account of the 19thC train shed jutting out to the side of the bridge.

London Bridge Until 1749 London Bridge was the only bridge to span the Thames in London. The first recorded wooden bridge was Saxon, but it is possible that a Roman structure may have existed here. In 1176 the wooden bridge was replaced by a stone structure, with houses, shops and a church built upon it, similar in appearance to the Ponte Vecchio in Florence. The heads of traitors were displayed on the spikes of the fortified gates at either end. In 1831 this bridge was demolished and a new bridge, by John Rennie, replaced it. A granite bridge with five arches, this soon became too narrow to meet the demands of modern traffic and because of structural faults could not be widened. A new bridge, constructed under the direction of the City Engineer, was opened to traffic in 1973. Built out of concrete, it has a flat-arched profile in three spans carried on slender piers. The McCulloch Corporation of Arizona paid $2,460,000 for the facing materials of Rennie's bridge, which has been reconstructed spanning Lake Havasu.

Blackfriars Bridge Blackfriars Bridge was built in 1760. It cost £230,000 and was mainly paid for by fines which had accumulated from men refusing the post of Sheriff. Replaced by the present structure in 1860. Note the pulpits, a reminder of the religious significance of its name.

Blackfriars Railway Bridge Built in 1886 for the London, Chatham and Dover Railway, this elegant iron bridge, with its high parapet and decorative coat of arms at each end, can best be seen from the road bridge.

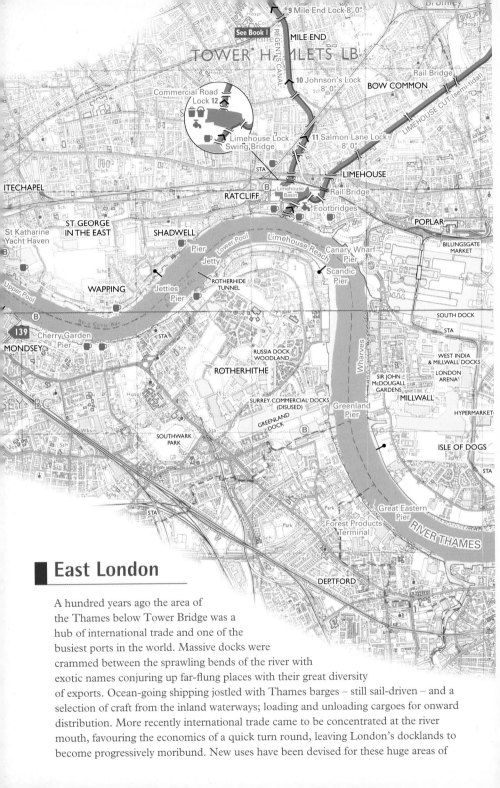

East London

A hundred years ago the area of
the Thames below Tower Bridge was a
hub of international trade and one of the
busiest ports in the world. Massive docks were
crammed between the sprawling bends of the river with
exotic names conjuring up far-flung places with their great diversity
of exports. Ocean-going shipping jostled with Thames barges – still sail-driven – and a
selection of craft from the inland waterways; loading and unloading cargoes for onward
distribution. More recently international trade came to be concentrated at the river
mouth, favouring the economics of a quick turn round, leaving London's docklands to
become progressively moribund. New uses have been devised for these huge areas of

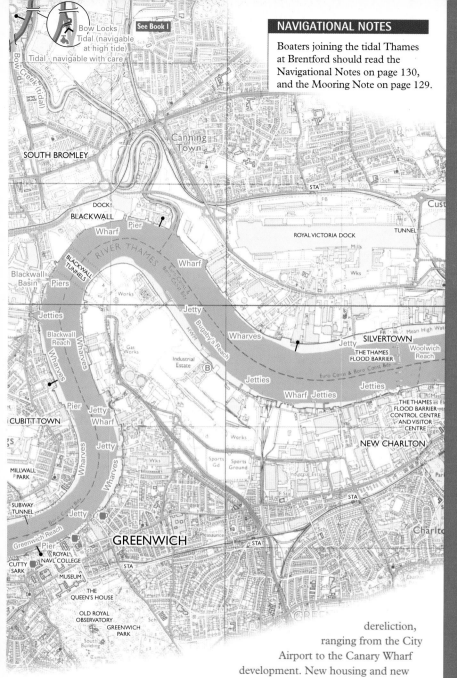

NAVIGATIONAL NOTES

Boaters joining the tidal Thames at Brentford should read the Navigational Notes on page 130, and the Mooring Note on page 129.

dereliction, ranging from the City Airport to the Canary Wharf development. New housing and new industry have been drafted in, often with scant regard for established communities and cultures. In converting redundant warehouses the value of these solid symbols of a previous prosperity and optimism has at least been recognised. However, they sit uncomfortably beside their futuristic counterparts that, in these times of commercial pessimism, still struggle to find tenants.

St Katharine's Dock St Katharine's Dock was the first of the docks to be rejuvenated. Built on 23 acres in 1828, from a design by Thomas Telford, the original docks were closed down in 1968. Five years later an £80 million building scheme was begun which included the Tower Thistle Hotel and the World Trade Centre. The magnificent warehouses have been restored and now house shops, apartments, offices, restaurants, a yacht club and marina. Visiting cruisers nestle alongside resident yachts and barges.

Tobacco Dock Pennington Street *E1*. Designed by Terry Farrell in 1989, this 19thC former warehouse has been converted into a shopping and leisure complex. Development work was carried out using original suppliers of materials wherever possible.

Butler's Wharf Transformed from narrow alleys, where Oliver Twist's Bill Sikes met his end, into a smart restaurant, shopping and office complex including the Conran restaurants – Le Pont de la Tour, the Cantina del Ponte and the Butler's Wharf Chop House.

The Design Museum Butler's Wharf, Shad Thames *SE1*. A fascinating introduction to 20thC design, technology and consumer culture.

Cherry Garden Pier Where ships sound their signal if they want Tower Bridge to be raised. Turner sat here to paint *The Fighting Temeraire* as she returned from the Battle of Trafalgar.

Rotherhithe Tunnel Built 1904–8 by Sir Maurice Fitzmarice, the tunnel is still used as a thoroughfare between Rotherhithe and Stepney. The top of the tunnel is 48ft below the high-water mark to allow for large ships passing above.

YHA Island Yard, Salter Road *SE16*. This prominent landmark on the south bank of the river is a luxurious youth hostel catering for families, groups and individual travellers.

Limehouse Basin *E14*. This used to be called the Regent's Canal Dock, and forms part of the Grand Union Canal system, which was opened in 1820 to allow barges to trade between London and Birmingham. The Limehouse Cut also provides access to the River Lea.

Royal Naval Victualling Yard Grove Street SE8. Founded in 1513 as the Royal Dock for Henry VIII's navy, the yard became the principal naval dockyard in the kingdom, rivalling Woolwich. Sir Francis Drake was knighted here after his world voyage on the *Golden Hind*, and it was from this yard that Captain Cook's *Discovery* set sail.

Docklands Stretching from Tower Pier to Beckton is London's Docklands. The area has undergone massive change from a thriving, commercial port through closure to regeneration. The London Docklands Development Corporation (LDDC) was set up in 1981 to create a new city for the 21stC incorporating riverside apartments, shops, restaurants and offices.

Canary Wharf Tower One Canada Square, Canary Wharf *E14*. Designed by Cesar Pelli, 1988–90, this 800ft building is the tallest in the UK. Clad in stainless steel and topped with a pyramid, the 50-storey building boasts a magnificent lobby finished in Italian and Guatemalan marble. Thirty-two passenger lifts operate from the lobby and are the fastest in the country. Canary Wharf itself is full of elegant architecture, stately streets, well-planted squares and outdoor spaces. Intended as office space, a large proportion of the complex has remained unoccupied, although several international companies have now taken up residence.

Isle of Dogs Until the industrialisation of the early 19thC, the Isle of Dogs was mainly pastureland and marshes. Windmills stood by the river. By 1799 the Port of London had become so overcrowded that Parliament authorised the building of a new dock on the Isle of Dogs, under the auspices of the West India Company. Built by William Jessop, the two West India Docks were opened in 1802. In 1870 the South Dock was added. It was built on the site of the City Canal which had connected Limehouse Reach and Blackwall Reach between 1805 and 1829. The Millwall Docks, the most southern, were completed in 1864. The West India Docks are also the site of Billingsgate Fish Market, which was moved here from its old site near London Bridge in 1982.

Island Gardens Saunders Ness Road *E14*. This small park at the south tip of the Isle of Dogs was opened in 1895 to commemorate the spot which Wren considered had the best view of Greenwich Palace across the water.

Greenwich Tunnel The Blackwall Tunnel, opened in 1897, was designed as a road traffic tunnel. In 1902 it was decided to build a pedestrian subway to link Greenwich with the Isle of Dogs. There was opposition from the watermen and lightermen who, rightly, feared for their jobs. The southern entrance to the footway is in Cutty Sark Gardens, Greenwich, and the northern entrance is in Island Gardens, Isle of Dogs.

Greenwich *SE10*. Once a small fishing village, the historic town of Greenwich marks the eastern approach to London. Its royal and naval past is illustrated by the magnificent riverside grouping of the Queen's House, the Royal Naval College, the National Maritime Museum and the Old Royal Observatory. From the Observatory the views are magnificent, spanning Docklands and the City right through to Westminster. Museums, bookshops, antique shops, and a daily street market make for a bustling village atmosphere away from the industrialisation of the Docklands area.

The Cutty Sark King William Walk *SE10*. One of the great 19thC tea and wool sailing clippers, stands in dry dock. The history of the *Cutty Sark* is displayed in drawings and photographs. Close by stands *Gipsy Moth IV*, the yacht in which Sir Francis Chichester made his solo circumnavigation of the world in 1966.

Greenwich Park *SE10*. The park, laid out for Charles II by the French royal landscape gardener André Le Nôtre, commands a magnificent view of the Royal Naval College and of the river. It contains 13 acres of woodland and deer park, a bird sanctuary and archaeological sites. Crooms Hill lies to the west of the park, lined with a wealth of 17th, 18th and 19thC houses, the oldest being at the southern end near Blackheath. Greenwich Theatre stands at the foot of the hill.

Old Royal Observatory Greenwich Park *SE10*. The original observatory, still standing, was built by Wren for Flamsteed, first Astronomer Royal, in the 17thC. Astronomical instruments and exhibits relating to the history of astronomy are displayed in the old observatory buildings and the time ball which provided the first public time signal in 1833 still operates. Home to the Meridian Line, interactive science stations and the largest refracting telescope in the UK.

Royal Naval College Greenwich *SE10*. Mary II commissioned Wren to rebuild the palace as a hospital for aged and disabled seamen. Designed in the Baroque style, it was completed in 1705. The Painted Hall, or Dining Hall, has a swirling Baroque ceiling by Thornhill, one of the finest of its period. The neo-classical chapel dates from 1789. In 1873 the hospital became the Royal Naval College to provide for the higher education of naval officers.

Queen's House Romney Road, Greenwich *SE10*. Now part of the National Maritime Museum, this delightful white house in the Palladian style was built for Queen Anne of Denmark by Inigo Jones, 1618.

Execution Dock At the entrance to Blackwall Tunnel. This is where, until the late 19thC, the bodies of convicted pirates were hung in iron cages until three tides had washed over them.

Blackwall Tunnel Built in 1897 by Sir Alexander Binnie. There are now two tunnels; the second opened in 1967. One is for north-bound traffic, the other for southbound.

Thames Flood Barrier The Flood Barrier is best seen from the river. As you round the bend, the steel fins rise up from the water. Completed in 1982, it is the world's largest movable flood barrier and is designed to swing up from the river bed and create a stainless steel barrage to stem periodically dangerous high tides. Each gate weighs 3000 tonnes and is the equivalent of a five-storey building in height. The structures housing the machines which operate the gates seem to have been inspired by the 'sails' of Sydney Opera House. Blackwall Reach, on the way to the Flood Barrier, was where, in 1606, Captain John Smith and the Virginia Settlers left on their journey to found the first permanent colony in America.

PAST PROSPECTS

Arguably, London was the hub of the sixties around which the rest of the world swung. Carnaby Street became the focus of the international fashion scene, the West End put on plays by angry young men and the city's parks echoed to the sound of bells and strange chanting; pervaded by even stranger aromas. Faced with this wealth of outdoor, brotherly peace and love how did the capital's more traditional meeting places – its wonderfully diverse range of public houses – continue to provide a meaningful experience? One hostelry, of great antiquity and still plying its trade by the river in Wapping, went through a phase in its illustrious history (possibly one that it might now rather forget) which, for sheer incongruity, must to this day be unrivalled in the licensed victualling trade. License – in its poetic form – perhaps best describes the Saturday evening's entertainment which took place in a bar, so crowded, that full pints had to be carried from the bar above head height, arriving as half pints at the drinker's allotted slot in the throng. It was less troublesome to throw the empty glasses through the open window, into the Thames, than to return them to the bar and this practice soon became de rigeur. As did the wearing of old clothing able to withstand the steady shower of spilling ale. By way of further diversion, a bronzed band, attired in natty South Sea island garb and twanging Hawaiian guitars, accompanied themselves and the assembled company, relentlessly singing rugby songs – the lyrics degenerating steadily as the evening wore on.

Coxes Mill (see page 148)

WEY & GODALMING NAVIGATIONS

MAXIMUM DIMENSIONS
Length: 73' 6"
Beam: 13' 10"
Draught: 3' 0" to Guildford
2' 6" above Guildford
Headroom: 7' 0" to Guildford
6' 0" to Godalming (at normal levels)

Locks: 16 (including Worsfold and Walsham
Flood Gates)

Navigation Authority:
The National Trust
Dapdune Wharf
Wharf Road
Guildford GU1 4RR
Visitor Services Manager: (01483) 561389.

Annual or visitor's licences are issued at Dapdune Wharf, or at Thames Lock. Rules and bye-laws are supplied with each licence.

The speed limit is 4 knots – in practice, slower. Watch your wash. Use only the correct Wey Navigation lock handle, available from Thames Lock, the NT Navigation Office or Guildford and Farncombe Boat Houses. When leaving locks, exit gates should be left open, but with all the paddles *down* .

As a river navigation, the Wey is subject to flooding, increasing the speed of the current and pull of the weirs. Under certain conditions, locks may be padlocked and craft should moor up in a sheltered place and seek advice.

The towpath side of the navigation is available for mooring. Respect private property.

In 1964 the Wey Navigation was given to the National Trust by Harry Stevens, its last private owner. In 1968 the Godalming Navigation Commissioners passed their section to Guildford Corporation, who in turn passed it on to the National Trust. It remains an artery of peace and tranquillity amidst the noise and bustle of Surrey, and will amply repay a visit.

Boats have used the River Wey since medieval times, but the present navigation dates from the 17thC. In 1651 authorisation was given to make the river navigable for 15 miles from Weybridge to Guildford. This involved the building of 12 locks and 10 miles of artificial cut. This early navigation had the usual battles with mill owners, but gradually trade developed, predominantly local and agricultural in character. More unusual were the extensive Farnham Potteries, who shipped their wares to London along the Wey. In 1763 the Godalming Navigation was opened, adding another 4 miles to the waterway, and by the end of the 18thC considerable barge traffic was using the river. This was greatly increased by the building of the Basingstoke Canal in 1796, and the Wey & Arun Junction Canal in 1816; the latter offered a direct route from London to Portsmouth and the south coast. This canal closed in 1871, but trade continued to thrive on the Wey and as late as 1960 barges were still carrying timber to Guildford. Grain traffic to Coxes Mill continued until 1968, with a brief revival in the early 1980s. Unfortunately this traffic was short-lived, and at present there is no commercial activity.

Weybridge

The River Wey Navigation leaves the Thames Shepperton Lock. The correct channel is clearly signposted. Just around the corner is the pound gate, used only when the water level is low or when a deep draughted vessel is passing through. The lock is in an attractive wooded setting, and the keeper here is available to advise you. Above the lock, beyond the weirs, smart houses and gardens line the east bank; the west is wooded, a rural illusion. There is a sharp westward turn (see Navigational Notes) followed immediately by Weybridge Town Lock, where Addlestone Road flanks the navigation on its way to Ham Moor. Just above the railway bridge is Coxes Mill, a very handsome and varied group of industrial buildings now tastefully converted into flats. Note the large mill pond to the west, now owned and managed by the Trust as a wildlife habitat. The Wey continues its quiet wooded passage south – look out for a Wey barge, used as a houseboat, its width looking quite massive on such a narrow channel. Much of New Haw consists of 20thC Georgian commuter retreats. Moored craft line the east bank above New Haw Lock (with its pretty lock cottage) as the cut makes a beeline for Byfleet, cowering under the massive concrete structures and earth embankments of the M25 motorway – there is no longer any peace to be had here. The Basingstoke Canal (see page 11) leaves the Wey Navigation in the midst of a flurry of bridges. Beyond Parvis Bridge the navigation becomes more rural – breaks in the waterside trees reveal open meadows and farmland.

NAVIGATIONAL NOTES

1 Thames Lock (01932 843106). Attended. Licences and visitor passes, lock handles for sale or hire. All those wishing to enter the lock should consult the lock keeper. Craft of deeper draught than 1ft 9in coming up from the Thames should advise the lock keeper – he may then use the pound gate to increase the water level before they enter the lock.

2 Weybridge Old Bridge – the navigation channel is clearly marked, and is the most westerly arch (furthest right) when coming upstream. The lock is immediately above the bridge. The River Wey is navigable for a short distance by small craft.

● **Weybridge**
Surrey. All shops and services, laundrette. A commuter town in the stockbroker belt, built around the confluence of the rivers Wey and Thames – the junction is marked by a pretty iron bridge of 1865. Weybridge represents the frontier of the suburbia which now spreads almost unbroken to London. Behind Weybridge lie the remains of Brooklands, the doyen of motor racing circuits in the early 20thC (see below).
Coxes Mill *Surrey.* Overlooking Coxes Lock is a magnificent group of mostly 19thC mill buildings, partly brick, partly concrete and partly weather-board, the best industrial architecture on the river.
Brooklands Museum Weybridge (01932 857381). A museum assembled around what remains of the Brooklands race track, the world's first purpose-built circuit, constructed by wealthy landowner Hugh Locke King in 1907. Its heyday was in the 1920s and 30s, when records were being set by the likes of Malcolm Campbell and John Cobb,

driving vehicles with wonderfully evocative names, such as the Napier, Delage, Bentley and Bugatti. It became very fashionable, and was known as The Ascot of Motorsport. It was also an aerodrome, and it was here that A.V. Roe made the first flight in a British aeroplane. The Sopwith Pup and Camel were developed here, and later the Hawker Hurricane and the Vickers Wellington were built here. The outbreak of war in 1939 brought an end to racing, and aircraft production ceased in 1987. Now you can walk on part of the legendary circuit, and see historic racing cars and aircraft in the museum. The Clubhouse is listed as an ancient monument. *Open 10.00–17.00 (16.00 Winter) Tue–Sun & B Hols. Closed G Fri & Xmas.* Charge.
● **Byfleet**
Surrey. EC Wed. PO, shops. Although buried by modern commuter housing, parts of the old village can be found. The church with its bellcote is mostly late 13thC, and the 17thC brick manor house is an elegant delight in the midst of so much dreariness.

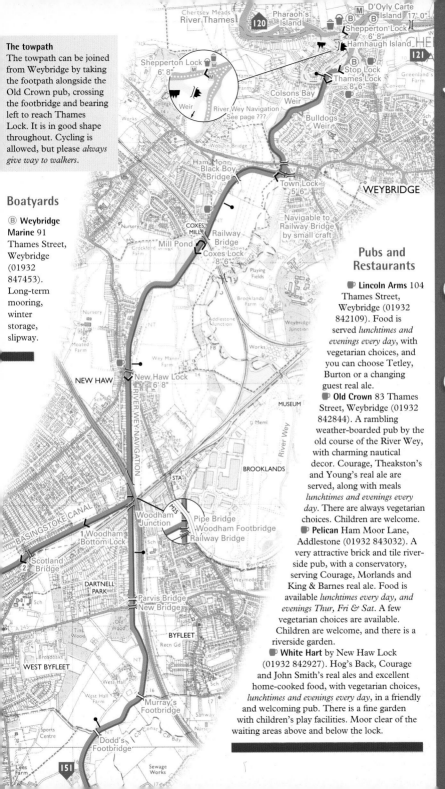

The towpath

The towpath can be joined from Weybridge by taking the footpath alongside the Old Crown pub, crossing the footbridge and bearing left to reach Thames Lock. It is in good shape throughout. Cycling is allowed, but please *always give way to walkers.*

Boatyards

Ⓑ **Weybridge Marine** 91 Thames Street, Weybridge (01932 847453). Long-term mooring, winter storage, slipway.

Pubs and Restaurants

🍺 **Lincoln Arms** 104 Thames Street, Weybridge (01932 842109). Food is served *lunchtimes and evenings every day*, with vegetarian choices, and you can choose Tetley, Burton or a changing guest real ale.

🍺 **Old Crown** 83 Thames Street, Weybridge (01932 842844). A rambling weather-boarded pub by the old course of the River Wey, with charming nautical decor. Courage, Theakston's and Young's real ale are served, along with meals *lunchtimes and evenings every day.* There are always vegetarian choices. Children are welcome.

🍺 **Pelican** Ham Moor Lane, Addlestone (01932 843032). A very attractive brick and tile riverside pub, with a conservatory, serving Courage, Morlands and King & Barnes real ale. Food is available *lunchtimes every day, and evenings Thur, Fri & Sat.* A few vegetarian choices are available. Children are welcome, and there is a riverside garden.

🍺 **White Hart** by New Haw Lock (01932 842927). Hog's Back, Courage and John Smith's real ales and excellent home-cooked food, with vegetarian choices, *lunchtimes and evenings every day*, in a friendly and welcoming pub. There is a fine garden with children's play facilities. Moor clear of the waiting areas above and below the lock.

Pyrford

The popular Anchor pub is close to the bridge at Pyrford, with Pyrford Marina opposite; just beyond is Pyrford Lock and many colourful moored craft. The navigation then passes Pyrford Place, with its lovely old Elizabethen summer house with a pagoda roof, beside a charming little riverside terrace. Except in times of flood you may pass uninterrupted through Walsham Flood Gates, overlooked by the quaintly business-like lock cottage. The large weir is to the east. The river then becomes wider and strewn with lily pads, before it splits to form a trio of islands at Newark, where the remains of Newark Priory can be seen at the water's edge. The lock cut continues to Newark Lock – above here the river winds towards Papercourt Lock, arguably the prettiest on the river, with its stepped weir and charming garden, jokingly called Costa del Papercourt. Factories and offices line the south bank as the navigation passes under High Bridge and approaches Cart Bridge, to the west of Send. It is, surprisingly, quite peaceful here – a relief considering the boundless activity all around. As you pass Worsfold Flood Gates, note the unique peg arrangement on the paddles. The restored National Trust Workshop is here, often with a few sturdy barges moored opposite. Then once again the Wey resumes its rural course, passing Triggs Lock, with its very pretty asymmetrical lock cottage. To the south east lies Send Church.

NAVIGATIONAL NOTES

1 All the locks on this section are unattended.
2 Walsham and Worsfold Flood Gates are normally left open, except in times of flood. When closed the chamber should be used as a normal lock.
3 Be wary of the cross current below Papercourt Lock.

● **Pyrford Village**
Surrey. Surrounded by water meadows and trees, Pyrford is still a real village, an oasis in the ever-spreading suburban web. Brick cottages overlook the church, an almost intact Norman building 'built of puddingstone, dressed with clunch'; such a thing is rare in the Home Counties and is thus an even greater pleasure. The north porch is half-timbered and dates from the 16thC. Inside are wallpaintings depicting scenes from the flagellation and the Passion, circa 1200: the pulpit is 17thC. There are many attractive 18thC houses.
Royal Horticultural Society's Gardens Wisley (01483 224234). By footpath south east of Pigeon House Bridge to Ockham Mill, then north east towards Wisley, or by footpath from Pyrford Lock. A 200-acre botanic garden acquired by the RHS in 1904 and famous for its trials and improvements of new varieties. Notable collections of old-fashioned and new roses, rhododendrons, camellias, heathers and rock garden plants. *Open 10.00–19.00 Mon–Sat (closes 16.30 or sunset in winter). Members only on Suns.* Charge.
Newark Priory The tall broken flint walls of this 12thC Augustinian priory stand in a meadow at the river's edge, an enticing and romantic ruin. Unfortunately there is no right of navigation up to the walls.

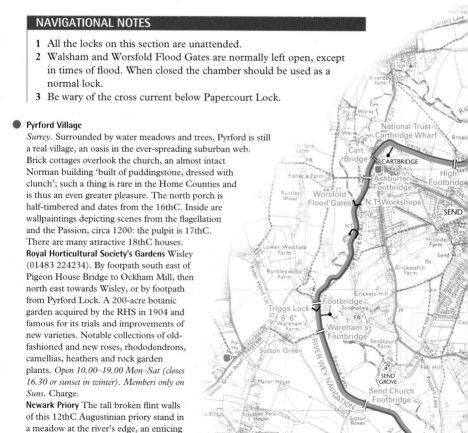

● **Send**

Surrey. EC Wed. PO, shops, laundrette. An unremarkable linear village useful for supplies. The church, a muddled affair of all periods, lies close to the River Wey and well to the south-west of the main centre. Although nicely sited amongst trees and 18thC houses, it looks at its best from the river.

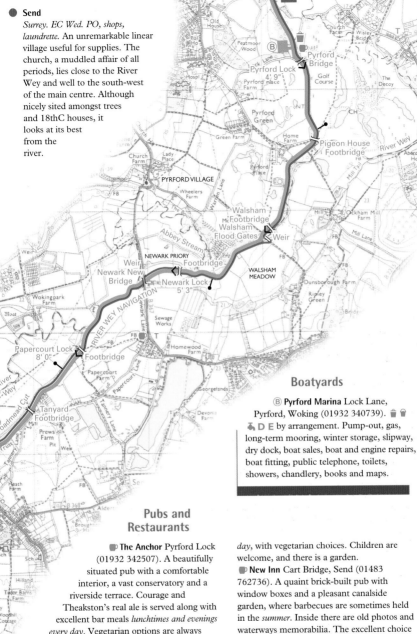

Boatyards

Ⓑ **Pyrford Marina** Lock Lane, Pyrford, Woking (01932 340739). 🛒 🛒 ♿ D E by arrangement. Pump-out, gas, long-term mooring, winter storage, slipway, dry dock, boat sales, boat and engine repairs, boat fitting, public telephone, toilets, showers, chandlery, books and maps.

Pubs and Restaurants

🍺 **The Anchor** Pyrford Lock (01932 342507). A beautifully situated pub with a comfortable interior, a vast conservatory and a riverside terrace. Courage and Theakston's real ale is served along with excellent bar meals *lunchtimes and evenings every day*. Vegetarian options are always available, and children are welcome.

🍺 **Seven Stars** Newark Lane, Ripley (01483 225128). An ivy-covered roadhouse serving an excellent choice of real ales, including Brakspears, Batemans and Hook Norton, along with meals *lunchtimes and evenings every day*, with vegetarian choices. Children are welcome, and there is a garden.

🍺 **New Inn** Cart Bridge, Send (01483 762736). A quaint brick-built pub with window boxes and a pleasant canalside garden, where barbecues are sometimes held in the *summer*. Inside there are old photos and waterways memorabilia. The excellent choice of real ale comprises Friary Meux, Thomas Hardy, Marston's, Wadworth and a guest. Food is served *lunchtimes and evenings every day*, with vegetarian choices. Children are welcome. There are shops and a laundrette to the east, also accessible from High Bridge.

Guildford

The navigation now begins to sweep around Sutton Place, and comes very close to the A3, with its constant rumble of traffic. Care should be exercised at Broadoak Bridge and Bower's Lock (see below). The approach to Stoke Lock is tree-lined, a blessing in that it alleviates some of the noise from the nearby trunk road, but it is now very clear that Guildford is being approached and the scene is becoming increasingly urban. A few willows overhang by Stoke Bridge, but soon all is back gardens, roads and factories. The scene gradually improves, and at Dapdune Wharf, the National Trust has established a visitor centre, with a fine barge amongst other exhibits. At Onslow Bridge the change of scene is completed: the town turns to face the water – and what a jolly scene it is – with riverside walks, a handsome mill, the theatre, a busy boatyard, pubs and restaurants, all overlooked by the castle. Note especially the rare treadmill crane standing on what was the old Guildford Town Wharf: from here the Wey Navigation becomes the Godalming Navigation and leaves Guildford in an ideal setting, with parkland to the east and pleasant private gardens glimpsed over high walls to the west. A footbridge marks the site of the old St Catherine's Ferry on the Pilgrims' Way, and a small stream spills into the river here below a pretty grotto, where those who pass are 'treading the path trod by Geoffrey Chaucer's Canterbury Pilgrims in the reign of King Edward the Third'. Just beyond is St Catherine's Sand, a favourite haunt of the local children during warm school holidays.

NAVIGATIONAL NOTES

1 At Broadoak Bridge pass through the arch closest to the towing path.
2 When approached from downstream Bower's Lock is to the left before the footbridge. When locking down, take the sharp blind turn to the right with care.
3 Keep clear of the weir above St Catherine's Lock.

BOAT TRIPS
Guildford Boat House Millbrook, Guildford (01483 504494). Regular trips on the *Harry Stevens* for up to 69 passengers, departing from Guildford Boat House or the Town Quay, from *Easter–end Oct*. Restaurant cruises on the *Alfred Leroy*, from *May–Oct*. Telephone for details.

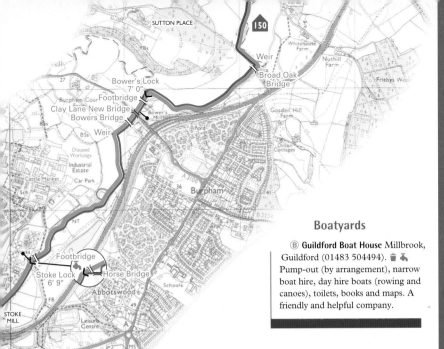

Boatyards

Ⓑ **Guildford Boat House** Millbrook, Guildford (01483 504494). 🚽 🚰 Pump-out (by arrangement), narrow boat hire, day hire boats (rowing and canoes), toilets, books and maps. A friendly and helpful company.

● **Sutton Place**
Surrey. One of the most important early Tudor houses in England, Sutton Place was built by Sir Richard Weston, a Knight of Bath, Gentleman of the Privy Chamber and Under Treasurer of England. He died in 1542. It is a brick house, with terracotta ornamentation, built originally around a square; one side was demolished in 1786 leaving the plan more open. The house is an interesting mixture of Renaissance and English styles, and was once owned by the late Paul Getty. Private.

● **Guildford**
Surrey. All shops and services. The town is built on the steep sides of the Wey valley and so its centre is very compact, overlooked on the west by the bulk of the cathedral, and on the east by the castle ruins. The best parts of the town are around the traffic-free cobbled High Street, which leads steeply down to the river, where there are interesting mill and wharf buildings, including the last tread wheel operated crane in existence. The High Street is rich with good buildings of all periods; facing each other at the top, the Baroque splendour of the 17thC Guildhall and the 18thC simplicity of Holy Trinity Church determine a rich diversity that characterises the street. Also in the High Street is the Tudor Grammar School. The University of Surrey has been developed on the slopes of the cathedral hill; the buildings show a better feeling for architecture than many other modern universities. The strength of Guildford as a cultural centre is shown by the modern Yvonne Arnaud Theatre, standing on an attractive riverside site, surrounded by trees but still in the town centre, and the number of festivals held here throughout the summer. Guildford seems to have been by tradition a popular and self-contained town, and this feeling still survives.

Guildford Cathedral The brick mass of the cathedral overlooks the town – it is an uncompromising and unsubtle thing, the last fling of the Gothic revival. Designed by Edward Maufe in 1932, it was only completed in 1961, and sadly reveals its period all too clearly. From the outside it is a mixture of cinema, power station and church; the inside is a complete contrast – a wealth of detail, and delicate use of shape and form, far more genuinely Gothic in feeling. Interesting furniture, fittings, glass and statuary. *Open 08.30–17.30 daily.* Gift shop, book shop and café.

Guildford Castle The huge motte dates from the 11thC, topped by a tower keep circa 1170. It remains an imposing ruin.

Guildford Museum Castle Arch, Guildford (01483 444750). Founded in 1898, the museum houses the largest collection of archaeology, local history and needlework in Surrey. *Open 11.00–17.00 Mon–Sat, and most B Hols.*

Guildford House Gallery 155 High Street, Guildford (01483 444740). A variety of exhibitions throughout the summer. *Open 10.00–16.45 Tue–Sat.* Free.

Dapdune Wharf Visitor Centre Wharf Road, Guildford (01483 561389). This was once the barge building centre of the River Wey Navigation, and has been tastefully restored with a stable, smithy, barge building shed and old cottages. Displays tell the story of the people who lived and worked here. Some handsome restored craft can be seen outside, including the barge *Reliance*, built 1931–2, one of 11 Wey barges built here by the Stevens family. It traded between the Wey and London Docks until it hit Cannon Street Bridge, in London, and sank. It languished on the mud flats at Leigh-on-Sea in Essex, until it was salvaged and returned to Dapdune for restoration. *Open 12.30-16.30 Wed, Sat, Sun & B Hols Apr–Sept.* Charge. You may visit by river bus from Guildford Town Quay or Guildford Boat House – details from Guildford Boat House, (01483) 504494.

Tourist Information Centre 14 Tunsgate, Guildford (01483 444007).

● **Shalford**
Surrey. EC Wed. A meandering village built along the main road. It is at its best by the river, which is flanked by old wharf and warehouse buildings.

Pubs and Restaurants

● **The Rowbarge** Riverside at Stoke Bridge (01483 573358). Pleasant garden and moorings, close to the Guildford Waterside Centre. Courage beers, coffee and *lunchtime* bar food. There are lots of pubs, restaurants and tea rooms to choose from in Guildford. The following are all close to the navigation.

● **The Plough** Guildford (01483 35610). A cosy one-bar pub offering Tetley's, Young's and guest real ales, and fresh home-cooked food *lunchtimes only Mon–Sat*, with some vegetarian options.

● **The Greyhound** Guildford (01483 300490). A locals pub serving Courage and a guest real ale. Discos are held *Fri & Sat evenings*.

● **The White House** 8 High Street, Guildford (01483 302006). A smart new pub in an attractive riverside building, with a shady terrace by the water. Meals are served *lunchtimes and evenings every day (but not Sun evening)*, with vegetarian choices. Children are welcome. *Sunday* is quiz night, and there is also live music on other evenings.

● **Scruffy Murphy's** Millmead, Guildford (01483 572160). Overlooking the lock, this handsome red brick pub has been converted into an Irish style bar, serving Guinness (of course), Kilkenny stout and Tetley's real ale. Food is served at *lunchtimes*, children are welcome, and there are seats outside overlooking the river. Plenty of entertainment, including quizzes, theme nights and live music.

● **The Jolly Farmer** Shalford Road, Millbrook, Guildford (01483 38779). A large riverside pub with conservatory and terrace. Real ales on offer include Burton, Friary Meux and Tetley's, and meals are available *lunchtimes and evenings every day (not Sun evening)*. There are lots of vegetarian choices, and children are welcome.

● **Ye Olde Ship Inn** Portsmouth Road, Guildford (01483 232343). Up the old Pilgrims' Way, this pub serves Friary Meux and Tetley's real ale, and food at *lunchtimes every day*. There are vegetarian choices, children are welcome, and there is a garden. Every *Tue* there is a music quiz, and once month a karaoke night.

Godalming

The river passes Shalford through flat meadow land, and by former riverside mills above the low Broadford Bridge. There are craft moored here and at Guns Mouth, the entrance to the unnavigable Wey & Arun Canal. A fine wooded stretch below Unstead Lock ends abruptly, an indication that the main roads are closer than you might think. The gardens of very smart residences line the Farncombe bank as the river approaches Catteshall Lock, the highest on the river and the furthest south on the navigable system. There are good moorings at Lammas

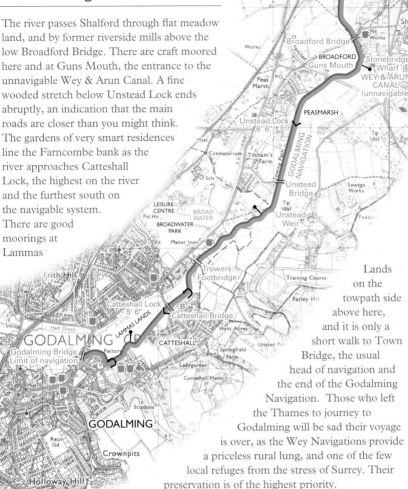

Lands on the towpath side above here, and it is only a short walk to Town Bridge, the usual head of navigation and the end of the Godalming Navigation. Those who left the Thames to journey to Godalming will be sad their voyage is over, as the Wey Navigations provide a priceless rural lung, and one of the few local refuges from the stress of Surrey. Their preservation is of the highest priority.

TRIP BOAT

Restaurant boat *Speedwell* is available for private charter from Godalming, for parties between 6 and 12 people. Bring your own wine. Details on 01483 421306.
Iona The Packet Boat Company (01483 414938/425397). Horse drawn trip boat based at Godalming.

NAVIGATIONAL NOTES

1. Broadford Bridge is low, with only 6ft 4in maximum headroom.
2. In Godalming, at the last winding hole, navigators are advised to wind with their bows to the towpath side of the navigation.
3. Small, shallow draught craft may be able to pass under Town Bridge to reach Boarden Bridge – but note that it is beyond the navigable limit, and there is a weir just above the railway bridge.

Boatyards

(B) **Farncombe Boat House** Catteshall Lock, Godalming (01483 421306). 🛏 🛢 ⚓ D E Pump-out, gas, narrow boat hire, day boat hire, long-term mooring, boat sales, boat and engine repairs, public telephone, toilets, books and maps, gifts. Riverside tearoom.

● **Wey & Arun Canal**
This navigation, built between 1816 and 1817, linked London with the south coast at Littlehampton, and Portsmouth, and has been romanticised as London's lost route to the sea. The first 100yds or so is still in water and used for moorings, but there is no turning space. A low bridge impedes further progress. Much of the rest of the route is still intact and The Wey & Arun Canal Trust is working towards restoration, a dream that one day may well become a reality. Meanwhile the canal makes a very attractive walk, linking the North and South Downs Way.

● **Godalming**
Surrey. All shops and services. The head of navigation is near the heavy stone bridge to the north-east of the town centre. By tradition a cloth-making town, Godalming has developed in a haphazard way over the years, but its confusion of streets have something to offer. The Market Hall, built in 1814 by John Perry, a local man, is a modestly handsome building with an open ground floor, and is ideally situated. The church of St Peter and St Paul, with its rare and tall leaded 13thC spire, gives the town an interesting skyline.

Pubs and Restaurants

🍺 **The Parrot** Shalford (01483 561400). East of Broadford Bridge. A Victorian pub by the green, which has been a winner of the Guildford in Bloom Pub of the Year award. You may choose from Ruddles, Wadworth, Courage and a guest real ale, and meals are available *lunchtimes and evenings every day*, with lots of vegetarian options. Children are welcome *until 19.30*, and there is a very attractive walled garden. Entertainment once a month – usually theme nights, such as lobster, Greek or French.

🍺 ✗ **The Manor Inn** Farncombe (01483 427134). A riverside hotel with a garden, serving bar meals *all day every day*, and restaurant meals *at breakfast, L & D*. There are always vegetarian choices, and children are welcome. You can choose from Boddingtons, Flowers or a guest real ale.

🍺 **The Leatherne Bottle** Catteshall (01483 425642). A small busy brick built pub, offering Hogs Back, Wadworth and Websters real ale, and meals *lunchtimes and evenings every day*, with vegetarian options. Children are welcome, and there is a garden.

🍺 **The Wey Inn** 1 Meadrow, Farncombe (01483 416680). North of Town Bridge. A friendly pub serving Courage and Fuller's real ales and meals *lunchtimes and evenings every day*. There are always vegetarian choices. Children are welcome, and there is a skittle alley, a games room and a garden.

🍺 **King's Arms & Royal Hotel** High Street, Godalming (01483 421545). An old coaching inn which was visited by Peter the Great in 1698. Real ales on offer are Friary Meux, Burton, Marston's, Tetley's and a guest, food is available *lunchtimes and evenings every day*, and there are always vegetarian choices. Children are welcome, and there is a garden. You might also like to try their theme food evenings, held once a month. Telephone for details.

🍺 **Woolpack** Godalming (01483 414003). A mock Tudor town pub, with an open plan interior. Courage and a guest real ale are offered, and food is served at *lunchtimes* in the pub, and *evenings* in the Stable Wine Bar, at the back. There are always vegetarian choices.

🍺 **The Sun** Wharf Street, Godalming. A lively pub, close to the Woolpack.

✗ **Sinclairs** 7–8 Bridge Street, Godalming (01483 418816). Excellent traditional fish and chips. *Open 11.30–14.30, 16.30–22.30 Mon–Wed (23.00 Thur & Fri), 11.30–23.00 Sat. Closed Sun.*

INDEX